Joseph Rykwert

Vittorio Gregotti & Associates
Gregotti Associati

1953–1968	1974–1980	1981–1995
Vittorio Gregotti	Pierluigi Cerri	Augusto Cagnardi
Lodovico Meneghetti	Vittorio Gregotti	Pierluigi Cerri
Giotto Stoppino	Hiromichi Matsui	Vittorio Gregotti
	Pierluigi Nicolin	
1969–1974	Bruno Viganò	
Vittorio Gregotti		

RIZZOLI
NEW YORK

Edited by
Maddalena Borasio
Paolo Colao
Heidi Hansen
e
Antonella Bergamin
Orietta Ferrero

Photography credits
Aaron/Esto
Amendolagine e Barracchia
Graziano Arici
Aldo Ballo
Gabriele Basilico
Dida Biaggi
Giorgio Boschetti
Giorgio Casali
Mario Carrieri

Vincenzo Castella
Giovanni Chiaramonte
Carla de Benedetti
Donato Di Bello
Daniel Faure
Luigi Ghirri
Mimmo Jodice
Andrea Martiradonna
Alberto Muciaccia
Antonia Mulas
Ugo Mulas
Peter Oszvald
Uwe Rau
Francesco Radino
Vaclav Sedy
Luciano Soave
Onelio Ventura
Paul Warchol
Pozzi & Romeo

First published in the United States of America in 1996 by
RIZZOLI INTERNATIONAL PUBLICATIONS, INC.
300 Park Avenue South, New York, NY 10010

First published in Italy in 1995 by
RCS Libri & Grandi Opere S.p.A., Milan

ISBN 0-8478-1951-5
LC 95-72947

Translated by Renee Tannenbaum
Designed by Carla Parodi
Typeset by Art Servizi Editoriali s.r.l., Bologna, Italy

Printed and bound in Italy

Table of Contents

This book is dedicated to all those who have worked with me over the past forty years: Lodovico Meneghetti and Giotto Stoppino with whom I began my activity and to the many people with whom I have collaborated subsequently; I wish to remember at least, for the respect that is owed to masters, Gino Pollini and Edoardo Detti; to the associates who followed one another over the last twenty years through the workshop of Gregotti Associati, and in particular Augusto Cagnardi and Pierluigi Cerri, with whom I have worked steadily since 1981. Finally this book is dedicated to the many young people who have worked with a generosity of ideas and diligence in our studio, to Spartaco Azzola, with whom I have worked for twenty-five years, and to Michele Reginaldi, who represents for me a continuity of ideas and principles directed toward the future.

But the debts accumulated over forty years of work do not end there; they must be extended to those who worked on the magazines *Casabella* and *Rassegna* and to my university teaching assistants at the faculties of Milan, Palermo, and Venice, with whom many design problems were discussed.

Finally there are debts to my teachers, including Ernesto Nathan Rogers and Enzo Paci, and to the historical, literary, and philosophical friends with whom I passionately debate and from whom I draw stimuli and ideas on a daily basis.

Vittorio Gregotti

Realignments

Vittorio Gregotti

Publishing a book on my own work, particularly since that body of work has accumulated over many years, is for me above all an operation of realignment: to verify whether what has already been built constitutes a ground for what is now being worked on and also to establish where that ground is less solid and must be abandoned to explore another. In this book Joseph Rykwert undertakes the task of making historical and critical material out of projects from years past; I, instead, would like to make out of these past projects material for the future.

In some way a monograph therefore is also a program for the subject. To write about one's own architecture is also, without solution of continuity, to write and rewrite that very architecture.

To write one's own architecture means to us (and this "us" refers not only to my associates and collaborators but also to the collective character of the artistic practice of architecture) to determine the inclination of the plane upon which to arrange the language of that writing and to choose families of words and establish relationships: it also means to some extent to invent those very words or to twist the existing ones to the point of making them new in order to resolve specific problems. Only in this process does the precision of the image open to the ambiguity of reading that in time constructs open interpretative chains. Such an image also fixes all the uncertain and contradictory viscosity of the present; it represents a hypothesis of the present, oriented by reorganization by means of the stability of the project. To write one's own architecture signifies, then, also to rewrite, one at a time, the rules of writing for a specific case starting from the present—in a nontransferable way.

Architecture never describes directly; it does not narrate; it sets the mechanisms in motion to discuss itself, its construction, and through this it produces things that may be objects of metaphorically narrative interpretation. Between symbolic will and symbolic results there is the wall of architecture: the two sides of the wall may correspond or not, but that has little to do with the construction of the wall itself.

This does not in any way signify that the empirical conditions of site, functions, and convictions are not the principal materials and the specific objects with which and of which the architectural project sets about eloquently to write: these remain, like dialogue or criticism, nailed into in the construction of the project even when the site is altered (altered first of all by the presence of the new architectural object), when the convictions change, and even when their function in the broadest sense of the word is forgotten.

Since it is my conviction that the structural character of our discipline, precisely insofar as it is an artistic practice, requires working with empirical conditions as project material, I attribute great importance to the discussion of their nature and meaning when I put together an architectural project. To recognize this means neither to legitimize nor to participate in such empirical conditions but to assume them as an object of criticism and, by means of the tools of our discipline, make them into project materials.

This naturally has nothing to do with transforming architects into pure technicians, managers, or cultural organizers, and even less into traffickers of politics, but, on the contrary, it has to do with resisting attempts that try to expel us from our universe of specific competencies or with combating those approaches to architecture that aim to exclude us from it, rendering it purely decorative.

To do this today is not simple and natural. It demands forceful and tenacious theoretical reflection. We architects have much difficulty finding a suitable plane upon which to place the question of theory, a plane as suitable as it was in the time of the architecture treatise. Until now we have not succeeded, and often our theoretical reflection is a subspecies of philosophical thought or a simplification of historical thought. Sometimes it is adopted as an after-the-fact justification of an architectural work, other times as a form of metaphoric interference among different languages that instead, precisely in order to communicate, must keep their different identities open and clear. Other times still the educated citation is also a means to acquire "symbolic capital" sufficient to conquer a recognized professional status.

During the last fifty years European culture has undergone the difficult divorce of the avant-garde from sociopolitical and scientific progress. It has experienced directly and painfully the contradiction between individual freedom and collective freedom, things that, in the modern tradition, have established ideal references of the utmost importance.

Many of us recognize in the separation between instrumentality and meaning the origin of the difficulty derived from the post-social hypermodernity in which we are immersed. From this also follows the idea of the end of the story that raises the social issue about "natural questions" of ecology and rejects any narrative concept of the human experience, activating the very destruction of the subject's meaning.

The absence of ideal common references, or rather the absence of these as ideal, leads to the consequence that we no longer have general rules and we must fight each time to establish them in a work, well aware of their temporary nature. For this reason also I declare myself a disciple of the principles of the modern project—a project incomplete by nature, capable of criticizing its own results and even its own premises, and therefore in a position to renew itself without losing the relationship among principles, objectives, and methods.

I believe that, in these last forty years, the most relevant transformation deriving from this "positive self-criticism" of the tradition of modernity in architecture involves recognition of the fact that materials come from a context, in the broadest sense of the word, like history or geography, and of the importance of the meanings of limited truth, specifics of the essence of the problem and the site. I believe this even if within the notion of context and the value of the relationship from which it comes misunderstandings of every kind are hiding.

The modern project, in the last forty years, has thus become conscious of its own nature of dialogue with what exists or better, of the modification of existing conditions. Not only the new, but the "suitable" new seems therefore to be what is called for. Contrary to what is practiced today, making something new that is both suitable and durable demands forgotten virtues such as simplicity, order, organic unity, and precision, and it is to these that I would like to refer in building a project. These words are outmoded, tied to a long and great European tradition of making architecture. They can pass as naive in a world in which "complex" means acting neurotic, replacing creativity within the increasingly rigid margins of mass society. It is also for this reason that I am fond of such qualities which, as opposed to the imperative "all and right now," are connected to ideas of slowness and endurance. Only these make it possible to withstand the constant concern about styles and to construct things that appear as if they had always been.

For me *simplicity* is not simplification, especially as a formal model: one can only arrive at simplicity with hard work. Architecture is not simple; it can only become simple through the complex development of a project.

Precision means that each work constructs its own rules that establish a specific order of modifications of what exists and of the discipline's tradition. It means that each organized act of the work, each part, must be wholly consistent with respect to those rules. It means finally that the work must be constructed with maximum economy of technical and expressive means in relation to what is necessary, that such means must therefore converge without residue in each element of the work, and that the subtlety of such means is proportional to their capacity to obtain a whole that is endowed with meaning.

Conceived in this way, precision is itself a way to demonstrate the need for *organic unity*. *Order* then is a word particularly opposed in our world, which glorifies deregulation as possibility. But order is the very structure of things, even if we have discovered that such structure is the result of the interrelation of many superimposed orders. For a project, order is the law of constituting the thing, selecting and organizing the elements that make it up; it is also the law of the new system of meanings that is being proposed and through which it is possible to see, that is, to order the world in a new way. Without meaningful order forms do not exist, only aggregations; rather, according to the famous saying of Louis Kahn, "Form is; order is form."

The words "order" and "rule" in architecture evoke one of the most feared ghosts of the contemporary world, that of the loss of identity through uniformity. That the terror of uniformity is directly connected to the structures of mass society is a well-known argument, for example, the notion that the simplest way to escape such a state is to embrace the different, the artificial, or the unnecessary—a system of differences so strong as to construct another type of uniformity. In fact, so many things, all whimsically different, produce that very faint sound of uniformity: that is the common experience.

The rule that comes from order is the opposite of repetition; it is that which allows rhythm and sequence to establish themselves; it is that which makes the identity of the project idea physical and therefore visible. The "idea" here is used in its original Greek meaning of the "visible form" of things, and the project is that which makes things significant, that is visible. That is not to underestimate at all the importance of architectural invention and of its irreplaceable value in appealing to what is not in any way present.

As the great musician Joseph Haydn wrote, music requires only a small phrase, a great structure, and a strong intelligence to produce variation. The "small phrase" is everything that has to do with the identity of the case, the "great structure" relates this identity to the "forms of the tradition of the discipline." Upon these two polarities and their rules the process of variation is woven: pleasure and the capacity for invention and harmonies, narrative metamorphoses, and the composition of scales and suitable hierarchies.

Architectural Narratives

Joseph Rykwert

"Does architecture have the same foundation as the other branches of the expressive arts, some have wondered; is there any stable ground for the practice of architecture as an art?" wrote Gregotti recently. His work over nearly half a century has been an attempt to answer that question, and to answer it affirmatively. Any account of the architecture—or indeed of the visual arts in general—in the second half of the twentieth century will have to come to terms with his work and his personality.

Gregotti was born in 1927 and began working independently in the fifties. His work has been primarily that of an architect-builder, but he has also been a prolific writer. Through the part he played in two institutions, the Milan Triennale and the Venice Biennale, he has also become a cultural impresario and an art critic. As the editor of the most influential Italian architectural monthly, *Casabella*, he has had an incalculable impact on the next generation of architects, for whom he has become a *maître à penser*, which means that his way of conceiving the problems that he has had to face—both as an architect and as a citizen—have become exemplary.

Because he is also a social thinker of some consequence, his position is unique in his generation. Parallels from earlier ones may be more confusing than helpful. He is not like Le Corbusier or Mies or Wright; he has not invented a new architecture and he did not need to—because they had already done so. There have not been such inventive masters in Gregotti's generation (which is also mine), nor even in the generation that separates them from us. Yet he is not a ringmaster or manipulator of a team (as Walter Gropius was) either, if only because he draws so much better than Gropius did. His teaching career has taken him through existing universities and has not prompted him to found a new one. A comparison to Siegfried Giedion is tempting—but Gregotti's vast number of executed buildings frustrates that also.

And he began building early. His father was a successful textile manufacturer in Novara (an industrial town between Piedmont and Lombardy), which has the usual feature of towns in the Po Valley: the plan of a Roman colony at the center, an Early Christian basilica, and a sainted bishop (San Gaudenzio). But in the nineteenth century, Novara produced one of the great eccentric architects of the time: Alessandro Antonelli, born in the nearby village of Ghemme (though he spent much of his life in Turin), considered himself a native of Novara. Antonelli entirely rebuilt that Early Christian cathedral and added a vast dome to the patronal church of San Gaudenzio. Although he occupied the chair of ornament in the new Royal Polytechnic in Turin, he treated the subject quite conventionally, drawing on the pattern books of the late eighteenth century. This conventional approach concealed a highly original conception of structure and a devouring desire to build as tall as the materials available to him (brick, granite, and wrought iron) would allow, and taller—taller, at any rate, than the users of new materials, of cast iron and even steel, could manage. From the masters of the eighteenth century, Antonelli also inherited an idea that he always managed to convey to his clients—namely, that point supports are always preferable to linear ones, that columns are better than walls. Combined with a foolhardy courage, this notion led him to achieve spectacular results, but also to court structural disasters. Gregotti, who was born and spent his early years—literally—in the shadow of that extraordinary three-leveled dome of San Gaudenzio, is almost his opposite: a prudent builder, but an adventurous planner and designer. And yet Antonelli taught him an early lesson which the Viennese masters were later to formulate more explicitly: that the vital innovation may often need to be hidden in the cloak of the ordinary.

Yet architecture was not what Gregotti set out to study: he enrolled in the Milan conservatory to learn piano and composition, and he still has an enviable (to me) ability to sing anything he chooses in tune. The passion for building could not be denied, however, and he moved from the conservatory to the Polytechnic, where, in the early years after the war, the teaching was conventional and the atmosphere stifling. Looking for some other approach to the work and life of an architect, he soon found his way to the most "advanced" studio in Milan, that of BBPR. The four, whose initials were the cipher of the studio, had begun to work together as soon as they graduated in the thirties. The war had inevitably dispersed them: Lodovico Belgioioso had been involved in the resistance and was sent to Matthausen concentration camp, as was Gian Luigi Banfi, who lost his life there (but whose initial was commemorated in the cipher). Enrico Peressutti was away on army service; Ernesto Rogers (as a Jew) had gone into exile in Switzerland. When the three survivors returned after the fall of fascism, their splendidly airy, vaulted office became a focus not just for the most interesting architecture, but for a resurgent Milanese intellectual life. The magnet was Rogers's personality and teaching.

He was a charismatic figure: insatiably curious—both intellectually and personally—Rogers was a brilliant speaker and a witty conversationalist. He was active in the Partito d'Azione which had grown out of the non-communist resistance, though, after providing the new republic with one prime minister, it was to have little future. The writers Elio Vittorini, Sergio Solmi, Leonardo Sinisgalli, and the philosopher Enzo Paci were friends, as were some painters and sculptors with whom BBPR sometimes collaborated—Marino Marini, Lucio Fontana, Fausto Melotti, Renato Guttuso—just as they did with a fellow student, Saul Steinberg, who had by then emigrated to the United States. Rogers was a rare commodity in those immediate postwar days, a cosmopolitan fluent in English, French, and Spanish. Around the studio and his other activities, a small group of younger men who would guide the architecture of the next generation came together: Marco Zanuso and Giancarlo de Carlo, and the younger Guido Canella, Francesco Tentori, Aldo Rossi, and Gregotti, of course. Many now see Gregotti as a *miglior fabbro*, but also as Rogers's natural heir.

While this group dominated the northern scene and was immediately given international airing through the review *Domus*, which Rogers edited with questing verve and elegance in 1946–47, a rather less cohesive Roman group formed itself around Bruno Zevi (who returned from his USA exile in 1943) with two of Rogers's Roman contemporaries: Lodovico Quaroni and Mario Ridolfi. Unlike Rogers, Ridolfi and Quaroni were obsessed with problems of practice and concerned with exploiting the materialities of building, while Zevi was interested in importing the notion of an organic architecture of democracy to free his contemporaries from the constricting pieties of the static, smug, Rome-centered official crust. Yet when Wrightian libertarianism was transplanted from its original habitat on the Wisconsin and Illinois prairies, it did not flourish in the Tiber Valley—for all the vigorous promotion through Zevi's brilliant teaching and his reviews, first in *Metron* and later in *L'Architettura*.

As in the rest of Europe, so in Italy in the immediate postwar period, the primary work of the architect had to be reconstruction and it overshadowed theoretical disputes. The war may have scarred Italy less than it did Germany or France and Britain, but the housing shortage in the cities, already acute in the 1930's, was exacerbated by the renewed influx of the rural population into the towns. Low-income housing was therefore as much an overwhelming priority in Italy as it was in the rest of Europe. Under Ridolfi's aegis, a manual of building practice was prepared which was distributed free to all architects. Later the state-financed building corporation, INA CASA (established in 1949; there were others, financed by local government or insurance companies), was to give wide currency to the popular house-types which Ridolfi and Quaroni had studied and used as the basis of their housing projects; in the first major one, the *quartiere Tiburtino* in Rome, they attempted to work out notions of neighborhood in terms of their research.

In the rather different Milanese situation, the moderate low-rise slab and the terrace house which had been developed and refined by the Italian CIAM group (who were also interested in industrial, and therefore labor-saving, building techniques such as prefabrication) provided a prototype for the housing project. A new Milanese district had been planned (and partly built) under the direction of Pietro Bottoni in conjunction with the first postwar Triennale (VIII Triennale of 1947). Called QT8, the district was considered a showcase of that approach. Although a part was ready for the exhibition, it was never completed, and building was to continue for several years until the original plan became irrelevant. For all its importance, many of the younger Milanese architects looked with admiration to Quaroni and Ridolfi as masters of a more materially sound and popularly based way of building. Their pragmatic attitude to planning and to a building technology which demanded labor-intensive building sites was popular both with the authorities and the trade unions. Many saw their approach as analogous to that of the new generation of neo-realist filmmakers, some of whom (such as De Sica) inevitably dealt with the horrors of the housing shortage. It could also be aligned with the doctrine of social realism (as it applied to architecture), which the Communist party was to enforce for a decade after the war.

But there were other centers, other masters: in Florence, Giovanni Michelucci was closer to the Romans than to the Milanese; in Venice, Giuseppe Samonà had become head of the school of architecture which was to dominate Italian architectural education, while Carlo Scarpa (who succeeded him) became the most assiduous and idiosyncratic of the Italian followers of Wright; the Neapolitans, Giuseppe Cosenza and Carlo Cocchia, were in some ways closer to the Milanese than to the Romans—the picture is complex, of course. Nor was the Milanese situation straightforward: the two best-known younger masters, Franco Albini and Ignazio Gardella, both flirted with historicism; the less familiar Gino Pollini and Luigi Figini remained faithful to their conception of modernity; the now largely forgotten but highly influential Mario Asnago and Claudio Vender developed an approach of quite breathtaking minimalist elegance. They were all considered teachers and role models, though the commercially successful modernity of architects like Gio Ponti or Marcello Nizzoli—even of Figini and Pollini—was seen as the set manner of an "establishment" sterility from which a recourse to history, with its implications of a popular appeal, paradoxically offered the excitement of an alternative approach to the problems of building.

At the time when Gregotti moved to study architecture, these alignments were important, but in the background a shift had occurred in the social situation of the Italian architect toward the end of the war. The key word, reconstruction, with its possible social and economic overtones, had a great deal to do with it. If in the thirties the law was the model of a university education—so that a young man or woman who had no definite aim but was thinking vaguely of business or corporate and state employment might take a law degree—in the immediate postwar period the subject chosen by many would have been architecture. Though the phenomenon is difficult to establish statistically, such a shift in mentality did seem to affect most Latin-speaking countries, and Italy perhaps even more than others. As a result, the schools produced far too many graduates for the profession to absorb, and moreover of such intellectual caliber that they could never bend to the discipline of the office and the site. This may explain the high number of industrial and fashion designers, film producers and journalists, even inventors or painters and sculptors who have suffered an architectural training. And because most schools of architecture were in universities (even if important ones, such as the one in Milan, might be in a polytechnic), the nature of the influx and the academic context almost inevitably fostered discussion and created a new, receptive, eager public for architectural polemics.

Many Italian architects did move into industrial design: this may have been incidental to their main task, but it caught attention abroad. The lira stood so low that Italian exports were relatively cheap; the export of smaller machine products, which a light Italian industry could produce very competitively, and fashion articles, as well as tourism and film therefore became an important source of hard currency. An Italian fashion was quickly established, first in Western Europe, then in the United States. The scooter provides a perfect instance of both fashion and product. Although such a mini-cycle was not without some precedent in the United States, the Vespa and the Lambretta conquered Europe first, then the rest of the world: light, agile, ridiculously economic in fuel consumption, they provided the commonest form of individual urban transport in the immediate postwar period. A number of other Italian industrial products had a perhaps less dramatic but equally diffuse impact. The Necchi electric table sewing machine and the postwar Olivetti typewriters,

both designed by Marcello Nizzoli, and the trains designed by Renzo Zavanella and Giulio Minoletti gave a rather seductive image of Italian industrial and economic realities to the outside world. It is true that the excellence of the packaging could often conceal mechanical imperfections, but, to many Italian critics, the over-optimistic and falsely harmonious view of the Italian situation which the design exports seemed to convey abroad was even more serious. What was not appreciated either by many of these designers or by their foreign admirers was the enormous advantage they derived from the late arrival of the industrial revolution in Italy, which had permitted the survival of a highly trained, traditional corps of craftsmen and building workers whose positions and skills were eventually to be eroded by the advance of some technologies, but whose talents were at that time still available. By the late forties the now-ubiquitous espresso machines (some of which were indeed designed by architects) had become as potent an emblem as the scooter.

The fall of fascism and the monarchy inspired an optimism which soon evaporated—it did not produce any radical change. The Italy of the New Republic was a hard, capitalist society in which the old contradictions remained unresolved; perhaps a bit provincial with respect to England and France, never mind the United States because of the delayed industrial revolution. The new leaders therefore fitted into the surviving structures of power very snugly.

Rogers's editorship of *Domus* belonged to the period of immediate postwar optimism. When the publishers withdrew the magazine from his control and returned it to its founder, Gio Ponti, it quickly recaptured the loyalty of its previous, smart but comfortable audience. For a while Rogers had no platform for his ideas—though when the same publisher, in 1953, offered to revive *Casabella* as a much more staid and professional periodical, the editorship was restored to him. He set up a study group to act as an editorial committee and selected Giancarlo de Carlo, Marco Zanuso (who had been his second-in-command on *Domus*), and Vittorio Gregotti. Later Gregotti became editor-in-chief, with Aldo Rossi as editor, while Gae Aulenti was responsible for layout. But, of course, Rogers did have other institutional support: his teaching at the Milan Polytechnic School of Architecture and his direction of the Italian branch of CIAM gave him direct access to the international architectural community, and this was confirmed when the first postwar CIAM conference was held in Bergamo in 1949.

At Milan Polytechnic, Rogers's more academic colleagues ensured that he remained a marginal figure. To his chagrin, he was not to achieve the status of full professor until 1962 when he had already lost his power of speech, so that his lectures had to be delivered from a script read by Gregotti and Rossi. Perhaps because of his teaching and his public persona, Rogers seemed, erroneously, far from professional practice, but he was in fact an essential and fully involved member of the BBPR office when Gregotti started working there in 1949–50. The office then was engaged on its first skyscraper, the Torre Velasca in Milan, whose critical reception was to become a *cause célèbre*. However, the first fruit of the collaboration between Rogers and Gregotti (together with the young Giotto Stoppino, who would become an associate of Gregotti), was a small but extraordinary show, "The Measure and Greatness of Man" at the Milan Triennale of 1951. The fully enclosed white room had a pebble floor and a black ceiling; on exhibit were rigid panels on which black-and-white photographs of different subjects were mounted and held in place by metal guylines and flexible joints, which, though fragmented, combined into an articulated space that was at once violent and harmonious—with great impact. It is always difficult to apportion responsibility in a partnership, but the hand of Gregotti—who would become the most brilliant, economic and expressive (if that is the word) exhibition designer in Italy—was evident in the Triennale exhibit. Startling as it was, that exhibit still had something of the unyielding optimism of modernity, though the coming fifties were to be a period of retrenchment.

One of the most discussed projects of the decade was the village of La Martella in Calabria, designed by a team headed by Quaroni, using technically low-grade materials and elementary building techniques. It was planned on rather Anglo-Saxon "neighborhood" lines to accommodate some of the inhabitants from the condemned rock dwellings at Matera, the troglodyte town which was then considered the very token of southern underdevelopment—even if it is now treated rather more respectfully by sociologists and anthropologists. As the village came to suffer various financial and social problems, it focused some of its disillusionment on those years of development. The situation was not specifically Italian; a vast number of buildings had gone up far too quickly in the decade after the war—and the many mistakes which had inevitably been made were becoming increasingly apparent. At the same time a new generation of architects was impatient to take charge.

In the BBPR office, most of the energy during the fifties was channeled into the Torre Velasca project, which Rogers was to regard as his masterpiece: a skyscraper whose thick concrete mullions rose twenty stories, to be transformed into slanting struts which sustained a much wider six-story crowning block covered by a pitched roof—a gigantic version of the medieval fortified tower. Gregotti had collaborated on the project at an early stage. The Torre Velasca was not the only BBPR project that indulged in this type of reinterpretation of the past. Rogers, for one, saw it as the taking possession of a past which was omnipresent and contiguous with current practice. Some of his critics, however, thought that it was a diversion from the realities of technological reduction and planning problems: plan and context seemed neglected in favor of an erudite and sumptuous play of surfaces.

The architectural changing of the guard was marked by the virtual dissolution of CIAM at its tenth conference in Dubrovnik in 1956; the eleventh one, in 1959 (at Oterloo in Holland), was really a meeting of its successor body, Team X. By then Italian historicism had gone further than the rest of Europe was as yet prepared to allow, and Rogers's presentation of the Torre Velasca at Oterloo was therefore greeted by an almost incredulous hostility by most of the participants. Seen from the vantage point of the mid-nineties, Rogers's approach does not seem to be a simple retreat into historicism, which many considered it at the time, but an urbane and reasoned warning about the inadequacies and the coarseness of a certain positive modernism. Rogers's work may still seem, in a certain sense, somewhat stilted and fallow, but it has none of the simulated rage and obtuseness of eighties postmodernism.

Gregotti's other work in the BBPR office was to take him in a different direction. Rogers (and, in varying degrees, his other Milanese contemporaries) was the most prominent member of the most cultivated group of architects: the assertiveness of the British and German, or even of the French modernists was not for them. If the most "advanced" among architects were "traditionally" of the left, other tendencies—existentialism and phenomenology—were attracting several of the Milanese group and transforming their dialectical position. Rogers's contemporary and friend, Enzo Paci, philosopher and historian of philosophy, was the most influential transmitter of the ideas of Husserl and of Merleau-Ponty. Political practice might support a populist assertion of the validity of customary types and the value of a labor-intensive building technique, but the perceptive complexity which architecture is called to address required some consideration of customs and history. For the next generation (which was Gregotti's), this change would bring about a transformation in their attitude toward the past. The past that mattered to them was no longer that of the monuments and historical styles, not even the immediate past of revolution and the avant-garde, but a past observed in the existing city fabric, seen as the context for a contemporary architect's work—the relationship between the architect's invention and the preexisting building texture rather than any specific reference to the past.

An enforced recognition of the normality, of the routine of architectural practice, was consistent with a drive toward a revaluation of traditional building types. The modernity of the Viennese masters, of Loos especially (but also of his enemies in the Wiener Werkstätte), became more vital, more immediately important than the radical "make it new" stances of some Bauhaus masters or even Le Corbusier. Moreover, the kind of questioning of the past which the philosophers taught modified the attitude of many architects.

Conscious of their historical role, such architects as the younger members of the *Casabella* group found themselves obliged to assume a position that was not without a certain irony. They considered the society in which they worked as the result of the immobility of a reestablished bureaucracy and bourgeoisie. It seemed that there could be no candid and consensual architecture: they were not building for a society whose conflicts had been resolved, in which national aspirations and belief in progress were reconciled, but they had to hold a distorting mirror to their patrons. The late nineteenth century was, for them, the epoch when bourgeois power had reached its apogee, so that the architecture of a postwar society had inevitably to measure itself against those great days of confidence and optimism. The publication in *Casabella*, in 1957, of the project for the bookshop Bottega d'Erasmo in Turin, and of other work by Roberto Gabetti and Aimaro d'Isola caused Rogers and Gregotti to redefine their rather different approaches to history and to modernity. If Rogers recognized that the modern movement no longer needed to assert itself stridently against history, having lost its inferiority complex, he nevertheless warned against any wholesale appropriation of motives from the past. The modern movement had too hastily, according to Rogers, identified modern design with the technology of steel and concrete: it was equally wrong, he continued, to link traditional building techniques, which had remained effective and vigorous, to old and threadbare forms which were inadequate to contemporary demands. Gregotti's rather more ambivalent attitude is clear in his comments: "The revaluation of history . . . sets us opposite a dilemma: either we shall reap the civic promise it offers to us, and narrate it, celebrating it for

our fellows and affecting them—or we shall be condemned to the terrible silence of a private perfection."

Gregotti had meanwhile established his own office in partnership with Lodovico Meneghetti and Giotto Stoppino in 1953. The office, called *Architetti Associati*, was to last until 1968. It initially flirted with historicist themes, particularly in some interiors and in furniture design, but the first major buildings—an office block in Novara and workers' housing for the textile firm Bossi—are exercises in the reworking of nineteenth-century Lombard rationalist (in the sense of Viollet-le-Duc) themes through a typological approach which owes something to postwar Roman exemplars, even if the detailing is firmer and crisper than it would have been farther south.

Five years later, Gregotti was to do more housing for the same firm, this time quite eschewing the historicism of the earlier project. But 1963–64 brought many changes. The Italian "economic miracle" had seen a great move of population from agriculture to industry, a drastic reduction of unemployment, and the return of emigrants. That boom had brought its own problems of imbalance and social blight, and by 1963 a mini-economic crisis seemed to signal its end. That *Congiuntura* immediately affected the building industry and led to a flight of capital, to Switzerland and beyond.

That year had also seen the formation of a group of writers and artists, to which Gregotti belonged, the *Gruppo 63*, perhaps the last consciously and convincingly avant-garde group in Italy or elsewhere: it is notable that of the manifestos reprinted for the exhibition, *The Italian Metamorphosis 1943–1968* at the Guggenheim Museum in New York, the last one is dated 1960. The Gruppo 63 was not, in fact, united around any aggressive proclamation, but focused on a number of technical interests: collage and montage, for instance—and on the radical consequences of the change in the artist's situation in a postindustrial world.

Although, as I said earlier, Gregotti draws too well to be only the leader of a team, he has always worked with others. In 1964, the XIII Milan Triennale, organized around the theme of leisure, gave him the opportunity for a breakthrough. The team he assembled for the occasion was rather startling: besides his partners, Stoppino and Meneghetti, there were the Swiss architect Peppo Brivio, the architect–graphic designer Massimo Vignelli, and the writer-philosopher Umberto Eco. With the help of painters (Lucio Fontana, Achille Perilli, Enrico Baj, and others), musicians (Luciano Berio and Cathy Berberian), writers (Nanni Ballestrini), and filmmakers (Tinto Brass), they produced a most memorable space—one of the most extraordinary, disturbing exhibition interiors I have ever seen. Its effect depended on the use of the spectator's passage through the show as a communicative instrument. Much of this past was lined with reflecting, silvered surfaces and articulated by the contrived but thematic deployment of projection and artificial light, including neon. Viewers were invited to consider, while meandering through the tortuous complex of staircases, the contrast between work and leisure and the choices the "leisure industry" offered them. The climax was a triangular tunnel; its mirrored surfaces reflected each other into a vast hexagonal hall—like the interior of a kaleidoscope—by the judicious use of projections (Tinto Brass's films), and the images replicated themselves as well as the figure of the viewer into a shimmering mirage.

The Triennale installation was symptomatic, but there were deeper changes than could be shown in interiors or individual buildings. It had become increasingly clear that for all the effort of bodies like the National Institute of Urbanism (INU) and the publication of detailed development plans for most Italian cities, social and financial power were quite beyond the planners' control. The old kind of town plan (and practically every Italian town had its *piano regolatore* which had been overtaken by events) was inadequate to the new urban situation. The English new towns, with their powerful state-backed development corporations and their design offices, were much envied. However, the Italian crisis reflected events elsewhere in the world—even the English new towns would not live up to expectations.

Toward the end of the fifties a number of projects had been published and discussed (such as the Dutch painter Constant's *New Babylon)* which proposed a "textural" handling of human settlement. Such manipulation had no place for individual buildings or even groups of them, but proposed human settlement as continuous patterns. These schemes owed something to the fantasies of R. Buckminster Fuller and Konrad Wachsmann, but even more to the realization that the old techniques of urban planning, as they had been applied since the end of the war during the years of reconstruction, were not adequate to the growth and diffusion of urban texture.

The term megastructure was coined about 1960, but several of the fifties projects had already suggested outsized horizontal complexes of mixed-use buildings; during that time, the English group Archigram gave the notion wide currency with a series of coarse graphic presentations that transformed the architects' and planners' frustrations into visions of their technological domination of some postrevolutionary society of the future.

Few such megastructures were actually built. Gregotti's approach to the situation was different—it was both lucid and innovative. He formulated it first in a special number of the review *Edilizia Moderna* (which he edited briefly in 1965–66) and expanded it into a book, *Il Territorio dell'Architettura*, which appeared in 1966, and which is all too little known outside Italy. A new interest in structural anthropology, prepared by his phenomenological readings, allowed Gregotti a reconsideration of the relation between society and its shelters and its territory. Perhaps because of his own interest in both geography and anthropology, he focused his attention on the way major built forms enter into relationships both with the natural phenomena of a site and the cultural (especially the agricultural) ways in which landscape has been shaped by humans. He saw clearly that nature "understood" must in some sense always be nature exploited.

For architecture to transform society in the way many of the avant-garde artists had hoped seemed a vain ambition to Gregotti. What did fascinate him was the notion that built form is always a permanent trace on the environment. The idea that human intervention might in some way be masked, camouflaged, or neutralized by natural phenomena, and then broken up into "organic" units is quite alien to him. His approach has always emphasized measurement, difference, definition, change. The relation to site and nature is established by recognizing the distinction between artificial and natural.

This approach is evident in a number of buildings of about this time. The earliest are perhaps the science departments (physics, chemistry, biology—then mathematics and geology) of the University of Palermo, on which Gregotti, leaving the old partners, worked with Gino Pollini, one of the great masters of rationalism, who was teaching there from 1968 on. The low-slung stepped blocks of the classrooms and laboratories which ascend the hill, following its contours—and include a small open-air theater—are crossed by decisive finlike service elements that give the complex a sharp definition.

In this same period in 1969, also in Palermo, Gregotti won, together with Franco Amoroso, Salvatore Bisogni, Hiromichi Matsui, and Franco Purini, a competition for a very high-density, low-rise housing development—the Quartiere Zen. Conceived as a series of closed blocks, "defended" by higher buildings whose interior courtyards act as a "heart" for each unit (of which there were to be eighteen), the project, which was also to include a sports stadium, was only partially and very unsatisfactorily built. It is very much a manifesto building, as an extension of the city grid and also its miniature, since

Palermo is crossed by its Roman *cardo* and *decumanus* more ostentatiously than any other modern city and its whole organization has retained its division into *insulae*. Above all, the Zen quarter is a denial of the suburb and a metaphorical dam against the outward movement of the urban fabric.

In 1973, with a team of younger architects, he won another competition, for the buildings of the new University of Calabria at Cosenza. This may be the most deliberately programmatic of all his projects. A long spine that reads like a megastructure in plan is in fact a three-tiered bridge which carries an access road over a level of service ducts, over an open pedestrian way. It spans the hilly landscape between an autostrada and a railway line. Along the bridge are strung the separate teaching, workshop, and laboratory buildings. This device allows the complex to accommodate itself to the awkward terrain of valleys and ridges. The height of the buildings above the bridge remains uniform, while their depth is regulated by the rise and fall of the site; they may be entered both from the ground and from the bridge. The construction does not damage the character of the landscape, which on the contrary determines its configuration. It is the first project displayed through one of those aerial perspectives (in that case the work of a member of the team, Franco Purini) that have become a characteristic of Gregotti's later presentations—and which were crucial to an appreciation of the nature of that particular design. Since then they have become almost a constant in his working method, a way of thinking visually about a project in the context of its territory. The University of Calabria has also had its problems of execution, political rather than technical. It is a crucial building both for its exemplary combination of geometrical assertion and elasticity, and for its adaptation to the landscape.

The group with which Gregotti worked on the University of Calabria became the nucleus of his second office, which was larger and more inclusive than the first, since it now included both Pierluigi Cerri, who is as much a typographer and graphic designer as an architect, and Augusto Cagliardi, who is an urbanist and planner. As the office has grown, so has the scale of the work. I will only speak briefly about some of the projects which seem to me most emblematic of the approach of the group during the last fifteen years.

It is especially important to point out how the experience of moving among diverse work environments, made possible on account of associate architects who were specialists in different fields, had characterized the group's work in a special way. Making plans for great cities like

Turin, designing fittings for large passenger ships, drawing the graphics for books and journals, and, at the same time, building edifices of various scales in a logical context of urban design—these constitute a texture of very personal, reciprocal influences, experiences that illuminate the various works in a very specific light. Gregotti loved to compare this interactive workplace with a Renaissance workshop, not only because of its efficient atmosphere and sense of craft, which were inhaled in the offices on Via Bandello in Milan, but also because of its didactic character, a place of encounter: something that he certainly remembered, although in other modes, as part of the atmosphere at BBPR in the 1950's.

The first commissions came from Venice: the new maintenance docks for the vaporetti on the lagoon side of Giudecca island; the development of Tronchetto Island at the entry of the city from the causeway, and the new housing north of the station, in the district of Canareggio, which is already completed and occupied. Completed, too, are the arrival and transit center for the Republic of San Marino, designed in 1981, and the housing on Lützowplatz in Berlin, designed in 1980.

Several of the later projects involved the proximity of great historical monuments: the new hotel in Vicenza (1986) was to neighbor Palladio's Palazzo Chiericati; at Uskudar, on the Asiatic side of Istanbul, the replanning of the square at the ferry landing (1987) involved the eighteenth-century Yeni Valide Mosque; at Nîmes (1993), the new building faces the ruined Roman amphitheater; the new railway link in Como is to pass between the fifteenth-century cathedral and Giuseppe Terragni's Casa del Fascio, or del Popolo (1984). Completed and exemplary are the additions to the fourteenth-century (and much rebuilt) Palazzo dei Priori (now Comunale) in Arezzo (1986). It is almost a surgical operation, one of inserting a new member to close the old courtyard of the palace with some dignity, while the neglected inner and subterranean spaces are brought back into use. While the new parts are clearly identifiable, they do not enter into conflict with the older buildings but are polite and helpful neighbors. The Arezzo building shows how impressive the Feltrinelli Institute (1974), which was to have occupied a site overlooking the Roman ruins between Via Brisa and Via S. Maria della Porta in Milan, would have been, and how ingeniously it would have been inserted into the eighteenth- and nineteenth-century texture which surrounds it.

From 1983 to 1985, the stadium in Barcelona was rebuilt for the Olympic games (in collaboration with the Spanish group Corma), and the new soccer stadium in

Genoa was finished for the World Cup. In 1986 came two crucial projects: Gregotti Associati won the competition for the revitalization of the Bicocca in Milan, the industrial district from which Pirelli had withdrawn, to provide a complex which would include a new technical university. It is now under construction and will be built over the next decade. It is certainly the most important of the group's projects today—decisive proof of the themes of urban design elaborated by Gregotti in the last twenty years.

The second project, much more concentrated and therefore already completed, was the project for the European Cultural Center at Belém, in Lisbon (done with Manuel Salgado). Both projects raised acute problems of context and urban texture: the Bicocca, because there was to be a multifunctional complex situated on the periphery of Milan in what was a rather desolate industrial complex; the Belém plan, because one of Lisbon's greatest monuments is its neighbor—the Convent of Los Jeronimós, a great Manueline church and monastery which, with the adjoining fortress tower, is the westernmost landmark of Lisbon. Owing to its situation, it was hardly affected by the earthquake of 1755 and is therefore one of the most important Renaissance remains in the city.

The square, with an elaborate fountain, the *Fonte Luminosa*, at its center, is bounded by the nineteenth-century extension of the monastery to the north and the railway lying between the square and the banks of the river Tagus to the south. On the eastern edge are gardens and the entry from the old city. On the western edge it was faced by undistinguished recent buildings traversed by a street, on the axis of the square. The new pedestrian entry avenue divides the two main blocks of buildings and recalls that street, which is a continuation of the approach from the old center. The glazed bridge which links them becomes a gateway to a civic space and leads up to the inner piazza of the complex. One of the crucial problems of massing was to resolve the location of the stage tower of the opera house, which is an integral part of the building. To have set it in the perspective of Los Jeronimós effectively restores equilibrium to the massive form of the great monastic church.

The stone surface and the stepped outline of the building give it an impassive quality, as if it had been conceived of a piece with its much older surroundings; the flat roofs of the lower exhibition spaces become internal promenades, mirroring the public square onto which they face. The spare detailing, recalling some of the best Milanese work of the fifties, enhances that quality.

In the nineties, there has been a further extension of work, with many projects of urban design such as the

prize for rebuilding Potsdamer Platz and Leipziger-Strasse in Berlin; and that for the Lehrter Bahnhof (train station), also in Berlin; a skyscraper that will be constructed on the "Ring" of Leipzig, exactly on the spot where Richard Wagner was born; and the towerlike building for the *Kenya Times* in Nairobi. A prize for a whole new city of 150,000 inhabitants on the Black Sea in the Ukraine has been won by Gregotti Associati; and, most recently, a plan for the forthcoming exposition area in Lisbon has been drawn up. At this point, another, slightly older project for the Paris exhibition, planned but then suspended by Mitterrand in 1989, may be instructive. Instead of the expected vertical feature, which would inevitably have had to rival the Eiffel Tower, Gregotti, as a member of the planning committee, proposed an inhabited bridge over the Seine and a reorganization of the two riverbanks. Of course he has designed, and built, high-rise buildings, but the genius of his work is horizontal. It is interesting in this perspective to look at some of his early houses: for the Poretti family in Varese, or the Magni house at La Sacca on Lago Maggiore. The architect whose work they most recall is Frank Lloyd Wright. Not in any obvious way: they have none of the familiar floating roofs or quasi-naturalistic siting. On the contrary, as Gregotti would later insist, these houses rise with pride off the ground, standing as artificial, man-made objects with no pretense to naturalness. However, their relaxed massing, the use of corner bays and projecting aprons, the way openings are inserted in the walls, recall some of Wright's early projects. And like Wright, Gregotti is constant in his fidelity to the square. It assumes the role of stabilizer in the most relaxed and spatially varied works, a stabilizer both in plan and in the patterns of fenestration, and offers that laconic formality which he considers the only stance allowed to the architect in our time.

Architecture is above all the manipulation of fixed forms, but the grid and the square have never dictated to Gregotti. He masters them through the management of transparency and the agility with which he disposes his volumes. He has remained faithful throughout all his work to the conception of modernity formulated with a fidelity analogous to that proposed by Louis Kahn. This fidelity can be summed up in three points: the construction of forms based on the nature of the materials; the conception of the building as an organism in which exterior and interior are interdependent; the legibility of the process of construction. To have maintained such a commitment through nearly fifty years of enormously varied and prolific designing and building, makes Gregotti one of the major architects of our time.

History and Tradition

I am convinced that Italian architectural culture specifically has had, in the discussion surrounding the importance of materials derived from history and tradition, a special responsibility and an overall importance. It has been at the center of positive criticism on the tradition of modernity which, particularly in Italy during the 1950s, was proposed and theorized and from which, in the years following and with many different interpretations, international culture has moved. Also in its distortions, first as nostalgia for the classical styles and then as nostalgia for the modern as style.

There are three different levels of historicity that converge in a project. One originates from the theoretical and stylistic tradition and the tradition of the discipline's profession; it confronts in different ways the themes of representation and expression, of narration and description in order to construct a new present. A second comes from the historicity of the site, which houses the new architecture of social, administrative, and cultural conditions, conditions of needs and behaviors connected to it like the project materials or their content. Finally there is the level of the memory of the subject, of its phylogeny, of the nature of the accumulation of personal memories that are formed like an interpretive grid to the world. All three of these levels are present in a project, but it is their hierarchy, and even their voluntary absence, that make up the essential differences in the procedures of a given project.

Naturally, reading historical depth of the materials depends also on historical hypotheses that are continually reformulated. The past is reached starting from the present; yet no past can be considered a form of legitimizing the present, nor can the present be deduced from the past. Only a description of a field of conflicts is possible, to which we add new questions with our project. History, and therefore the history of architecture, cannot be directly imitated, just as a painting or a novel cannot be copied, except as a learning exercise. Precisely on account of this independence and specificity, as well as its seriously grounded creative character, it is for us architects an extremely precious material for thought. It is precious material for reflecting on the condition of respecting its integrity, on the condition of avoiding transposing concepts, methods, and hypotheses with too much ease, if not with the precise awareness of the metaphoric limits that such concepts, methods, and hypotheses assume in their transposition.

History, for an architect, is a way to become aware of the nature of the ground upon which we walk, but we must not be under the illusion that it can teach us the art of walking.

A project is a dialogue with conditions, with the site, and with their history through the subject and its memories. The dialogue is possible only among subjects that must recognize themselves as different, distant. For this reason, a project is change, establishment of difference, construction of a new thing in the historical flow.

The quality of the project is the quality of this difference. Coincidence and conciliations are not possible today. The project measures only the critical distances of the existing, required for the establishment of the new thing.

Regarding the use of history one can cite the famous passage of Wittgenstein: "From my propositions it is clear that he who understands me recognizes in the end that these propositions lack meaning when, through them and by means of them, he has risen above them (he must, so to speak, throw away the ladder, after climbing it). He must surpass those propositions; then he will truly see the world."

From Vittorio Gregotti, *Il territorio dell'architettura* (Milan: Feltrinelli, 1966)

Residences for Employees
of the Bossi Textile Industry

Partners: L. Meneghetti. G. Stoppino
Cameri. Novara 1954–56

The three duplex apartments are part of a larger project of nine dwellings located opposite the factory and bordering on the open country. The small piazza on which the three duplexes converge would have been finished with two other buildings, but these were not constructed. The structure is faced with brick, with sandblasted brick at the top. In the corners and at the sides of the windows, green ceramic tiles (6 × 6 m) are inserted. Windowsills, thresholds, and balcony accesses are of white prefabricated cement. The sheet-iron eaves are painted dark red, while the basement is concrete. The roof is terra-cotta tile.

1

2

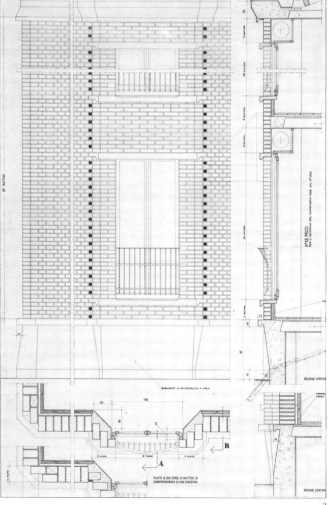

3

1. Main front
2. View of side toward garden
3. Detail of facade

Buildings for Residences and Offices

Partners: L. Meneghetti, G. Stoppino
Novara 1957

The complex is situated at the margin of the historic urban nucleus, along the trails of the seventeenth-century bastions and aligned along the low road that follows its walkway. The ensemble is formed by three blocks of equal length, two of which are contiguous, intended for mixed use, offices and residences. The unified design of the facades is the result of the system of curtain walls made of prefabricated panels of cement and gray gritstone. Each unit occupies three bays: the central one is covered with a grill and screens the loggia onto which the bath and kitchen face. The string course is constructed at the same time as the casting of the structure in reinforced concrete, with an interaxial constant of 3.5 meters.

1

1. Street front
2. Detail of side facade
with ladderlike
ground-floor doorlock

2

Office Building

Partners: L. Meneghetti, G. Stoppino
Novara 1960

Integrated among the historic alleys of the old city, the building assumes the vertical rhythm of nearby facades; accentuated by ground-level access and crowning eaves, it freely reinterprets the composition of the dimensional modules, of the framework, and differentiates in the choice of materials. A play of light, which alludes to ashlar surfaces, opens the entire glass front to a dialogue-comparison with the nearby buildings. On the ground floor, the building houses a bank office and on the upper floors, business and professional offices. The reinforced cement structure is covered with hammered grayish rose gritstone, like the prefabricated slabs of the eaves. The continuous jutting facade is made of glass and painted iron. The ground floor, enclosed by a secondary framework of iron, is recessed with respect to the outer line of the building, where the frames and curtain walls are set in slabs of serpentine.

1. 2. View and detail of facade
3. Front elevation

1

3

2

Giangiacomo Feltrinelli Foundation

Milan 1974

The complex occupies what was almost an empty city space, a legacy of wartime destruction, between S. Maria alla Porta, via Gramsci, and via Brisa. Here lie the ancient ruins of baths and an imperial palace from the Roman era, in addition to a medieval tower and the seventeenth-century entry portal to the court of the Gorani palace.

Recapturing traces of the historical appearance and at the same time adapting to the presence of a fragmentary building on the west side, the project places at the center of the area five square-based towers with sides of approximately 11 meters and heights of 19 meters; these establish a dialogue with the ancient Gorani tower, which now becomes an integral part of the complex.

The new towers define the limits of a paved piazza, which represents the distributive core of the entire complex: work rooms and a "book tower" with a trapezoidal base face the piazza. A basement, functional in the definition and completion of the building curtain, houses the meeting and reading rooms.

The entire complex is faced with bricks with metal frames.

1

1. Perspective view
from via Brisa
2. View of model
from west

2

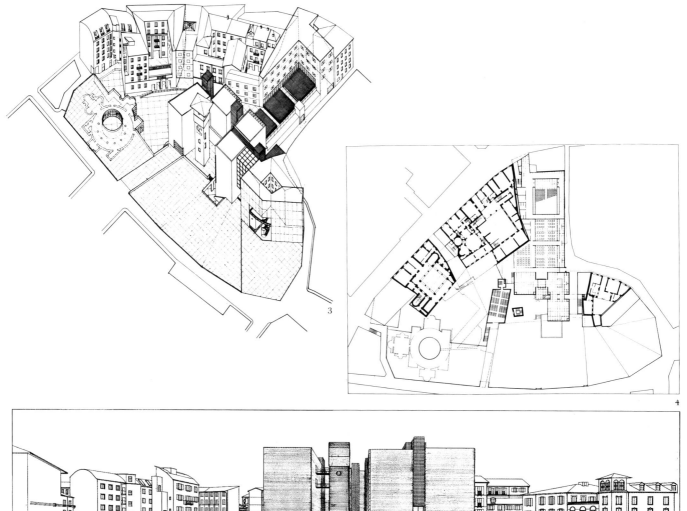

3. Axonometric view
of project
4. Ground-floor plan
5. Elevation from west
on via Brisa

Restructuring and Enlarging
the Palazzo Comunale
(City Hall)

Arezzo 1984–90

In Arezzo's old city, the intervention includes the restoration of Palazzo Sabatini and the layout of the city-owned buildings along via Montetini. Through integration with several new building structures, new relationships are introduced among the different preexisting elements, making the most of the connecting routes and enriching the possibility of fruition for the entire complex. The project provides for the roofing of the former Tani building, creating a 120-seat conference room, accessible from the former Stinche Lane, and the construction of an underground area connected to the courtyard around the Palazzo Comunale. The essence of the intervention is the redefinition of this courtyard, which becomes an actual city plaza, parking, passageway, and link between the different parts of the city. The layout, starting at the level of the portico of the city hall, allows for the change, through the introduction of stairs, ramps, and walls, the use of entrances to the adjoining property, and definition of a new face on Via Montetini. The open spaces are paved in brick laid on edge between square patterns outlined with slabs of stone, while the new building structures, in partitions of reinforced concrete, are faced with cut stone slabs (34 × 20 cm) and paved with jagged slabs (30 × 30 cm).

1. View of project from west
2. Plan of town complex with new crossway
3. 4. Views of new pedestrian courtyard between original building and extension

1

PIAZZA DELLA LIBERTA

2

3

4

Interventions in Piazza Madrice

Menfi, Agrigento 1984–95

The project concerns restoring Piazza Madrice and the complex formed by the Chiesa Madre (mother church), the Palazzo Comunale (town hall), the Pignatelli Building, and the Torre Federiciana after the damage caused by the earthquake of 1968. For the new church, a single nave was placed perpendicular to the existing one, keeping the entrance near the piazza and including the remains of the baroque construction. The building is a volume regulator of the surrounding space; from its roof, accessible for religious functions, the sea is visible in the distance.

The modulation of light, which is quite strong, was key in the restoration of the Torre Federiciana, and a new relationship with the piazza is established through double access: a large empty space includes the ruins adapted as halls for city offices, and a new staircase, placed in the passageway with the adjacent Pignatelli Building, leads to the mayor's office and the council chamber. The expansion of Palazzo Comunale provides for the restoration and re-erection of the adjacent storehouses, intended for offices and multipurpose rooms. The church and the Pignatelli Building improvement are still in progress.

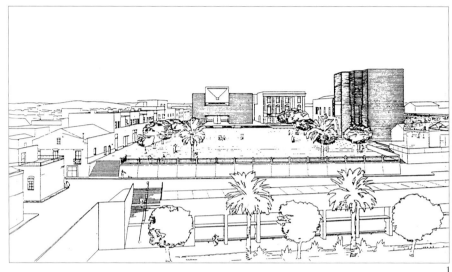

1

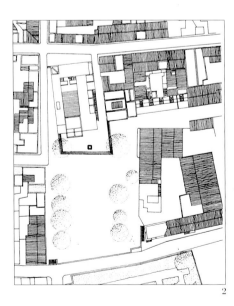

2

3

1. Perspective view from south of piazza with project buildings
2. General plan of piazza
3. Detail of Torre Federiciana
4. View of Torre Federiciana from piazza with remains of ancient fortification

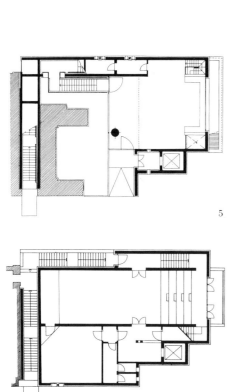

5

6

8

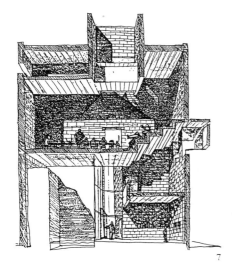

7

9

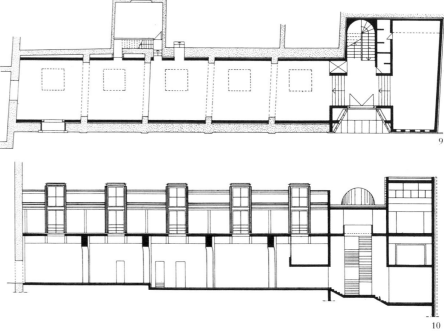

10

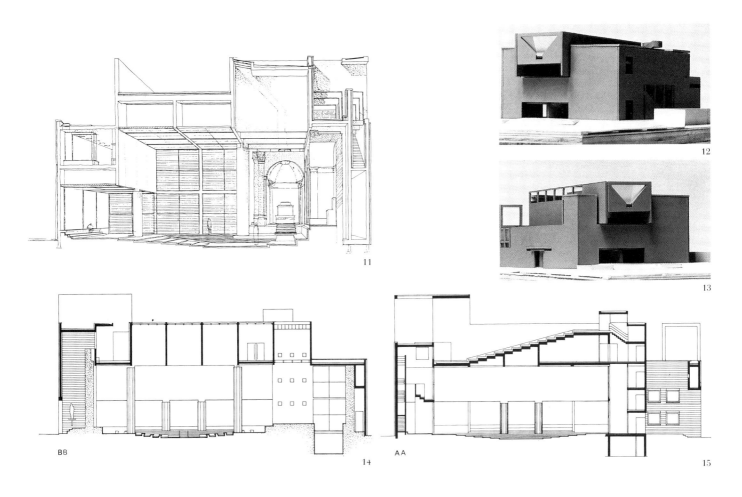

11

12

13

BB
14

AA
15

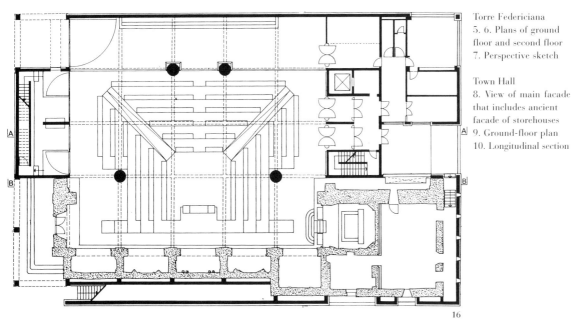

16

Torre Federiciana
5. 6. Plans of ground
floor and second floor
7. Perspective sketch

Town Hall
8. View of main facade
that includes ancient
facade of storehouses
9. Ground-floor plan
10. Longitudinal section

Chiesa Madre (Mother
Church)
11. Perspective section
12. 13. Views of study
model
14. 15. Longitudinal
sections
16. Ground-floor plan:
marked are the
surviving parts of the
Baroque church

New Location for Offices of the Marche Region

Ancona 1987

In an area at the foot of the city's ancient fortifications, the project unfolds along the ridge of the hill, following the progression of the land, respecting the contextual condition, but, at the same time, appearing with a strong identity in keeping with the character of a public building.

The construction is divided into four levels. The lowest forms a large pedestrian piazza-bastion at a height about nine meters above the main access road; under it are the parking lots.

The part of the building that looks onto the piazza is given a continuous portico all along the front, and its roof, which is accessible, is covered in greenery.

Five narrow service areas that contain the elevators, hallways and main stairways define and divide the office areas, arranged around interior patios. The central area contains the main entrance through which to access also the 480-seat auditorium and the Regional Council Chamber, both connected directly to the outside toward the garden on the hill.

In the office area, the natural light is assisted by interior patios measuring 12 meters per side. The structural fabric, made of continuous partitions in the service areas, is, in the office zones, in pillars of reinforced concrete, placed according to a modular fabric of 6 × 6 meters.

3

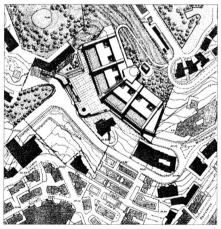

4

1. Study sketches
2. View of entire hill with ancient fortifications and new office complex

3. Main front and cylindrical bastion with pedestrian access ramp to raised piazza
4. Bird's-eye view of plan
5. View of main entrance

5

6. View of one of the porticos that border the elevated piazza
7. View of one of the side service yards
8. Transverse section of complex

6

7

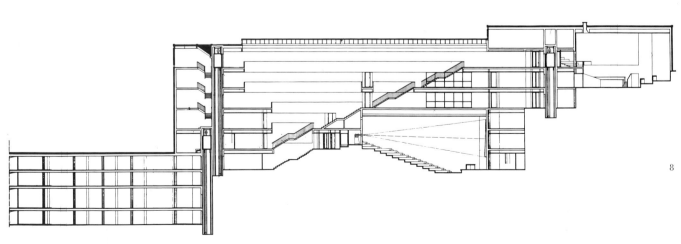

8

New Office of the Monte dei Paschi Bank and the Chamber of Commerce

Invited international competition
Siena 1988

Placed at a pivotal juncture and interrupted by a series of heterogeneous elements between two installation scales—that of the city and that of the surrounding countryside—the project is measured first of all against solutions to three main problems: the strategic urban position, the question of the image of the old city in this area, and the considerable quantity of space required as defined by the competition.

Searching for a new connection with the western part of the city, the project uses the opportunity presented by the relocation of the bus station as an important element of connection with the height of the project area.

The suggested location for the Monte dei Paschi Bank is on Piazza Gramsci, in an elongated space without any defined role, located between the site of the ancient walls and the Lizza, thus preserving the sixteenth-century Palazzo Ciacci, where the ancient garden is to be restored, and the adjacent Limonaia building.

With the new Chamber of Commerce buildings on Piazza Matteotti, an ensemble of buildings of varying sizes is formed that recalls a small-scale urban arrangement to organize the dimensional relationships between the new edifice and the main installations of the old center.

Near the Lizza a newly defined piazza is created out of a semicircular structure placed on axis with Via San Bernardino, following a spatial typology of recurring closure of road axes in Siena.

On the opposite side of the area, a new backdrop to Piazza Matteotti is created by two towers, 47 meters high, that contain the offices of the Chamber of Commerce and a low, square space to hold its equipment. The towers and the square structure are joined by a wooden bridge, an element of formal reference for whoever comes up from the square below.

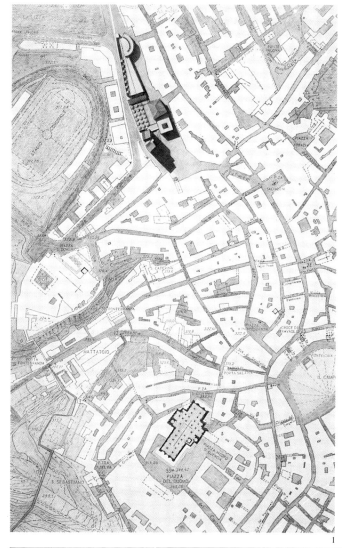

1. Plan of project and surrounding area
2. Ground-floor plan

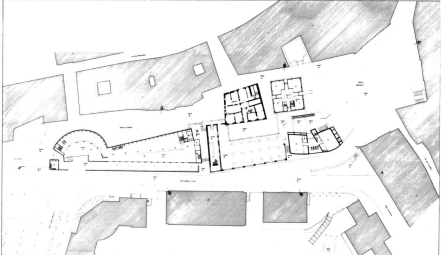

2

3. View onto Piazza
Gramsci
4. View onto Via Cozzi
5. View of old city from
west
6. Study sketch for
front and layout near
the Lizza
7. Study for exit area
of bus station
8. View from Piazza
Matteotti

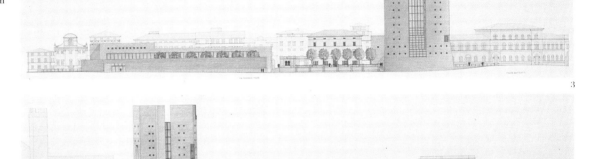

3

4

5

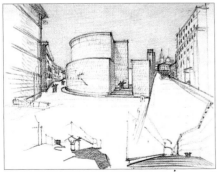

6

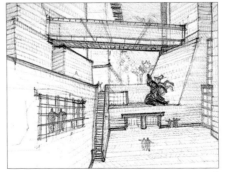

7

8

Restructuring the Offices
of *Corriere della Sera*

Milan 1988

The project can be related to a process of urban revitalization, resulting from technological conversions and productive redevelopment of many of the industrial activities present inside the historical envelope.

The works of transformation that the project envisions refer to the demolishing of buildings added in recent years and to the resulting rebuilding of industrial plants and buildings that originally housed the offices of different newspapers. The project intends to remedy the present disjointed image of the complex which has come about from numerous interventions over the course of many years and return the architectural image to its former unity. The design theories plan for an interior courtyard of 2800 square meters, with the objective of transforming a space without identity into an urban site, thanks to the recomposition of the internal views. The external views will be subjected in turn to works of maintenance or partial modification, with the exception of the building on the south corner, where the considerable change from printing house to editorial office will already cause a morphological transformation.

Plaster, which re-creates the character of the original complex, was used for the restoration, while the newly built walls were covered in prepainted gray aluminum panels. A metal grill was designed to cover the mechanical level of the roof in order to mask the various installations.

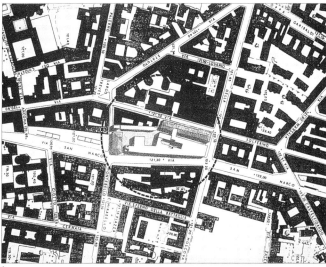

1. Drawing of interior courtyard
2. General plan
3. View of model from west

Rearrangement
of Piazza Matteotti

Invited competition
Vicenza 1986–87

Built on the possibility of establishing a project to transform isolated points while still connected to an idea of the whole that is articulated through the specificity of the single solution, the project extends the thought to the problem of transforming one part of a city, hypothesizing a system of roads that suggests the discovery of a relationship between the city and the orographical condition from which the installation draws its origin.

The four main areas of the intervention are arranged on a renewed system of pedestrian walkways made possible by strengthened circular roads and by planned parking lots.

To the north, for the block of Santa Corona, the completion of the cloisters is proposed with the arrangement of museum activities, the reconstruction of street fronts, and the creation, using the height differences of the existing levels, of a 250-space parking lot whose roof will become a public square.

Spanning the Bacchiglione River, in a strategic position with respect to the road system, the existing Angeli Bridge, altered, also houses a parking lot. Thus, a new relationship to the water is introduced through

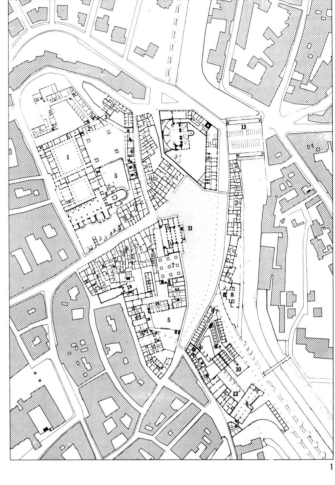

1

1. General plan of the piazza and its environs
2. Perspective drawing of Piazza Matteotti from north
3. Sectional view of Santa Corona complex
4. Perspective drawing of Angeli Bridge
5. Perspective drawing of area of former Macello along the Retrone River

2

the separation between vehicular and pedestrian traffic, bringing to completion the architectural definition of the office fronts that recall elements of the context's morphology.

The intervention on Piazza Matteotti aims to eliminate every visual obstacle with the goal of restoring the relationships among the monuments that face onto it, to lower the ground height of Palazzo Chiericati to its original level—in such a way as to restore its proper form and location—and to construct, along one side, a new museum.

A new building intended as a hotel is placed at the hinge between Viale Giurgolo and the piazza, in front of the former public baths that face the Bacchiglione. In memory of the ancient relationship with the water, the restoring of the original ground height of Palazzo Piovene and the architectural redefinition of the nearby Retrone River are proposed.

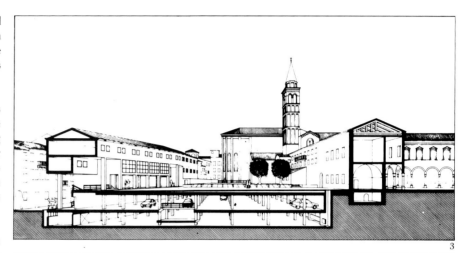

3

4

5

Restoration and Expansion
of the South Bank Centre

Invited international competition
Partner: Ove Arup Associates
London 1994

The South Bank Centre occupies an area of the south bank of the Thames opposite the Strand. The project aims to reinforce the urban characteristics of the site, establishing relationships with the other side of the river. Transforming existing bridges into paths with an urban character is one means. Waterloo Bridge is planted and endowed with a portico on both sides, while a linear walkway-garden, superimposed onto the railway bridge, connects pedestrian traffic to Charing Cross, Waterloo East-West station, the new international terminal, subway lines, and the cultural center. Two portals mark the new entrances to the area. Moreover, the project envisions removal of the footbridges that connect the Royal Festival Hall, the Royal National Theatre, Queen Elizabeth Hall–Hayward Gallery, and the film center; built in the early 1950s, these form a pedestrian system that connects to the boardwalk along the river; in this way a series of squares link the theater district to the railway station and to the opposite riverbank. Respecting these preexisting elements, the project plans a large glass hall that connects the level of the automobile bridge with the open square near the river. Support services at the cultural center and entrances to various organizations are laid out in an arcade that descends in successive terraces.

1. Axonometric view
of complex
2. Perspective section
of new hall
3. View of new hall
near central pedestrian
piazza
4. Study sketch
for structures of new
glass hall
5. Perspective study
of new central hall
6. Foreshortened view
of the Thames

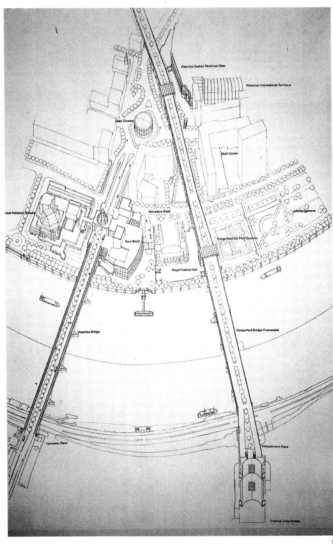

1

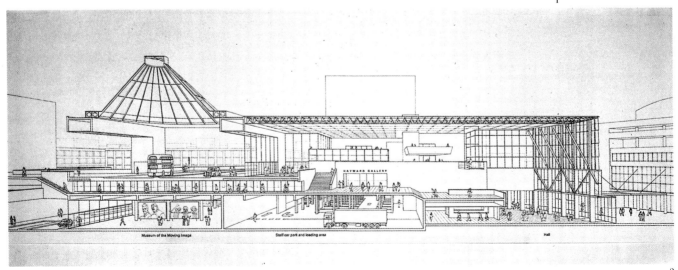

2

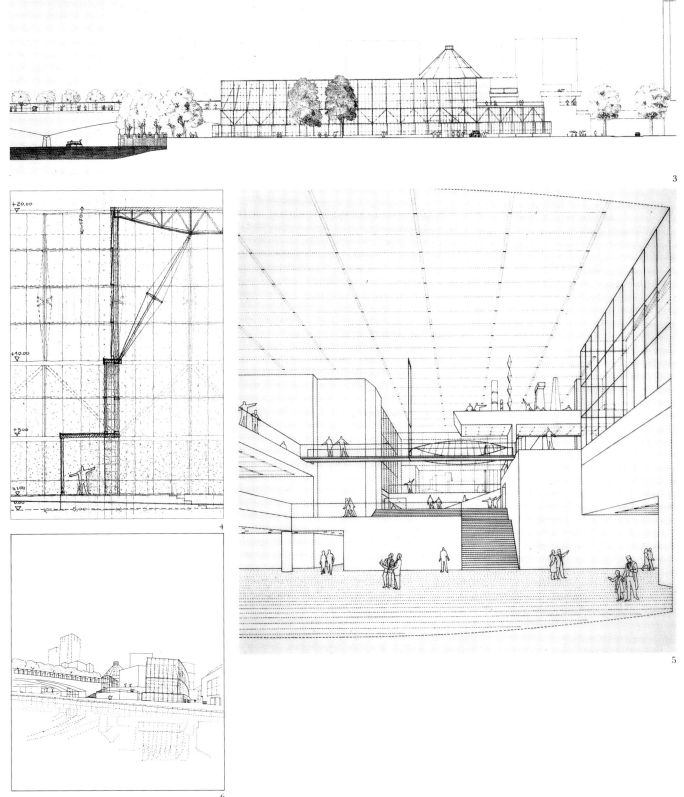

3

4

5

6

Building at Place des Arènes

Invited international competition
Nîmes 1993

The building, located in front of the Roman arena, introduces a series of relationships with the ancient construction through the adoption of several common elements, such as the height, the stone finishing of the facades, and the arrangement of the openings. The top floor opens into a large loggia, while the two floors underneath have large spaces that group four windows together as a single architectural element. The second floor, intended for offices, is lit by a continuous band of windows, which signals the mass of the base or ground-floor level, slightly protruding with respect to the edge of the facade. A wide opening on the axis central of the building leads to an octagonal courtyard covered by a high wooden structure that protects it from the sun. The use of natural wood returns in the trim on the facades facing the courtyard and emphasizes its intimate and protected aspect. The courtyard was planned as a public square, a place of access to the commercial spaces on the ground floor and the parking level along the path that recovers the layout of the ancient walls, following them from the Place des Arènes near the interior garden, where archeological finds of considerable interest are located, to the Porta Romana, on the opposite side of the block. Great attention has been placed on roofing materials. Besides wood, Barutel stone is proposed for the exterior facades, used for the arena and for all the historical buildings, while slabs of Roc Mayer stone have been selected for the paving, already used for the urban road network.

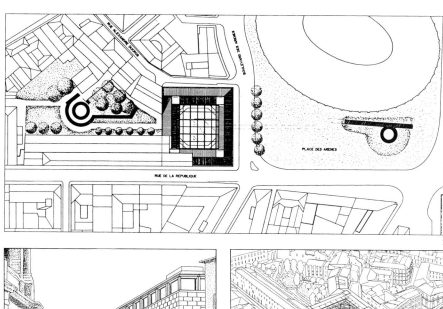

1. Plan of project
2. Perspective view along Boulevard des Arènes
3. Bird's-eye view from east
4. Perspective section on central pedestrian courtyard

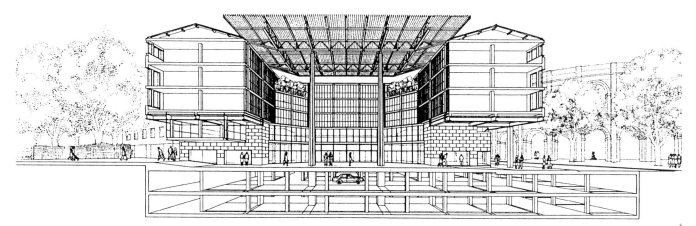

The economic expansion at the beginning of the 1970s deeply changed the social framework of a considerable part of Italy, which was approaching a brand new form of social consumption.

The mechanization of domestic work, television communication, the homogenization of languages and behaviors, the transformation of social ideals, and the progressive decline of local identities of rural culture are all consequences of these changes.

The theme of "free time" and of the criticism of its use and organization was at the center of the XIII Milan Triennale. The collaboration of new artists, filmmakers, poets, philosophers, musicians, and scholars, all connected by a common cultural experience—identified in those years by the discussion of the relationship between ideology and language promoted by Gruppo 63—contributed in a decisive way to its visual organization that followed a spatial sequence to construct a story, or rather, multiple stories. The experience of "Plug-in City" in 1963–64 developed out of these themes of change, the technological aspects rather than the sociocultural and political ones.

On the subject of architecture, the introductory section of the XIII Triennale exhibited several experiments. These included collage processes using heterogeneous materials, linguistic barriers and spatial slippage constructed through reflection and multiplication, and in general, multimedia ways with which to create a total environment, endowed with multiple possibilities of interpretative crossovers and necessitating the active participation of the spectator.

The principles of the XIII Triennale were accompanied by the image of the passage from the concept of space to the concept of place and environment, from that infinite geometric neutrality of the first to the non-homogeneity of the second. It drags with it the complex debris of memory and forces the examination of specificity and differences in conditions. This opened up the doors for us to procedure characterized by the conception of the project as a dialogue with empirical conditions and as an operation of continuous acquisition of a decentralized view of reality, capable of avoiding the circularity of utopia. This operation has accelerated over the last thirty years, bringing into question the very stability of our discipline and starting, in our field as well, the tiring task of turning completely around. This represents resistance to the "mediatization" of architecture and its reduction to consumer product, put into play to some extent by us at the beginning of the 1970s.

Introductory Section
on the Theme of "Free Time"
for the XIII Triennale

Partners: P. Brivio, U. Eco, L. Meneghetti,
G. Stoppino, M. Vignelli
Milan 1963

The dominant theme in the introductory section at the XIII Triennale was the debate on the quality of free time, its specificity, and its historical evolution. The arrangement intended to introduce "scenic time" that would accompany the visitor during the journey: abridged, explanatory captions proposed pictorial, graphic, and audio impressions and offered alternative routes and meanings that were enjoyable at different levels.

All the journeys departed from the *Terminal of Exaltation*, a multicolor place resonating with invitations to free time; through the *Decompression Chamber*, in which electric machines offered illusory alternative programs, the path led to the *Room of Containers*, where flights of stairs were reproduced, overturned, and multiplied by mirrors in such a way as to nullify any sense of geometry or dimensional relationship to the location. The *Corridor of Captions*, characterized by topical subjects, led finally to the *Room of the Kaleidoscope*, made of a triangular prism, enlarged and extended infinitely by the mirrors on the walls. The play of simultaneous images and sounds, alluding to the unreal possibility of the genuine freeing of time, was created through the simultaneous projection onto the mirrors of two films, one on free time and one on work time.

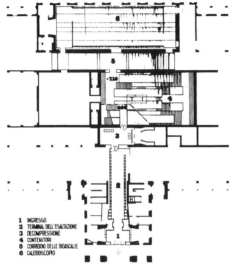

1. Plan of the
introductory section
  1. Entrance
  2. Terminal of
  Exaltation
  3. Decompression
  4. Containers
  5. Corridor of
  Captions
  6. Kaleidoscope
2. Transverse section
3. View of model

1 INGRESSO
2 TERMINAL DELL'ESALTAZIONE
3 DECOMPRESSIONE
4 CONTENITORI
5 CORRIDOIO DELLE DIDASCALIE
6 CALEIDOSCOPIO

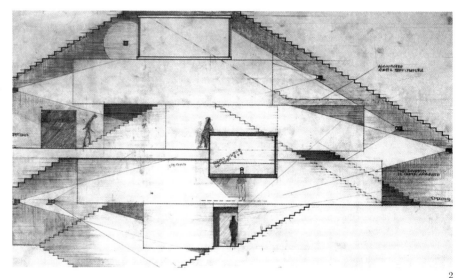

2

3

4. 5. Views of the
Room of Containers

4

5

6

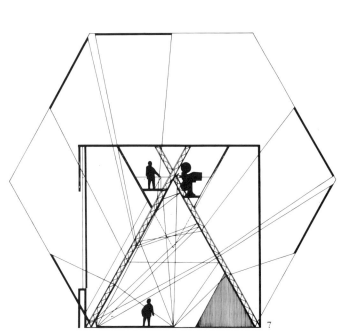

7

8

Room of the Kaleidoscope
6. View
7. Transverse section
8. Corridor of Captions
9. View of Room
of the Kaleidoscope
10. Longitudinal section
of Corridor of Captions

Toward a Mass Society

9

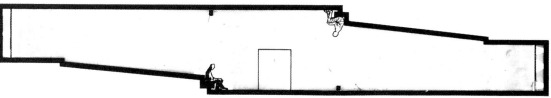

10

11

11. Container
of "Free Time"
(Fabio Mauri)
12. Container on
theme of technology
(Enrico Baj)

12

Harold Rosenberg wrote several years ago, with respect to minimalism, that each modern work shares in the idea from which its style draws its origin, and that, we architects would say, is the result of a theoretically based project. Later, Rosenberg added, "Rather than derive principles from what it sees, teach the eye to see the principles." Minimalism is for us a form of this relationship, of this way of conceiving the creative work. However, especially in our case it is a suggestion of meaning that we want to interpret freely here from the point of view of architecture. Someone wrote that minimalism, especially the American minimalism of great displacements of material, is essentially representation of symmetrically opposite signals, with respect to the spiritualist and rebuilding tension of the "abstractionism" of the period from about 1910 into the 1930s.

We are not dealing with reestablishing the reign of geometry as representation of the absolute (a common problem, even if developed in different ways, of countless artists and architects of the first avant-garde), but rather with restoring meaning to the original and fundamental gesture of placing, arranging, taking off, accumulating, and dividing.

Neither resolutive nor surprising, not even progressive, power has been attributed here to technology (if not to science). Technology for minimalists (but also for several architects of recent years) exists without wonders; it is neither to fight nor to exalt; it is the natural ground of actions but certainly not an instrument of freedom or a model to which to refer formally and methodologically.

If all this holds true for our architecture, it is even more characteristic of the procedure that regulates the designs of objects beginning in the mid-sixties. The previous experience, intensely directed at criticism of the conditions of industrial production of the object and its independent significance, has forced us to take definitive cover from what took place later. In general, in fact, the form of the object of use has tended, in recent years, to reconnect instead with the temporary, decorative nature of the fashions dependent upon the incentive of the market, and also to be seen as a symbolic value of a society that claims to be endlessly flexible and completely secularized, in which the dynamics of competitive interaction between groups aim to colonize the entire social system. This is accomplished also by approaching visual arts experiences; these too seem to move toward an increasingly marked aestheticization of the everyday, like a central obligation of their activity.

We are probably dealing with a much broader refunctionalization of the visual and applied arts and with their restored organic unity with the metaphorical convictions of a very homogeneous society in the choice of its own hierarchies of value.

Modern art is, rather, critical art and not organic with respect to reality. For this reason the modern project is not completed, nor could it be, especially as a project that is critical, first of all of itself and of the tools of criticism of those same forms of rationality. It is important, therefore, to describe the existence of the new condition in which the world of the construction of objects moves. To recognize in it its deep-rooted place in society, as it is today, is the first indispensable step toward the establishment of that critical distance that renders us necessarily modern.

From Vittorio Gregotti, "Editoriale," in *Rassegna*, no. 36, December 1988, monograph dedicated to *Minimal.*

1. Installation for the exhibit *La casa abitata* (*The Lived-in House*), Florence 1965
2. Apartment in Novara. Cavour armchair, 1959 (production Poltrona Frau, 1986)
3. Bronze door handle, 1956
4. Game table in curved solid woods, 1955
(1, 2, 3, 4 with L. Meneghetti and G. Stoppino)

5. Silver coffee service
for Cleto Munari, 1985
6. Floor lamp
for Arteluce, 1964
7. X Triennale chair
in recut plywood, 1954
(6, 7 with L. Meneghetti
and G. Stoppino)

5

6

7

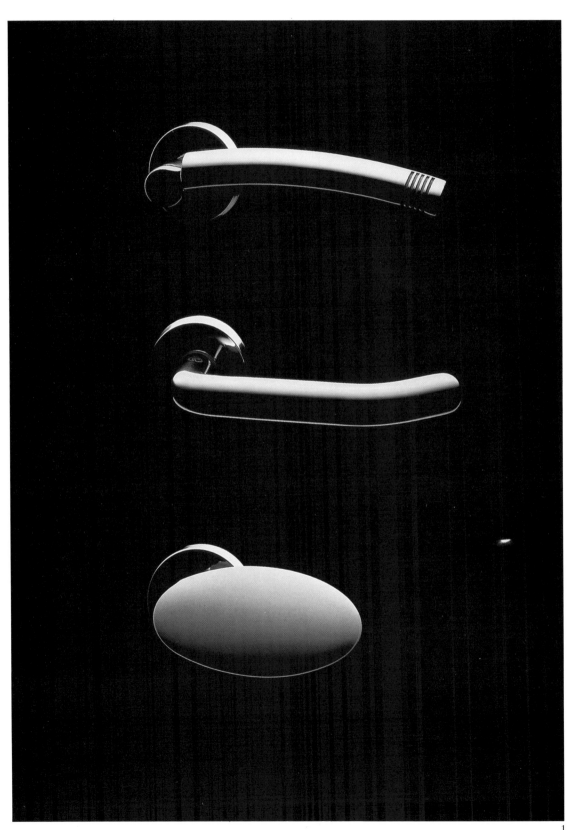

1. Handles for
Fusital, 1980–90
2. 3. Layout for
Naos office
for Unifor, 1994

2

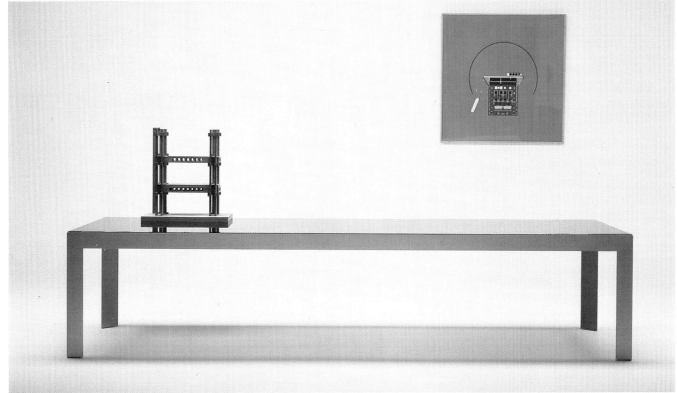

3

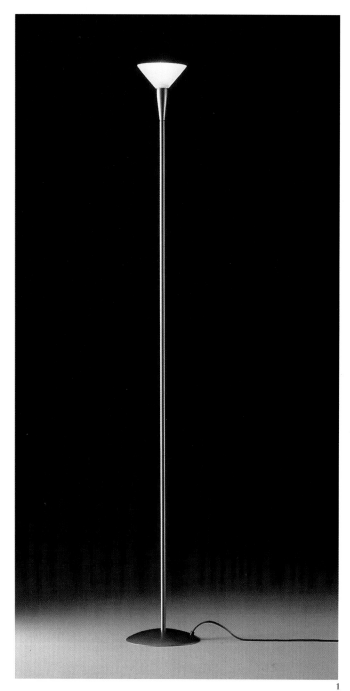

Lighting
elements for
Fontana Arte

1. Segno Uno
(Sign One), 1984
2. Tea, 1988
3. Sara, 1993

1

2

3

Visual communication is a subject that seized its own content.

Theorized as an activity belonging to the humanitarian methodology of the project in the twenties, it has been in some way flooded by the expansion of its own tools in the fields of electronics and mass communications. The ideology of technological modernization has managed to become preeminent, thanks also to the extent of the economic bases on which it relies. The speed of its changes (necessary for its commercial survival) has included an important part of these same figurative arts—not for no reason are they defined today as "visual arts."

The poetics of minimalism, of the reduction to the essential, that we are trying to practice, is a way to assume a critical attitude toward these phenomena. A critical attitude does not mean rejecting the instruments but rather trying to rearrange them at the level of means, related to the specificity of a "graphic design" and of its tradition—even the most ancient. Besides, the related exploration of small variations that is one of its specific characteristics stimulates the use of detail, the control of the value of the slightest movement in every dimension of the planning.

Walter Benjamin wrote in *L'abbecedario di cent'anni fa* [*The Primer of One Hundred Years Ago*]: "No building[. . .] no multimillionaire cottage has been the focus of a thousandth of the love of ornament that has instead been directed to the letters of the alphabet in the course of the history of culture." This is for us the very symbol not of visual communication, but of the visual value of human communication.

Graphic image for
XXXVII Biennale,
Venice 1976

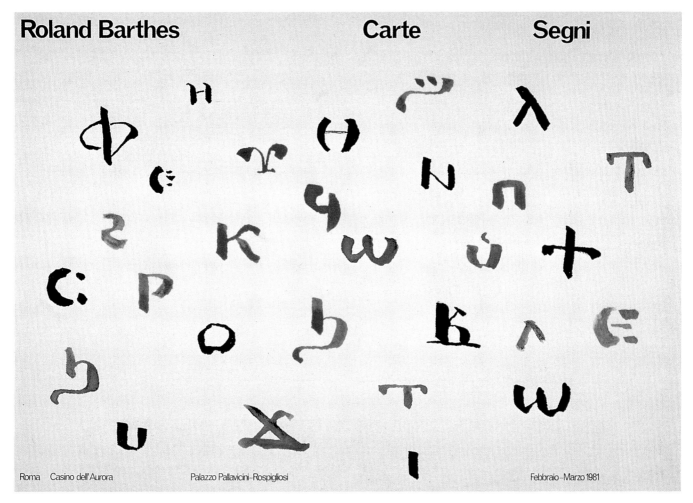

Poster for exhibition
Roland Barthes.
Carte. Segni
Palazzo Pallavicini
Rospigliosi,
Rome 1981

1. Poster for *Mario Merz* exhibit, Peggy Guggenheim Collection, Venice 1989

2. Poster for *Mario Merz* exhibit, Solomon R. Guggenheim Museum, New York 1989

3. Graphic image for exhibition *Futurismo e futurismi*, Palazzo Grassi, Venice 1986

4. Graphic image for Kunst-und Ausstellungshalle, Bonn 1992

1

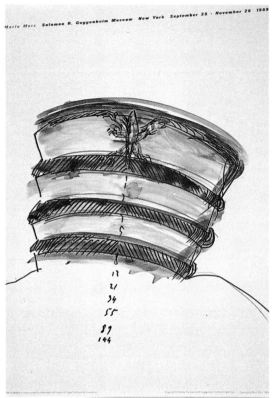

2

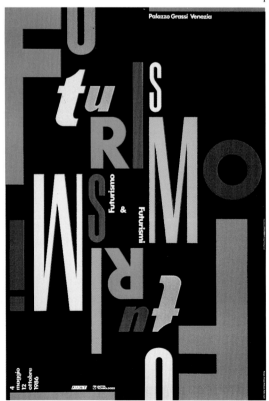

3

4

5. Poster for Polaroid
promotional campaign,
1988
6. Poster for conference
*Asiago: orientare il
futuro*, Asiago 1994
7. Graphic image
for Giuseppe Verdi
Symphony Orchestra

of Milan, Milan 1994
8. Poster for exhibition
*Ein Stück Großstadt
als Experiment,*
Deutsches Architektur
Museum, Frankfurt
1994

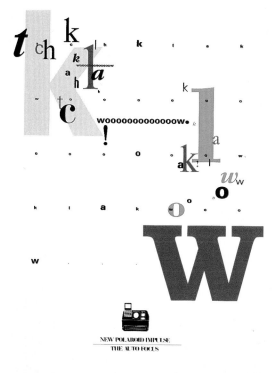

5

7

6

8

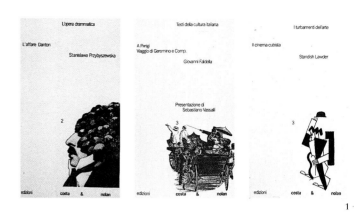

1

(Piet Zwart: L'opera tipografica 1923-1933/Piet Zwart: The Typographical Work 1923-1933)

(Architettura nelle riviste d'avanguardia/Architecture in the Avant-Garde Magazines)

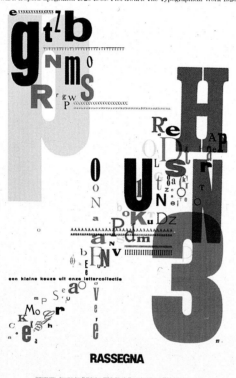

2

1. Book series for Costa & Nolan publishing company, 1982

2. Graphic project for magazine *Rassegna*, 1978–95

Raymond Queneau
Zazie nel metró

EINAUDI TASCABILI

Michel Tournier
**Venerdí
o il limbo del Pacifico**

Nuova edizione completa

EINAUDI TASCABILI

Miguel de Cervantes
Don Chisciotte della Mancia

Con un saggio di Eric Auerbach

Illustrazioni di Gustave Doré

Volume primo

EINAUDI TASCABILI

3

4

3. Book series for
Einaudi publishing
company, 1993
4. Graphic image for
Electa publishing
company, 1976–88

1. Logo for *Semiotic Studies* conference, 1973
2. Logo for book series *Hokuspokus*, Emme Edizioni, 1980
3. Logo for Textile Society of Como, 1981
4. Logo for O'Tool textile company, 1982
5. Logo for theater review
6. Logo for "Napoli 99" Foundation, 1984
7. Logo for exhibition *Civiltà delle Macchine*, Lingotto, Turin 1987–88
8. Invited competition for stamp of the XVII Triennale of Milan, 1985
9. Invited competition for stamp for Credito Industriale Sardo, 1988
10. Image for traveling exhibition *Achille Castiglioni*, 1984
11. Logo for book series *Lettere*, Rosellina Archinto publishing company, 1986
12. Logo for Piano Regolatore Generale (General Town Development Plan) of Turin, 1986
13. Logo for Fidis, 1988
14. Logo for Cosmit, 1989
15. Logo for Micheli Foundation, 1993
16. Logo for Palazzo Grassi, 1984
17. Logo for "EncycloMedia," 1994

1

2

3

7

8

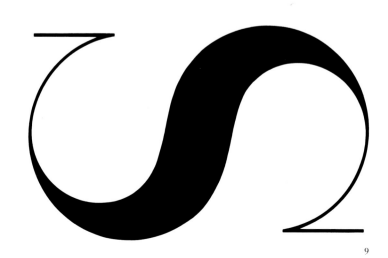

4

5

6

9

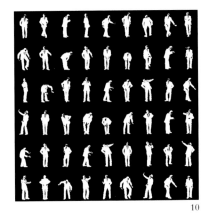

10

11

12

13

14

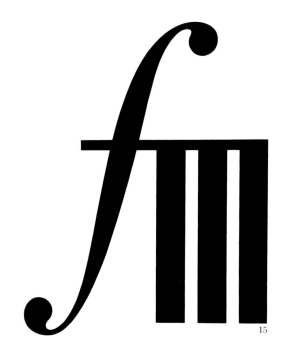

15

PALAZZOGRASSI

16

17

1

2

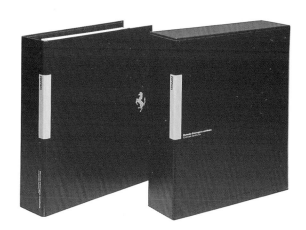

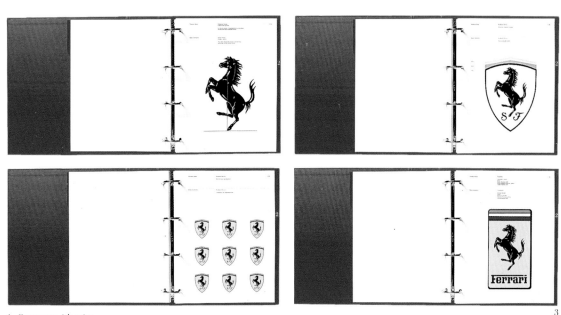

1. Corporate identity
manual *Pitti Immagine*,
1988
2. Manual for
coordinated image of city
spaces for *Italia 90*,
1988
3. Corporate identity
manual Ferrari Auto,
1994–95

3

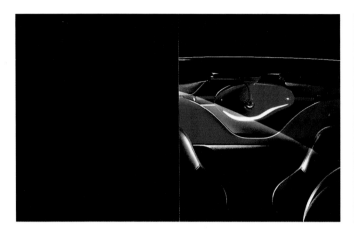
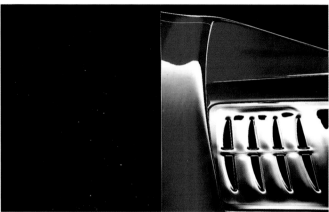
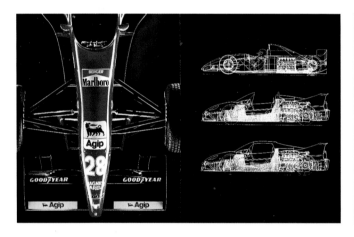
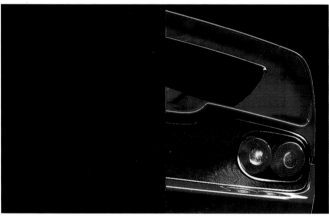

Corporate image for
Ferrari Auto, 1993–95

Coordinated image
for Unifor, 1982–95

Images for exhibit *Venti
progetti per il futuro
del Lingotto* [Twenty
projects for the future
of Lingotto], Lingotto,
Turin 1983

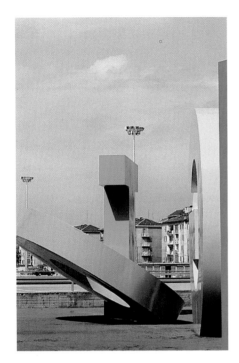

Geography, History, and Installation Principles

Starting in 1963, our firm turned to themes related to the notion of the installation principle and of context like geography and history. Coming into focus were questions that dated back to the mid-fifties and were connected to the discussion around the themes of tradition and belonging.

The constructed environment that surrounds us is, we believe, the physical manner of its history, the way in which it has been accumulated, according to layers and different meanings, to form the specificity of the site, not only how that environment appears visually but also what it is structurally. A place is built out of the traces of its own history.

If geography is the way to describe the solidification and overlapping of signs of history into a form, the task of architecture is to reveal, through the transformation of that form, the essence of the geographic-environmental context.

The environment then is not a system in which to dissolve architecture, but on the contrary, a supporting material for the architectural project; through the notions of site and the installation principle, it is the essence of the architectural operation. From this point of view, new principles and methods become possible which place in the foreground the strategy of relationship and placement, the means of putting oneself on the ground in direct confrontation with the specific area, having a knowledge of the context through its modification.

The "modification" also reveals the consciousness of being a part of a preexistent whole, the transformation induced in the whole system from a change in one of its parts.

Through the etymological root that associates it with the concept of size, the modification then joins with the geometric world of regulated things. It is this modification that, through the rules of geometry, recognizes and transforms the place into a thing of architecture, that establishes the original and at the same time symbolic act of connecting with the soil, with the idea of nature as a totality of present things, through the construction of the installation principle.

The origin of architecture is not, as we have repeatedly stated, in the hut, or in the cave, or in the mythical "Adam's house in Paradise." Before transforming the support into a column, the roof into a tympanum, before laying stone upon stone, man put a stone on the ground in order to recognize the place in the middle of the unknown universe—to measure it and modify it. Like each act of measure, it requires gestures of drastic, apparent simplicity.

From this point of view, there are only two great ways to place oneself in relation to the context. The tools of the first way are mimetic imitation, organic assimilation, clear complexity. The tools of the second way are measurement, distance, definition, the overturning within the complexity.

We believe in this second way for the very reason that, through the specific tools of the discipline, it does not propose impossible reconciliations between the natural and the artificial, between the new and the preexistent, but it establishes its own sense of the quality of that specific noncoincidence. This way is based on a series of acts of restless division: raise a wall, construct an enclosure, define areas, produce a tightly articulated interior that compares with the fragmentation of the compartments or a simple exterior that is offered as a measure of the complexity of the great level of architecture of the environment, great not in the sense of physical dimension but in how it possesses a great capacity for contextual change.

In order to construct the project it is necessary first of all to establish a rule. This has to do essentially with the tradition of the style and the profession and with its advancement. That which gives architectural truth and concreteness to the rule, however, is its encounter with the site: only the experience of the site gives birth to the exceptions that unfold to form architecture.

From Vittorio Gregotti, "L'architettura dell'ambiente" [Architecture of the environment], in *Casabella*, no. 482, July–August 1982; reprinted in *Questioni di Architettura. Editoriali di "Casabella,"* edited by G. Vragnaz (Turin: Giulio Einaudi Editore, 1986).

New Seat for the Università degli Studi

Partners: E. Battisti, V. Gregotti, H. Matsui,
P. Nicolin, F. Purini, C. R. Clerici, B. Viganò
Invited competition
Cosenza 1973

1

A linear structure 3200 meters long intersects the hills of the Crati Valley, containing, according to the installation principle of alignment and discontinuity, the buildings of 21 university departments. Their square-plan blocks are connected above ground level at the height of the beams of an outfitted metal bridge, which also links the projected station to the two main railway lines and to the connection between the north–south and east–west highways. The plan of the departments is built on a module of 25.5 × 25.5 meters which extends to a depth of two modules on the sides of the organizing axis.

The high blocks, connected at the bridge on three levels—pedestrian, mechanical, and carriage services—by a thin, vertical service structure, vary from five to two floors and are closed by partitions that support a system interlaced with metal beams. The natural light of the interiors is obtained by windows and skylights, screened by sun-dispersing elements. The 250-seat, stepped lecture halls are suspended between two side-blocks, maintaining in this way the continuity of the natural slope and of the underlying routes. The university service areas are placed at the intersections of the bridge system and the roads on the ridge perpendicular to it, where the structure widens to form four large piazzas. This arrangement establishes a significant relation between the didactic system, the residential units, and the service areas.

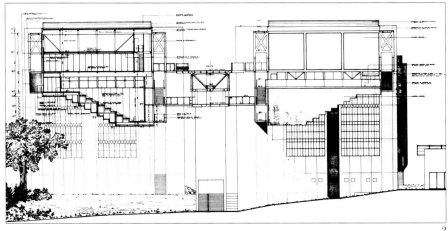

2

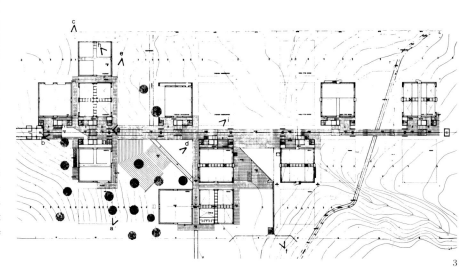

3

1. View of several
departments
2. Transverse section
of a block of stepped
lecture halls
3. Plan of several
departments
4, 5. Views of study
model for a standard
block
6. View of chemistry
department
7. General perspective
of Crati Valley

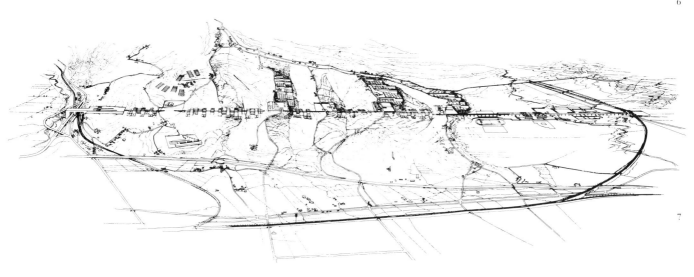

8

8. Stepped lecture hall
of chemistry department
9. Perspective drawing
of bridge near
humanities department
10. Side view of
humanities department

11. Perspective drawing
of chemistry and
humanities departments
12. Interior view
13. View of pedestrian
level of bridge

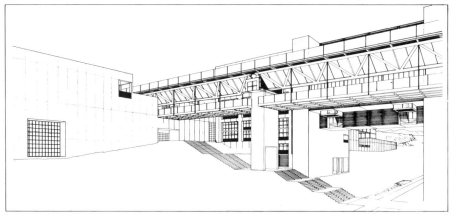

9

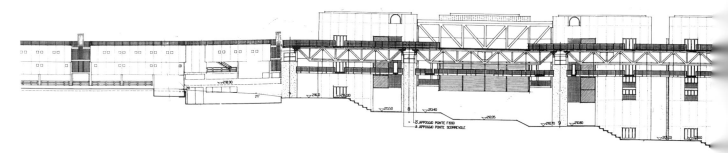

11

12

13

10

12

13

11

Archeological Park
at the Imperial Forums

Partner: L. Benevolo
Rome 1984

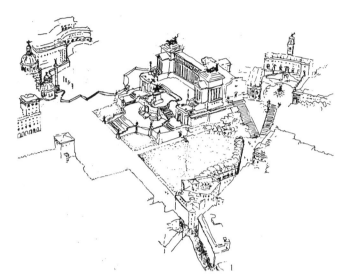

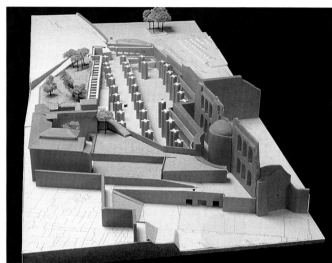

The intervention is part of a comprehensive project that includes the areas of the Imperial Forums, the Forum Romanum, the Colosseum, the Circus Maximus, and parts of the Oppian, Celian, and Palatine hills. Interpreting the superimposition of the three urban fabrics—imperial city, papal city, and post-unification city—the projects of the seventeen "problem areas" into which the intervention is subdivided lead to a historical-philological reflection on those relationships, on the design of parks and border areas, toward a clarification of general morphological rules. The intervention on the area of the Colosseum is an exemplary case. On the large open area determined by the opening of the Via dei Fori Imperiali, the volume of the ancient Velian hill is reconstructed to cover the new archeological museum. The roofing, restored to its original garden state, and the entrance fronts of the museum become functional as links to the different contexts that are present. Toward the area of the Colosseum the proposed layout redesigns the open spaces, eliminates automobile traffic, and

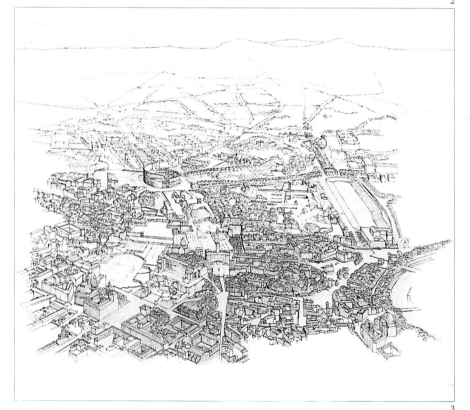

1. Sketch for layout
of area between
the Campidoglio
and the Ara Coeli
2. Study model
of museum
3. Overall view from
northwest
4. General plan
of forum area
5. Study sketches
for museum
6. Zenith view
of model

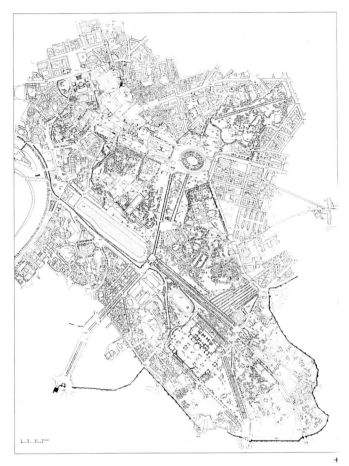

rearranges, inside a continuous surface of green, the spatial system of the surrounding large monuments. The entrance levels to the museum (+17m toward the Foro della Pace [Forum of Peace] and +23m near the Colosseum) determine the base heights of the longitudinal crossing of the interior space, conceived as a large continuous room whose roofing is supported by a series of large cruciform pillars faced in brick, with interaxials of 15m. The exhibit space, totaling 8600 square meters, projects 3600 square meters of storage and services, at a height of +27m, situated near the entrance of the Foro della Pace. From the inside, the height of the overlooking garden is revealed by the zenith light that descends along the cut that separates the ancient wall near the Basilica di Maxentius from the roofing.

Another element of connection is formed by a passageway that, cutting across the museum, connects the great terracing of the Basilica di Maxentius, integrated into the exhibit space, the Villa Rivaldi complex, and on the opposite side, the offices of the Sovrintendenza (the archaeological service) in Santa Maria Nova.

4

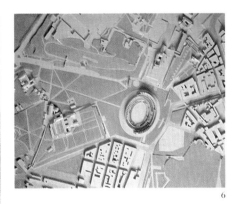

6

5

Plan for Low-income Housing

Cefalù, Palermo 1976–79

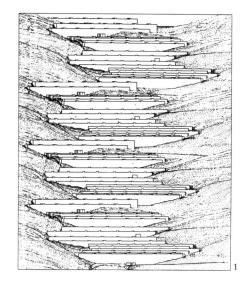

The area envisioned by the zoning plan for the installation of 3500 inhabitants extends along the S. Elia gorge on a surface of approximately 26 hectares [about 64-1/4 acres], with a linear development of 700 meters north–south on a gradient of 100 meters. The project takes advantage of the site's mountainous terrain, arranging a system of buildings transversally to the valley, as if to protect the fabric of the old city from the fringing of the suburbs. The location was chosen to rebalance development near Palermo, reassigning a fundamental role to the historical buildings and to the stronghold. The new installation establishes a complex relationship between natural support and artificial construction: repeating the buildings sequentially at successive heights, the total size is determined, from which the architectural scale of individual buildings is derived. The eight screenlike structures are made up of two parallel bodies, with an interior interval of 15 meters; neighborhood services form a margin asymmetrical to the central street, whose constant incline sets the counterpoint to the installation rule. The typical unit is a longitudinal building 155 meters long with a depth of 12 meters. It rises one story off the ground, against which the ends of the units are supported, defining the number of accommodations which are connected two by two by a stairway. The roof is intended as a parking garage or as a park for public use.

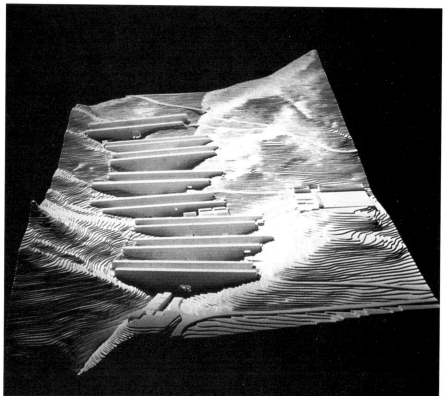

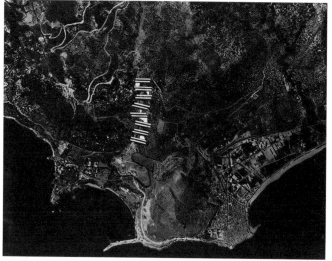

1. Perspective sketch of valley
2. View of model
3. General plan (photomontage)

72

Tourist Terminal
and Restructuring
of the Roadways

Republic of San Marino 1981

Not wishing to provide an exclusively technical response to the problem of traffic, the project transforms the empty urban space under the Porta di San Francesco into an arrival-landing for the city. Here the bus station, the multilevel parking garage, the public buildings, and the commercial services are involved in defining a new architectural organism that must morphologically and typologically confront the specific configuration of the place, assuming both urban and territorial value. The strong differences in height between the various parts of the city are overcome by ramps and mechanical pedestrian lifts placed in the two retaining walls which contain and emphasize the sequence of piazzas. Beneath them the car-parking areas are located. The only part actually built is the public services building on the area of the former Silo Molino Forni. Placed as the top of a high building spine, the new edifice consolidates it and defines the front, assuming the generative elements of the original project through the elevated placement and favorable panorama.

1. Axonometric drawing of tourist terminal
2. View of service building
3. Bird's-eye view from east

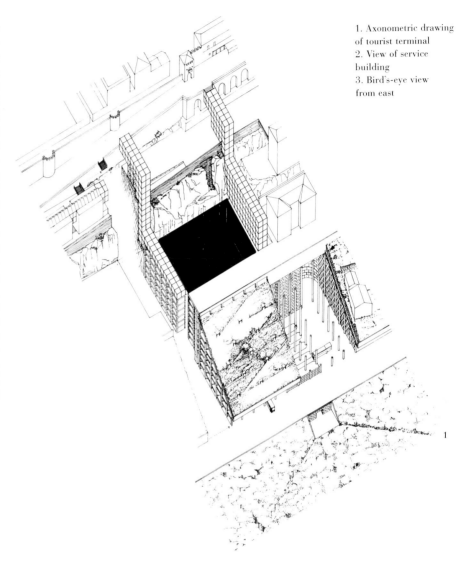

1

2

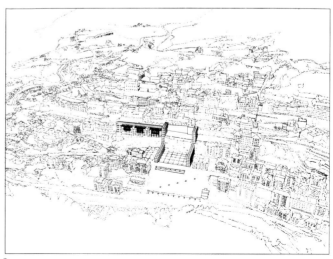

3

IBM Technology Center

Santa Palomba, Rome 1986

1

The project works toward the identification of completed parts and hierarchies of identifiable spaces in the various stages of the complex's development. With the same objective, the small existing tracks, the rows of trees, the opportunities offered by the gradients and slopes, and the relation to nearby shops designed by Marco Zanuso are all taken on as supporting elements of the project.

Planned for the first stage of the complex's execution are the main entrance, office block, calculation center, and cafeteria with general services. These four elements refer to a triangular central piazza, defined near the ridge of the hill by the main entrance structure and the curve of the cafeteria. The building of the calculation center is perpendicular to the existing factory and is built on axis with one of its towers. Provided with two floors and endowed with lateral and zenith lighting, it houses on the lower floor the power stations of the installation, accessible at the level of the factory. The office building is arranged around four cloisters; its interior arrangement is characterized by double-height spaces lighted from above and by stairs arranged axially. The access road that ends at the main entrance building gradually reaches the height of the piazza, embedding itself in the natural ground and in this way blocking the view of the parking lot, which is placed at the height of the natural ground and densely planted.

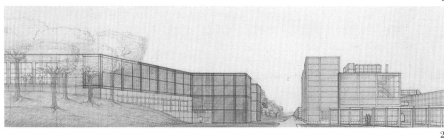

2

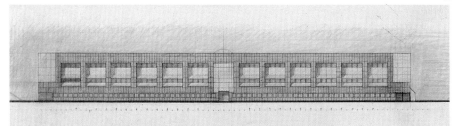

3

1. Drawing of new complex from south
2. Drawing of area between plant and technology center
3. Study of south facade
4. View of model from south

4

Study for the Reorganization of the Colle Cidneo

Brescia 1988

1. General plan
2. Plan of layout
   of castle area
3. Plan and section of
   reorganized ascent from
   San Giorgio church

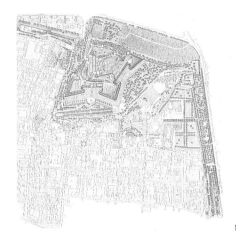

1

The study considers the possible function and significance that the city must have assigned to the Colle Cidneo, the defensive stronghold and very ancient, central settlement area.

The area dominated by a castle—approximately one-fifth the expanse of the walled city—has a marginal role today in the life of the city; it is the location of facilities that are random with respect to the place, like sports facilities or secondary facilities like a zoo and parking. The project takes off from a reflection of a wide spectrum that assesses different possible options, entrusting to the entire area and to the castle the function of place in the historical memory of the city.

Refuting a destination as a fully equipped park, the proposal suggests, within a horizon of civic and cultural references, a destination for the hill as a historical park, a place of reflection and memory. Thus making the layers of the city apparent, the project envisions the extension of the size of the park with the aim of making a public park having totally new attributes: separated from city traffic, with improved pedestrian accessibility and a better physical image. The hill will be freed from inappropriate functions; it will be uncrowded, recreating a historical expressivity formed by various parts now linked by the new condition of the park.

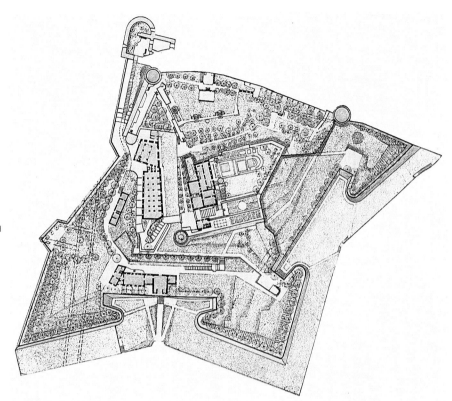

2

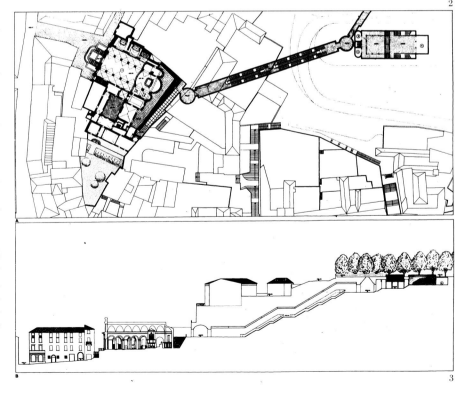

3

75

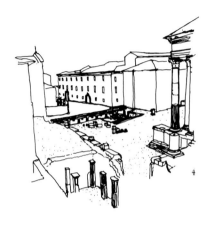

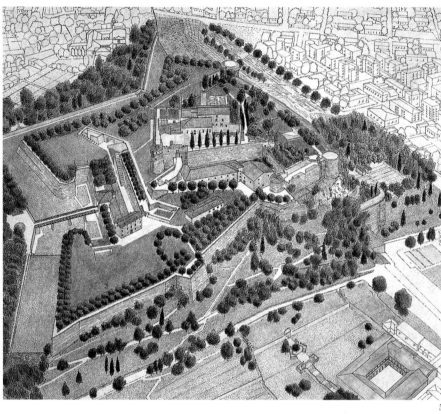

5

6

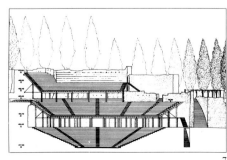

7

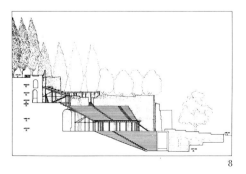

8

4. Study sketch of
archeological remains
near forum piazza
5. Perspective of castle
from east
6. 7. 8. Study
sketch and sections
for reconstruction
of Roman theater

Reorganization of the Ascent
to the Old City

Potenza 1991–93

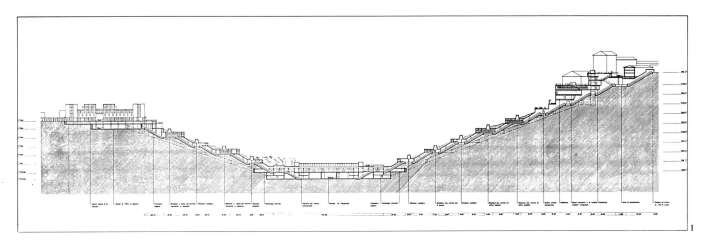

The project for connecting the districts of Portasalza and Cocuzzo, at the two sides of the Vallone di S. Lucia, and the need for connection with the suburbs assume a value of a guiding sort, with the prospect of transforming the Vallone [gorge] itself into a city park.

Outside the consolidated historical nucleus, which preserves a specific urban identity notwithstanding post-war enlargements, peripheral nuclei are formed whose nature is characterized by chance arrangement and by the absence of urban poles of reference. The resulting dispersion is accentuated by the topographic complexity, whose qualities were not used to their full advantage. One of the principal concerns during the planning process was to construct a guiding, connecting structure, which would utilize the steep terrain without being dishonest and at the same time would offer that element of order to one part of the city system.

To reach such objectives the project provides for the construction of a connecting structure that, first of all, does not jeopardize the future city park of the Vallone of S. Lucia and allows the greatest number of routes and points of view possible. It also enriches with small differentiated services the two structures at the top and bottom of the valley in such a way as to establish two points of the city from well-defined morphological and environmental identities.

The project of connection is therefore made up of system of mechanized routes that will put the bottom of the valley in contact with both the old city and the Cocuzzo district. Thus a two-fold objective is reached: the first, to construct a new access to the city, which resolves the problem of traffic and parking in the old city, creating a new "door," away from the center but able to represent a valid alternative relative to both parking and the presence of services of common interest; the second, to devise a new possibility of pedestrian movement between the two parts of the city, through a convenient and quick route, but at the same time measured by that richness of opportunities and events usually typical only of central places in cities.

1. General section
2. Plan

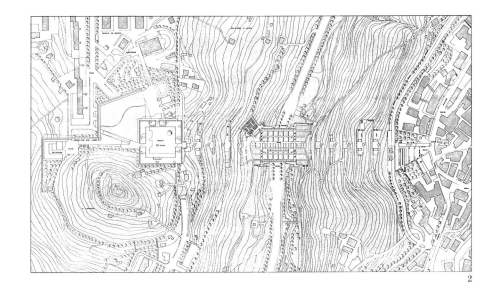

2

Project for a New City of 150,000 Inhabitants

Partners: C. A. Barbieri, C. Bertelli, P. Gelmini,
G. Martinotti, B. Secchi, D. Siniscalco, G. B. Zorzoli
Invited international competition
Ukraine 1992

Communication and accessibility, small advanced production, connection with the university, and environmental livability characterize this new place. Planned are an intercontinental airport and a railway pole from which depart the connection system to the new urban areas; functions relating to exchange and business line up along a central axis, which reaches the new harbor. The city is arranged around this structural axis like an archipelago of towns of approximately 30,000 inhabitants each. Two are flanked by the axis and three others protrude toward the existing bordering installations. This leads to an open configuration, turned toward a large central park (Peace Park) in which the city's most representative activities are gathered. Around the administrative seat and government office are arranged the main churches of the different religions, the places intended for shows, and the international learning centers. Each town, organized on a regular network, is characterized by the presence of a specific collective function, but integrated with the entire city (university, sports, health, etc.). With the exception of the harbor areas, the coast remains unchanged and for pedestrian use. Energy is produced by cogeneration power plants; solid waste is collected mechanically and transported to a recovery and energy production plant; collected liquid waste is carried away to a water purifier. In the central axis an underground distribution system for goods is also planned. The crown of outer forests and the parks inserted within the towns ensure a far-reaching biological protection and a strong wind barrier.

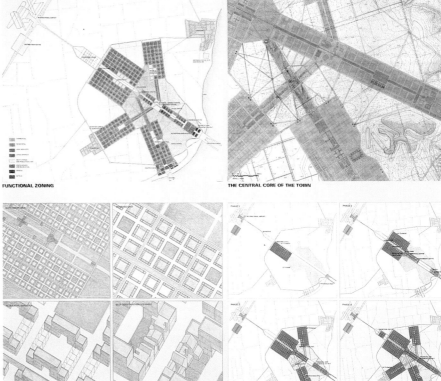

FUNCTIONAL ZONING

THE CENTRAL CORE OF THE TOWN

1. Localization of project
2. Plans for constructing settlement
3. View of model from southeast

3

4

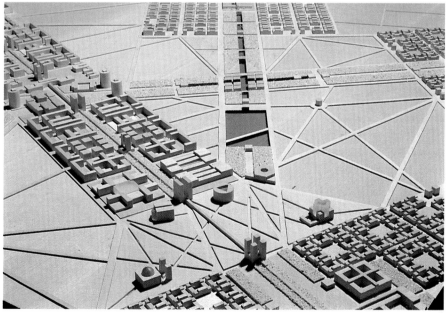

4. Sketch plan
5. Bird's-eye view
of central area

5

Cultural Center of Belém

Partners: Risco, M. Salgado
Invited international competition
Lisbon 1988–93

Placed in proximity of the shores of the wide estuary of the Tagus, in direct confrontation with the large monastery of Los Jeronimós and with a small and fragile urban fabric, the Cultural Center of Belém faces the problem of installing a large architectural project between a monumental edifice and a preexisting urban fabric.

Seat in 1992 of the Presidency of the European Economic Community, the building, with a longitudinal extent of 400 meters, exhibits a predominantly horizontal spread, which connects it with both the monumental zone of Belém and the tower of the same name on the banks of the Tagus. An axial pedestrian walkway

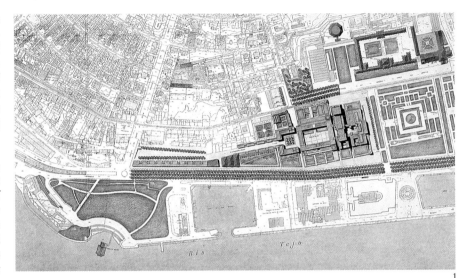

1

2

1. Plan
2. View of main front
on Praça do Imperio
3. Detail of side near
the Tagus

4

4. View of main front
5. Central pedestrian
walkway near Praça
do Imperio
6. Study sketch for side
of theater

7. View along central
pedestrian walkway
with skylight of
museum entrance hall
8. Exhibition center
square

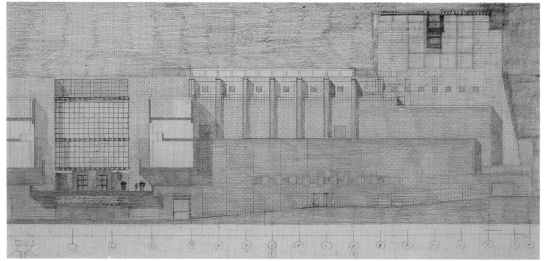

5

7

8

9. General plan at
height of +9.00m
10. Transverse section
of theater center

11. Transverse section
of exhibition center
12. Longitudinal
section along
pedestrian walkway

on multiple levels organizes a system of spaces which suggest urban complexity while maintaining the sequence of open spaces, the predominant characteristic on the river front.

A sequence of functional blocks, arranged perpendicularly to the main route, find their morphological tie to the contextual conditions through a series of transversal connecting streets. The main pedestrian walkway is characterized by the rhythm of the sequence of differentiated spaces and by the lateral foreshortened views on the service streets that intersect it.

The dimensions of the main front to the east conform to those of the monastery of Los Jeronimos, while the facade itself represents the characteristics of the institution to be housed. In fact, in this building are found, divided into three blocks, the EEC Council, consulting rooms of the prime ministers and commissioners, meeting rooms, all necessary services, a large auditorium, a 1500-seat opera house, and an exhibition center.

The pedestrian walkway leads to the cornerstone of the intervention in the large public square of the museum. Spaces for temporary exhibitions for a total of 8000 square meters are found beneath the square, while the permanent museum rooms are placed in the buildings forming its perimeter. The garden terraces, facing the river and the city, hold the outdoor exhibits. At the western end of the complex, the hotels and complementary furnishings include an eighteenth-century building that faces Rua Bartolomeo Diaz to the north.

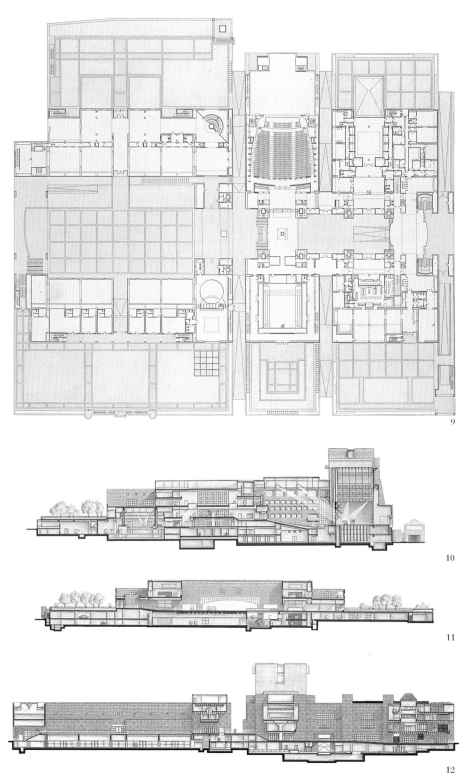

9

10

11

12

13. Auditorium
14. View of interior
layout of conference
center
15. Foyer for theaters

Geography, History, and Installation Principles

13

14

15

16

16. 17. Opera house
18. Foreshortened view
of an exhibition space

17

18

Multi-fuel Off-Shore Power Station

Partner: Ismes
1987–90

The theme of the project concerns the architectonic configuration of a large electric power station of 660 MW, to be placed in the open sea at a distance from the coast of approximately 12 miles. Preceded by a complex interdisciplinary feasibility study, the morphological definition is addressed on two lines of research. The first proposes a general plan with three different solutions regarding the protection dam for the docking of ships. Complying with Enel's standard for production parts, the entire system is "fitted" with concrete panels mounted on a steel structure. The large hall of the turbine-alternators is redesigned, while the services are arranged inside a slab lit from above and endowed with inside patios. The entire power station is floating, assembled on land on large platforms (160 × 199 × 21m) transported, submerged, and resting on the bottom. The second course of work was directed toward the total morphological aspect, establishing an articulated division between pier, island, and the space of the calm basin. The proposal institutes a dual order in the scale of perception: one at a great distance, regulated by the elements of the production parts of considerable height and two, the order of perception of the containment dam. The project is directed to regulate the relationships of scale in the comparison between the very large size of the manufactured structure and the abstract surface of the sea.

1. Zenith view of model
2. Perspective drawing

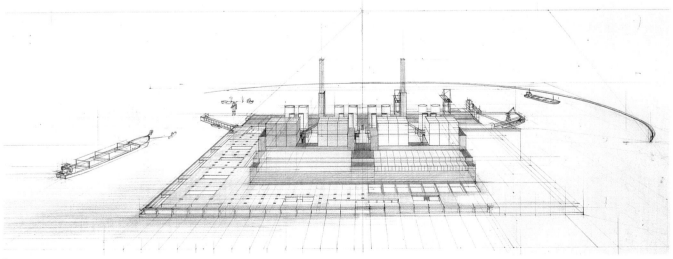

2

Studies for several parts
of the plant

Typology and Context

This attempts to be, to use a rhetorical term, a "demonstration to the contrary." Starting from three samples of the same typology, the insufficient relevance of type in architectural planning today will be demonstrated.

Beginning from the particular edifice, the stadium, for example—until today the engineer's domain—I would like to show the need and urgency for architecture to reacquire large-scale technical objects and, more generally, to reopen a dialogue with the culture of the new engineers.

Beginning with the very important discussion of the empirical-technical contents, such as material for the construction of the project, we wish to point out their indispensable effectiveness but insufficient respect for foundation of the installation.

Beginning from the idea of the inseparability of project and construction, I claim in the first place the rights of the project as disciplinary theory and, through it, as judgment and theory about social conditions. The stadium is a cult place for mass society and at the same time the space where imitations of its personal and collective conflicts are played out: the very metaphor of war. It is the symbol of the fixation of immediate action by means of image in its truth and, at the same time, of the interpretative falsification that completes the amplification of communication.

Rejecting the edifice and replacing it with an event scenario that demands, in a particularly evident way, a general reflection on the architecture of the city and territory as stage scenery, decoration, and background to, rather than as representation and witness of, social events: this is a role that naturally I refuse, but one whose diffusion I cannot not observe.

Since for us the initial act of architecture is not the construction but rather the delimitation—the marking of the place with a trail, an edge, a border—the stadium, a three-dimensional enclosure, is identified with a distant form, a form of apparition in which the primary value of the installation principle is at one with its spatial expression.

Finally, the publication of these stadiums may pose the problem of comparison of the architect's social statute in different European countries during these years and of the importance of conditions of institutional and productive advancement in relation to the successful execution of the project. In addition, there is a need for understanding the technical task of the architect and his position in the cycle of building production.

From a different point of view it would also be important to discuss the possible role of architecture in intellectual thought and in social transformation, even if this is not very fashionable. This does not at all mean to judge an architectural work on the basis of its intentions nor to look for its truth in critical or poetic interpretations. It means only to consider that it is the concrete expression of the capacity for organized creative thought, produced by complex arrangement, like a theatrical or a cinematographic work: in any case, the outcome of an extensive, patient, multiple, and conscious effort that more easily carries through or away the impure debris of an entire historical stratum of the social contexture. It is an age-old question, interpretable in different ways but structurally inescapable.

Cf. Vittorio Gregotti, "Cinque paesaggi urbani," in AA. VV., *Cinque dialoghi necessari*, Quaderni di Lotus, no. 14 (Milan: Electa, 1990)

Olympic Stadium

Partners: Corma (C. Buxadé, F. Correa,
J. Margarit, A. Milà), Inco (S. Zorzi)
Invited international competition
Barcelona 1986–88

The competition project for the center for the 1992 Olympic Games included the existing stadium, the sports building, the physical education center and the press center through the layout of a large enclosure that would have arranged these elements symmetrically around a central space 430 meters long, completed by outdoor playing fields and swimming pools. The only part that was actually built is the stadium.

Preserving the facades designed in 1929 by Domenech y Montaner Jr., the total capacity was increased, taking it from 20,000 to 65,000 seats plus all the related services. Lowered by 12 meters, the field accordingly redesigned the stands in the lower part beginning from the track, while the upper part follows the linear progression of the preexisting structures on the perimeter.

Particular attention is placed on the design of the interior spaces under the bleachers. In the upper stand made of precompressed reinforced concrete, these are characterized by a series of circular forms which allow the light to filter into the foyers below and by a vision of the surrounding countryside, illustrating the complex relationship between the new parts and the preexisting structure.

On the outside, the large white metallic roofing of the main stand, suspended from two longitudinal beams of 65 meters of light, is the only element indicative of the transformation that took place.

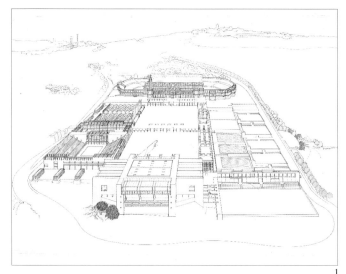

1. Perspective drawing of project for Olympic athletic installations (competition project)
2. Detail of side from south
3. Bird's-eye view from southwest
4. 5. Plans of middle and upper levels of bleachers

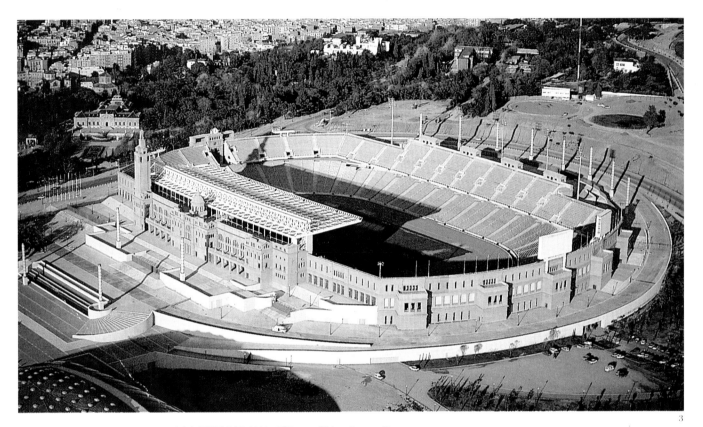

3

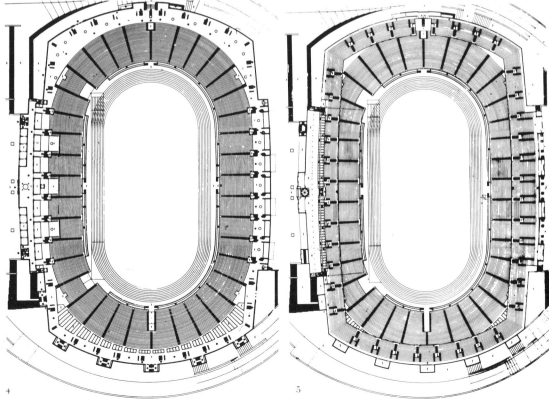

4   5

6. View of hall under
main stand
7. Foreshortened view
of foyer under bleachers
to south
8. Transverse section
of main stand
9. View of layout under
bleachers

6

7

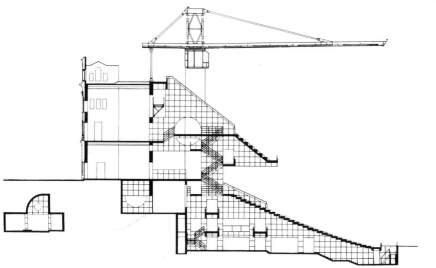

8

9

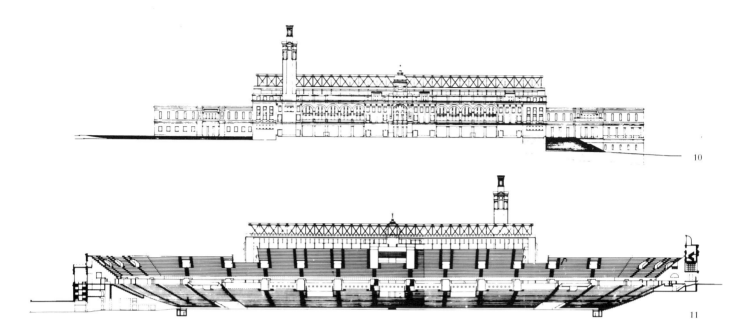

10

11

10. View of west side
11. Longitudinal
section toward west
12. "La Puerta
de Maradon"
(Marathon Gate)

12

Restructuring
the Luigi Ferraris Stadium

Genoa 1986

The project takes into consideration a complex series of limitations and objectives. These included rigorous adherence to the boundaries of the area occupied by the previous stadium, construction in stages to allow it to function during the building, provision for multiple services in the area, and an overall capacity of more than 44,000 covered seats. Inserted into the tight fabric of the city, the stadium is redefined in relation to the urban texture in which it is located, pursuing the goal of a strongly unified image. Four piazzas improve the systems of pedestrian descending traffic and the relationship with the functions on the ground, allowing at the same time reabsorption of the different planimetric and altimetric geometries of the stands. The four towers which are attached at the corners of the piazzas become, like the metallic roofing, an important element in the formal unity. The rationalization of security systems finds a solution in ample colonnades on the ground floor from which it is possible to enter the small gymnasiums and area services.

1. Bird's-eye view from north
2. Section of stands
3. Plan of ground floor with proposed partial covering of the Bisagno stream
4. View of west facade
5. View from northwest
6. Detail of one of corner piazzas
7. Foreshortened view of east facade

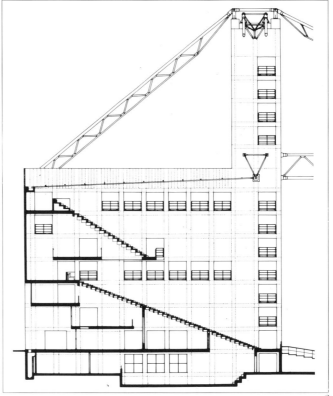

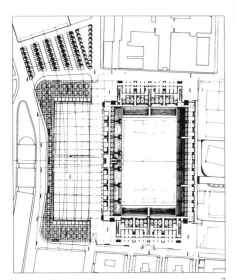

5

6

7

8. View of corner tower
9. 10. 11. Details of
bleachers and layout
under bleachers

8

9

10

11

Sports Complex

Partners: March Chausse, Beterem
Invited international competition
Nîmes 1986

Originating from an idea about the typological tradition of the stadium, the project rejects the characteristics of monofunctionality, standardization, and indifference to context and proposes an integrated body in a position to respond to the demand of continuous use.

Located in an area of recent urbanization, the new building strengthens the new urban layout founded on diagonals that depart from a central hemicycle.

The steps of the stadium, created on an elevation in the ground that was outside the original urbanization project and left under grass, connect with the ground level and are defined by four buildings, each 13 meters high, that house the vertical routes, service areas, and complementary, integrated functions.

Physically and functionally independent of the stadium, in a separate piazza in front, are the ticket-selling areas, a large gymnasium, a fencing room, a billiard hall, and an exhibition space.

The project is completed by a sports palace for 5000 spectators, equipped with gymnasiums and areas for nonathletic activities; it is located on the same axis as the stadium, recovering planned geometric principles as organizing elements for this area.

Next to the sports palace, a small pavilion for temporary fairs and exhibitions was erected in 1994.

1

1. View of northwest corner
2. Foreshortened view of north facade

2

3. Overall view of south
facade
4. General plan
of project
   A Stadium
   B Sports palace
   C Pavilion for
   temporary fairs
5. Detail of stands
to south
6. View of north facade
of sports palace

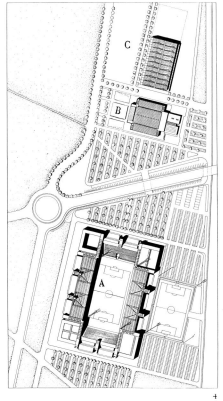

4

5

3

6

7

Sports Palace
7. Interior view
8. Detail of front
toward stadium

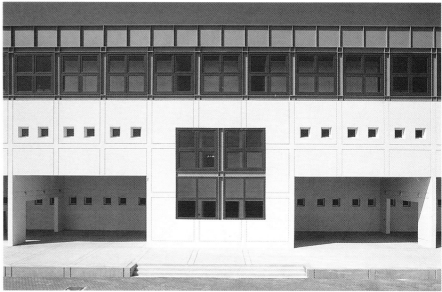

8

Two Cities

Sometimes it happens that an architectural study deals repeatedly with cases in one city, intervening at many points or constructing theories on the whole body of important parts of that city. Considering the character but also the difficulty of the city, two different ways of confronting this situation may be consolidated: to manage the decadence of Venice as an ancient city or to attempt to rebuild the central area there within a different urban and territorial framework. People considered sensible seem traditionally connected to the first way; different attempts at speculation seem connected to the second. But it is not like that, the truth has long since been more complicated.

In the first case we are dealing with emphasizing the characteristics of the city-as-museum, of the tourist-administrative monoeconomy, until having to drain the access to the old city: the same services necessary to this perspective will be forced into a gradual displacement outside the area of the old city. The result will certainly be able to ensure to a substantial group of inhabitants a secure and satisfactory income. This would be a city to visit on fixed schedule, a city with gates that close in the evening, where it would be necessary to engage, in the most common parts, in a kind of theatrical disguise so as to make them completely consistent with the client's dream.

A second vision is one of conceiving of Venice as the heart of a much more robust and complex spread-out city, from Mestre to the outer canal of the Lagoon, from the Lido to the city islands, whose possibilities and activities would first of all have to be divided in a synergetic way and then to be used in a plan suited to the specific qualities of the environmental conditions. These conditions today allow a wide range of possibilities of simultaneous activity, precisely as a function of the environmental quality and of the kind of life that we can think of constructing there. In this perspective, which is certainly more risky, it is not only the use of the different parts of the city that assumes a new logic and possibility—including providing Mestre with a decent urban appearance, attributing several central functions to the city islands, reorganizing the harbor activity without hoping for too much, and rendering a project for tourist activity—but also the same question of residences in Venice is presented from a new point of view: not only to fill a need but to become an important element in reversing a trend.

Since the early seventies, Berlin has been at the center of interest of study, with historical work on the subject of the architecture of expressionism in 1960 and then, on various occasions, of seminars or debates that unfolded after I.B.A. shows. Beginning from the construction, in 1981, of the apartment building of Lützowplatz, a fragment of a larger reorganization project of the area, the competition projects to which we were invited were numerous. In 1990, with Berlin Morgen, we tried to propose a complex contribution to the reconstruction of the central part of the city, a contribution on which the different individual projects depend.

Berlin has become one of the most intensely literary cities in the European consciousness. Focused on it is the most radical sense of the rending of the urban unity of the European old city through the events of the last half century. In the context of our discipline it is certain that Berlin will be decisive proof of the capacity of architectural culture to imagine the urban design of the European city of the third millennium. It will be necessary from one side to be able to exploit thoroughly and in the collective interest the exceptional public patrimony of the former East Germany, which will offer occasions of historical redesign if it is able to withstand the ideology of the marketplace as an absolute positive value. Planning and articulation must be able to marry in the interest of the monumental and environmental historical patrimony, avoiding the blackmail of both conservative and ecological fundamentalism, while making a point of strength and reference for renewal out of that patrimony. It will be necessary to avoid monumental modernism such as stylistic decorativism, as well as certain technological attitudes such as the purely formal self-referential experiment.

New Shipyards for the Venice Municipal Transport Industry

Venice 1980

The project, located on the area once occupied by the Naval Docks and Workshops of Venice, is intended as a connecting system between typologically differentiated elements.

The entrance to the shipyard, facing the city front, is created out of a preexisting building. The front toward the Lagoon, the workshop building, arranged on a square module of 15 x 15 meters, and the roofing system for the manufacture on water of large naval ships recall the characteristics of industrial construction in bricks and iron, typical of the island of the Giudecca.

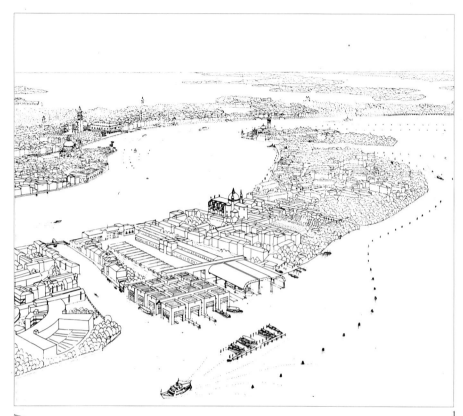

1. Bird's-eye view of project at the island of Giudecca
2. Foreshortened drawing along interior canal

3. Perspective section of workshop
4. Plan

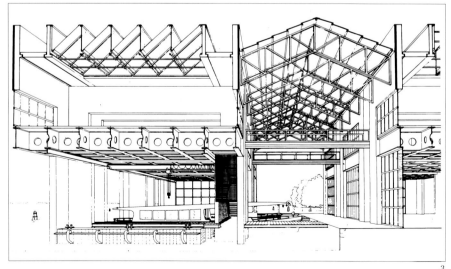

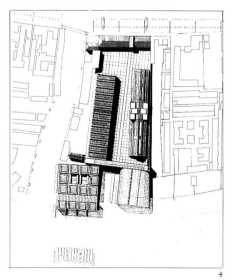

Study of Accessibility
and Detailed Plan
of Tronchetto Island

Venice 1980

1

The proposal for the detailed plan of Tronchetto Island is part of broader study for the reorganization of access to the Lagoon city: its objective is to use the potentials of the infrastructural system in reorganizing the disjointed image of the eastern area that lies near the cross-lagoon bridge.

A linear bridge structure passes over the railway office, doubling back to Santa Lucia station and connecting for pedestrians the district of Cannaregio with the system designed for Tronchetto Island. In this way the problem is solved of the external circular lines of public navigation, presently obstructed by the Ponte della Libertà, ensuring the closure of the lagoon-route ring, decongesting the Grand Canal, and distributing the tourist traffic throughout the areas that border the old city.

A new structure connects to Tronchetto Island, redefining the fragmented edge of the city's outskirts and completing the Grand Canal with the image of a continuous portico on the water, analogous to the San Marco basin.

The new street connection is presented with a complex section that includes the main pedestrian walkway, with small commercial facilities and a pier for docking boats.

2

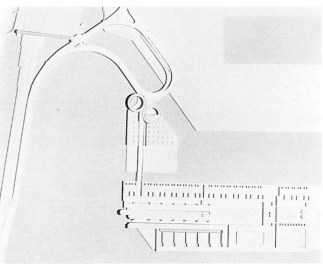

3

1. Perspective from
new bridge
2. General perspective
3. Zenith view
of model

Residential District in Cannaregio

Venice 1981–94

The project is based on the completion and strengthening of the existing structure, characterized by a combed building arrangement on the Cannaregio canal, emphasizing the role of interrelated, open spaces, and order. The extended courtyard typology is consistent with the establishment of a hierarchy following the characteristics and dimensions of the "calle" (Venice's narrow streets), joining to the Campo Lungo (the regulating element of the connecting systems), the main pedestrian walkway and public space rich in commercial activity and public services. Other building units are defined on it with their own special elements, like the building to the south, placed on the border of the area, characterized by the double-height portico on the axis of the Campo. The configuration of the open spaces, the "calle," Campo Lungo, Campo Verde, and the canal, and their architectural control become the real regulating elements of the system, the principles for the architectonic definition of the buildings. They develop an idea of architecture that assumes the concept of difference as the specificity of individual solutions in relation to their context. Attachment to the ground becomes the opportunity for maximum articulation of the buildings in relation to the contextual conditions. The completion of upper parts is also an opportunity for development of the Venetian theme of the roof-terrace. Particular attention is directed toward the typological study of lodgings, thereby benefiting the relationship between interior and exterior through the adoption of zone-day passages, the care for the private exterior spaces, the solutions in the points of similarity between the structures of the project and pre-existing buildings.

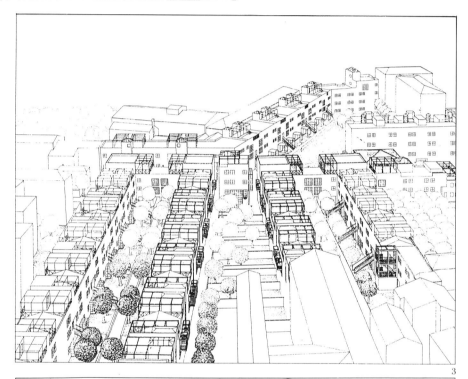

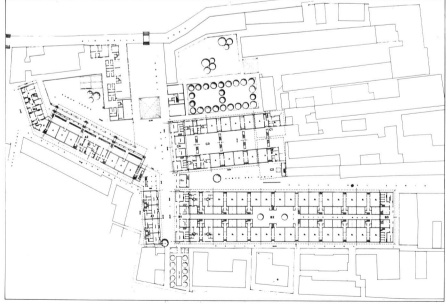

5

1. Zenith view of area
2. General plan of
district of Cannaregio
3. Perspective
bird's-eye view of project
near Campo Verde
4. Plan of project
5. 6. Foreshortened
view and detail
of interior courtyard

6

7

8

7. 8. Foreshortened
views of building
on Campo Verde
9. Detail of front of
building on Calle Lunga
10. View of front
on Campo Verde
11. Detail of
double-height portico
near Campo Verde
12. View of top
of building

9

10

11

12

Proposal for the Reorganization
of the Port Area of the Old City

Partners: G. Creazza, G. P. Mar
Venice 1990

The project involves the reconnection of the maritime areas with the island of Tronchetto, seat of the large parking area for Venice, by instituting a series of outfitted roads as far as Piazzale Roma, the point of vehicle arrival on land and the beginning of the historical city.

The harbor functions would be rationalized in the unification on dry land of all commercial activities, transforming the landing places on the insular area exclusively for tourist purposes. Greenery ia planned for the triangular area of the Campo di Marte, facing the connecting waterway between the Grand Canal and the Giudecca Canal. The elimination of a series of railway bridges and tracks on the long levantine pier allows for its reorganization as a park with athletic facilities and the subsequent integration of appropriately restored existing buildings. The top parts of the large pier are defined by two hotel complexes: following a process of "urban microsurgery" alignments are recomposed and the front is brought once again up to the measure of the historical fabric behind, defining new spaces and circles for the university. A continuous pedestrian walkway joins the island of Tronchetto to the top hotel center toward the city, up to the bridge that leads from terra firma to the piazza where automobiles park.

A wide area, facing the marine station, is described by a building curtain in which a multipurpose auditorium, offices, and a commercial center are situated. From here the pedestrian walkway connects to the railway station.

The marine station, related to the pedestrian walkway in height, is formed from a principal body, in which halls for the public are located, and two extended wings on the piers, which allow for the movement of passengers at the entrance level for transatlantic ships, separating it from the loading and unloading that occurs at a still lower level. Functions of public interest enrich the station and make it a new focal point between the insular old city and dry land.

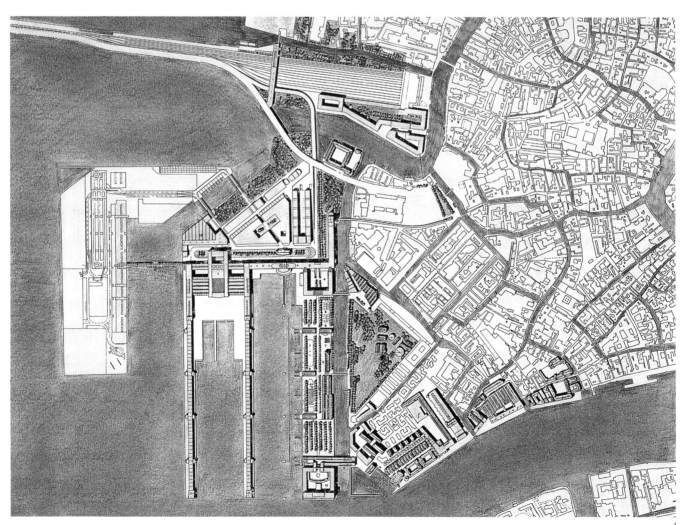

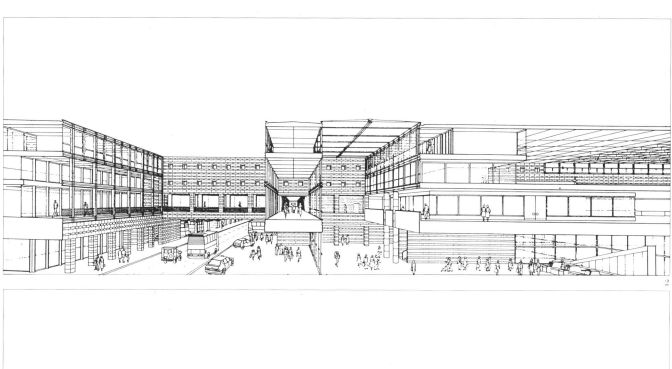

1. Plan
2. Perspective section
of entrance hall
at marine station
3. Perspective drawing
of basin with pedestrian
gangway for access
to cruise ships
4. View of model

Residences in Lützowstrasse

Iba. invited international competition
Berlin 1981

Applying the principle of consolidation of urban fragments and of recomposition of the parts to a superior scale, the project, placed between Lützowstrasse and the Landwehrkanal, seeks to restore a logical installation between several factories and a series of recent buildings in a formation without a precise system. The whole is defined by a curtain characterized by two entrance portals to the interior yards and defined by two tower blocks. The relationships between building parts and reticular metallic structures, the materials used, two-tone revetment klinker and the gray-blue of the metallic structures, are

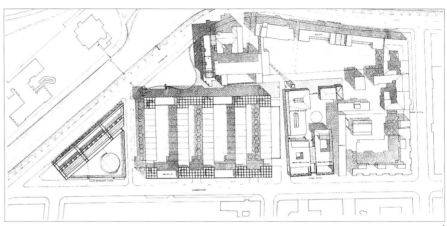

1

2

3

4

reconnected to the Berlin tradition of the 1920s. The environmental qualities of the Landwehrkanal are emphasized in the formation of a piazza defined by the northerly front of the residential complex and by a factory structure arranged on the diagonal, framing a preexisting smokestack. In the square is proposed a reconstruction of Walter Gropius's famous monument to the fallen of the Weimar Republic. At the extremity of the area a building for youth services is projected, triangular in plan. The only built part of the entire project is that near Lützow-strasse.

5

6

7

1. Plan (competition project)
2. Bird's-eye view of complex
3. Perspective drawing along Lützowstrasse
4. Entrance portal to interior courtyard
5. Detail of portal
6. Foreshortened view of front along Lützowstrasse
7. Perspective of the square on Landwehrkanal

Berlin Morgen

Invited consultation
Berlin 1990

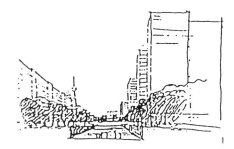

1

The project for the urban redesign of Berlin moved from an international consultation, launched a few months after the fall of the Berlin Wall, to the rearrangement of this city that, more than any other, represents the scars on the unity produced by the events of the last half-century of the historic European city.

The proposals drawn up for the different areas are part of a general reflection that confronts the problem of redesigning the city and its parts at different levels different scales of intervention.

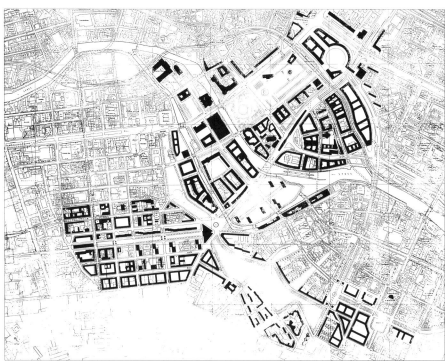

2

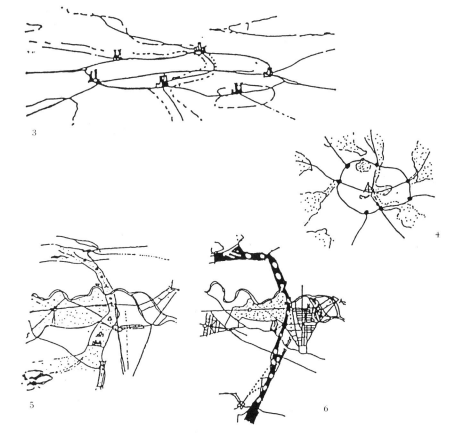

1. Study sketch
for revitalizing
Leipziger-Strasse
2. General plan
of project for central
areas of Berlin
3. 4. Hypothetical
development for a
polycentric Berlin
5. 6. Study sketches
for large park and new
railroad line that cross
city from north to south

Rearrangement
of Leipziger-Strasse

Invited international competition
Berlin 1992–93

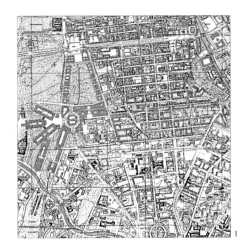

Following the wartime destructions and the reconstruction in the 1950s, Leipziger-Strasse lost its character of an historical street, becoming an exception within the urban structure of the Friedrichstadt. Defined by tall buildings, the new section of road reaches a width of 60 meters compared to its original 22 meters.

The project provides for the articulation of the large existing space into a series of piazzas lowered with respect to the street level and covered by glass arcades, defining a system of public spaces onto which commercial businesses face. This plan restores the character of an urban axis to the street. At the front a T-shaped building, 22 meters high, defines the passageway between the linear glass structure and the Spittelmarkt.

The roofing is interrupted, corresponding with the streets that cross Leipziger-Strasse, by the tops of the buildings which, destined for administrative purposes, are 22 meters high, the height of Berlin's historical buildings.

The two streets that define the glass arcade allow a reorganization of road conditions, returning the street sections to their original dimensions and integrating the layout of the new streetcar. The entire system does not compete with the high buildings that characterize this portion of Leipziger-strasse and therefore leaves to the arcade the problem of reconstructing an urban space at the scale of the Friedrichstadt.

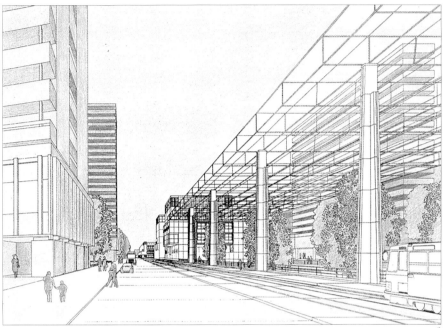

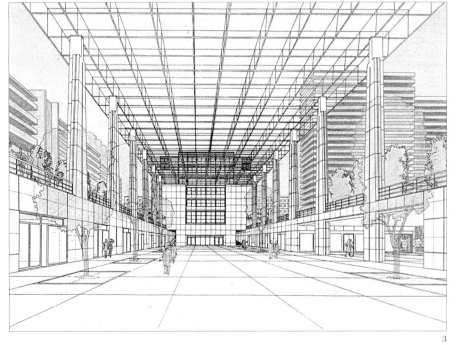

1. Plan of central area with insertion of projects for Potsdamerplatz, Leipziger-Strasse, central park, and Alexanderplatz
2, 3. Perspective views of proposed rearrangement of Leipziger-Strasse

Reorganization of Potsdamer Platz Area

Invited international competition
Berlin 1991

Potsdamer Platz is one of the places most symbolic of the rending of Berlin, which resulted from the destructions of war. The large empty space, for a long time crossed by the Wall, between the Brandenburg Gate and the area of large railway freight yards, has, with reunification, become an area of fundamental importance.

The project suggests a rereading of historical remains, reinterpreting them on different scales for forming autonomous building systems while connecting them to a reconstructed fabric that recalls the nineteenth-century city. The axes that join Leipziger-Strasse with the Kulturforum, historical Potsdamer-Strasse and the railway area of Potsdamer Bahnhof, Potsdamer Platz and the central park of Tiergarten—these establish the references for systems built as *insulae* that span these same axes.

From Potsdamer Platz, transformed into a large elevated pedestrian square, the area that leads to the Kulturforum offers the occasion for a great pedestrian space on different levels. The volumetric variations establish relationships not only within *insulae* themselves but also in comparison with park areas they define. Great importance is assumed now by the design of open spaces, the sequences between the spaces with trees, the piazzas, water basins, and green areas that reconnect in the north to the Tiergarten or in the south to the unused railway areas.

Restored to its original form, a glass building for commercial services connected to the subway station is placed at the center of Leipziger Platz. The large triangular empty space between the Brandenburg Gate and Leipziger Platz is defined from two built fascias, for which are fixed several installation rules. Viability has been assumed as the ordering scheme, reproposing typical street sections of Berlin, creating a network that distributes traffic onto the streets parallel to Leipziger-Strasse, and connecting the piazza to the pedestrian system that extends to the Kulturforum.

1. Sketch of plan
2. View of model from south

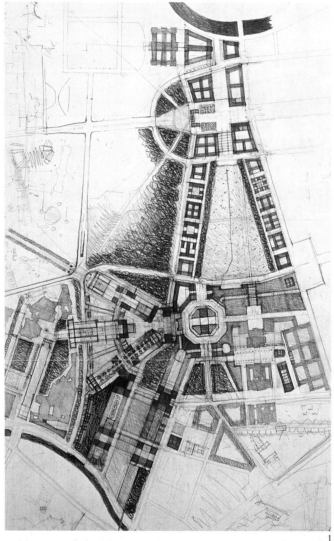

1

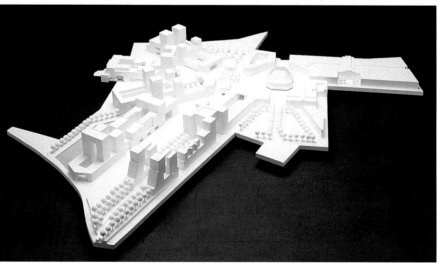

2

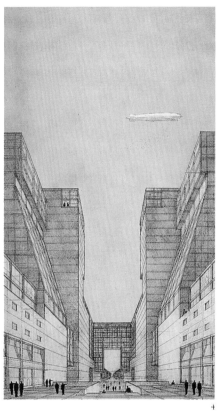

3. Perspective view
of Leipziger Platz
4. Perspective view of
a pedestrian courtyard
connecting with
the Kulturforum

3

Rearrangement of the
Lehrter Bahnhof Area

Invited international competition
Berlin 1994

The construction of the new central station marks a transformation of great importance that will affect not only the development of the surrounding zone to the north of the bend of the Spree, but also the infrastructural organization of the whole city. The area included between the bend of the Spree River and the curve of the railway, like the one north of the Invalidenstrasse, is characterized by large blocks in continuity with the fabric of the city. The new fabric follows the orientation of Invalidenstrasse, and the articulation of individual blocks takes into consideration the different functions, predominantly residential to the south and administrative to the north of the railway track. A system of three tall buildings is superimposed onto this urban fabric. Circular in plan, they are placed at the vertices of an equilateral triangle that is established as a scale element. For the area included between the bend of the Spree River and the projected station building, the project involves predominantly residential blocks, characterized by transversable public spaces onto which commercial and collective activity face. On the central axis is placed the first of the three tall administrative buildings, facing Humboldthafen. Around the station a raised slab forms a continuous commercial front on Invalidenstrasse. The administrative complex to the north of the station is organized beginning from a central axis on which are located a triangular piazza and a series of courtyard blocks. A triangular building that relates to the Hamburger Bahnhof Museum and a second tall building, intended as a hotel, are located to the north of Hamburger Bahnhof. Along Invalidenstrasse, toward the east, is the third building that closes the triangular system.

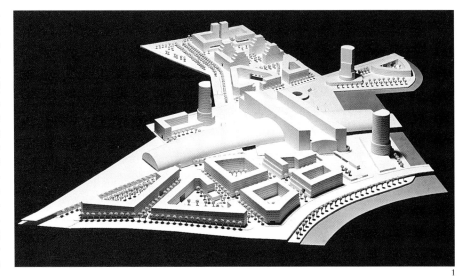

1

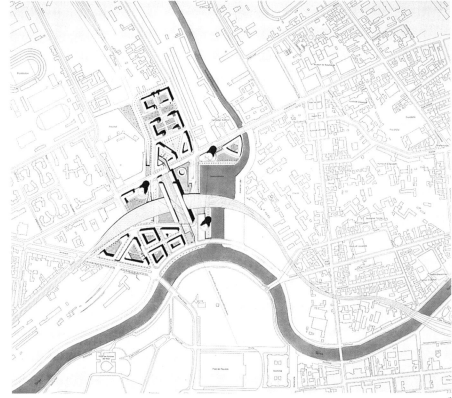

2

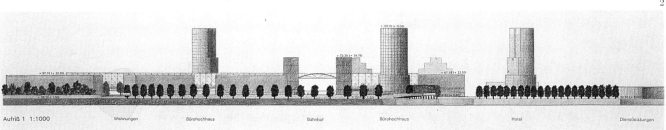

3

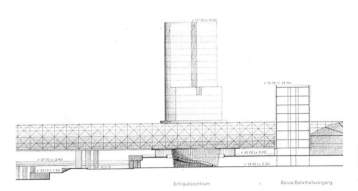

Einkaufszentrum   Büros/Bahnhofseingang

4

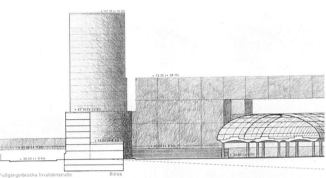

Fußgängerbrücke Invalidenstraße   Büros

5

6

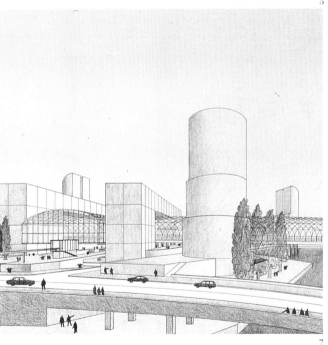

7

1. View of model
from southwest
2. Plan of project
3. Profile along
the Spree
4. Section of
commercial slab along
Invalidenstrasse

5. Transverse section of
administrative building
on Invalidenstrasse
6. 7. Perspective
drawings from
Invalidenstrasse and
Humboldthafen

Plan for a New District
in Biesdorf-Süd

Invited international competition
Berlin 1994

The project for a neighborhood to the northeast of Berlin's downtown is characterized by one green strip, perpendicular to the subway station, it represents the element of continuity of open spaces from north to south and stands out as a principal morphological system. The installation principle is determined by orthogonal street networks parallel to the curve of the elevation. The result is an urban structure of blocks with a average height of four stories and with dimensions that derive from their purpose and location. Four towers for administrative purposes are arranged in relation to the subway station and mark the center of the new installation. A commercial center is positioned on axis with the station and connects toward the north with the park. Commercial, administrative, and craft activities are located along the two tree-lined streets that parallel the subway and connect the system of parks to the east with the Biesdorf lake.

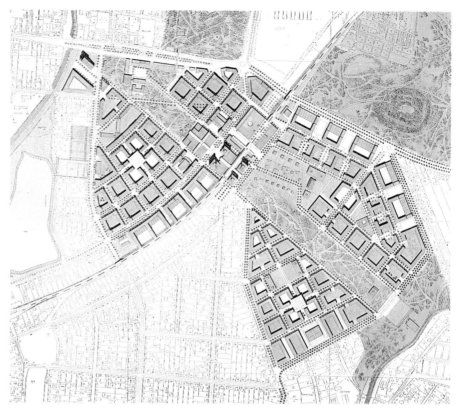

1. General plan

Residential Buildings
in Spandau

Berlin 1994–95

The theme of housing is interwoven into the problem of intervening in a plan already developed by a municipality that sets the rules for general orientation. On two lots that define at the east and west this new housing, two buildings, both square in plan and 6 stories high, are planned. Toward the east, the first building defines an elevated piazza onto which the commercial activities and the neighborhood services face. The square forms a basement upon which the buildings rest. The ground floor is reveted in klinker brick while the upper floors are whitewashed with blue shutters. The top floor is characterized by a pergola also faced in klinker.

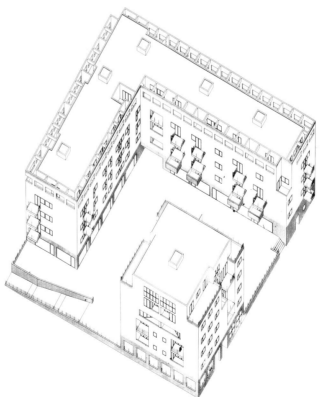

1. Axonometric view
of one of two parts
in construction

Plan and Project

More than ten years have passed since we proposed a new angle of discussion on the relationship between plan and project. That discussion wanted first of all to reaffirm the importance of the interaction between two approaches—the value of the plan as important content (even if it is not unique) of the architectural project and of the architectural project as concrete proof of its value. Such discussion cannot be separated from the process that in the last twenty years has brought out the theme of context as the preeminent material of an architectural project and, therefore, a conception of the project itself as a critical dialogue with what already exists. This position, which represents for us the most important and concrete positive criticism of the tradition of modernity as a structurally incomplete project, has had as a consequence a new attention to the constructed city and to the historicity laid waste in the land.

Perhaps the results of urban-design experiments that ripened in the 1980s did not give the outcomes that were hoped for on the disciplinary and social levels. Many are incomplete, however, or poorly realized; many owe their unsatisfactory results to dreadful management; several have exaggerated in trying to imitate the existing stratified city; others have perhaps tried to impose orders that refer to a social utopia that is absent in reality.

Since our task as architects is not to describe the crisis (if it is a relevant content it will insinuate itself in any event into the narrative structure of our materials) but to offer a remedy, since the positiveness of the theory and of the proposal is an inalienable disciplinary bond, the absence of a real or ideal reference represents an important obstacle to an operation like that of urban design. It is our task to bring together, in a sufficiently objective way and for a long time, socioeconomic efforts, complex morphological principles that involve recognizable strategies.

If, on one hand, the problem of giving physical form to the perspectives of social organization exists for us architects, on the other hand, urban design must bring into account the historicity of the existing city, with its resistances and stratifications; from yet another perspective, urban design must cope with the long duration of architecture and, therefore, with its character as witness. Urban design is, therefore, first of all, an act of mediation between these different conditions. Its task is to give meaningful form to the city and to its parts, starting from what I define as "project of the present." With this definition we intend to place the stress (metaphorical and concrete) of the project on two questions.

The first is a placing into discussion of the coincidence (and obsession) of the future as preeminent objective of the project. The accent goes, instead, on an interpretation of the project fundamentally as a *search for the truth of the present:* without illusion about its possession but without a renunciation of the tension toward it.

The second, directly illuminated by the first, is a recalling of the fact that the structural character of our discipline, as artistic practice, is to work with the empirical conditions such as unremovable material, criticizing it.

Urban design as project in the present imposes several qualities that are, at the same time, suitable means and preeminent specific ends of the discipline. Such qualities are specifically those that can make the urban morphology available to social use. Contrary to public opinion, we believe that the more ordered, precise, simple, and organic the result, the more it will be available to collective interpretation in time. We must not forget that monuments and urban structures of quality endure much longer than the motivations that produced them, even if such motivations were essential for their architectural quality. As Gadamer says: "They are hammered into them."

The New Urban Residential Center in Badia

Scandicci, Florence 1982–86

Among the primary objectives of the new general town plan is reinforcing the urban identity of Scandicci, redeemed from its subordinate position as a Florentine suburb. This is the context for the new town center. Four blocks with different purposes are connected to the existing road network, urban and extra-urban, adjusting it to the new regularization. The sequence of blocks makes up a pedestrian walkway that receives the traffic from nearby urban functions; the walkway crosses (in order): a town square upon which join all the new public functions (administrative, services, leisure); a commercial square; a large public garden onto which face four residential towers; a theater square connected to the nearby school.

New residences are planned in the hamlet of Badia San Colombano to offer alternative lifestyles. The new buildings, in two-story formation, are aligned with roads dating from the Roman centuries. The surrounding territory remains as productive countryside or park land where the ancient Badia di Settimo stands out.

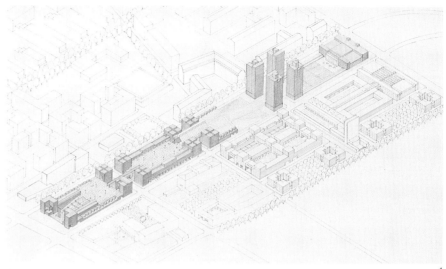

1

1. Axonometric view of new city center
2. Plan of Badia San Colombano with new residential typologies

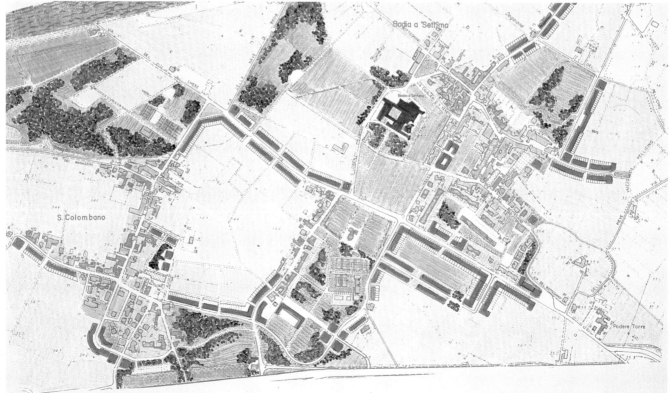

2

Reopening of the North Gate:
The Walls

Arezzo 1986–1987

Particular attention, in the drawing up of town planning proposals, has be given to the question of the public spaces and services: the planning search had aimed to define the most continuous plot possible for public areas upon which to articulate a variety of city places and functions in support of the interventions of urban renewal.

The first proposal intends to restore the city walls and the Medici fortress (Fortezza Medicea): arrangement of parks and removal of services gravitating onto the circuit of the walls restore to the city a high road on the bastion and a low one outside the walls: both take advantage of the "monumental" permanence of this urban document. In particular, the North Gate is redefined in relation to the fortress through a functional system tied to the exposition: at the fortress, spaces for exhibits and shows, at the gate a subterranean archeological museum enriches the Prato that ideally reconstructs the plan of the Roman Forum.

1. Plan of study for city walls project
2. Plan and longitudinal section of North Gate

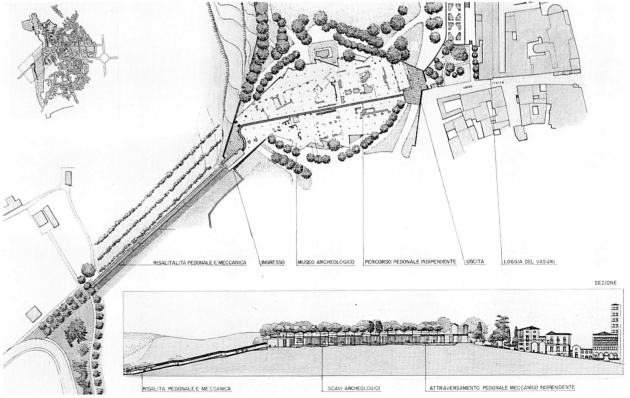

1

RISALITA LITA PEDONALE E MECCANICA   INGRESSO   MUSEO ARCHEOLOGICO   PERCORSO PEDONALE INDIPENDENTE   USCITA   LOGGIA DEL VASARI

SEZIONE

RISALITA PEDONALE E MECCANICA   SCAVI ARCHEOLOGICI   ATTRAVERSAMENTO PEDONALE MECCANICO INDIPENDENTE

2

The Gardens
La Cerniera (The Hinge)

Arezzo 1986–87

A transformation of public areas, which the general town plan deems of strategic value for urban renewal, forms a hinge between the old city and the new city near the railway station. Around the new park are arranged residences, administrative and commercial services, a cultural building, and an exhibition garden. The park system becomes the qualifying feature of the city: new city parks complete the area. On the territorial scale the general town plan projects new "gardens." Land reorganization and a new irrigation network allow for the realization of a vast park system to the north of the city center. A network of bike-pedestrian routes and agriculture service roads allows for recreational uses of the land.

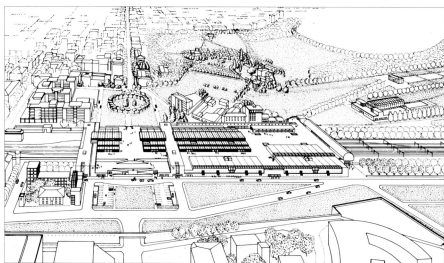

1

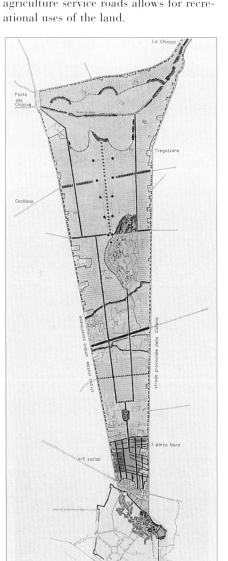

3

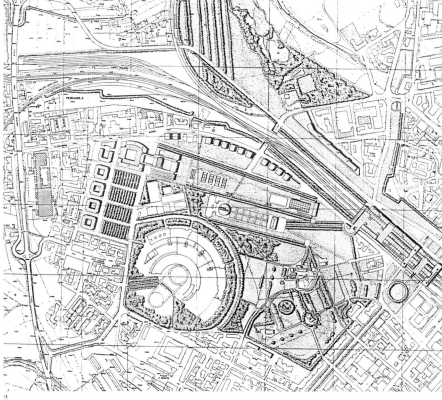

2

Study of the project
for La Cerniera
1. Perspective drawing
of old city
2. General plan

3. Plan of study
for gardens project

New Residential District
in Ceciliano

Arezzo 1986–87

The study for Ceciliano demonstrates different conceptions for residences contained in the new general town plan. The project indicates alternatives for living that aim to respond to the needs of the whole municipal territory, introducing choices that modify the rigid separation between urban and rural dwellings. The new installation of Ceciliano, planned for 1300 spaces, extends over the hill surrounded by the existing suburbs. It develops in a line along a hilltop route that defines the structure. The houses line this road to a depth of two rows, so as not to fall off the slope. At specific points in the road, again marked by particular attention to the design of public space, the main urban places are connected: public services, centers for cultural and social activity, and for limited amounts of administrative activity. These are the facilities that structure the quality of the "city" as well as the suburban towns, to which the new installation connects appropriately via a branch of the central road.

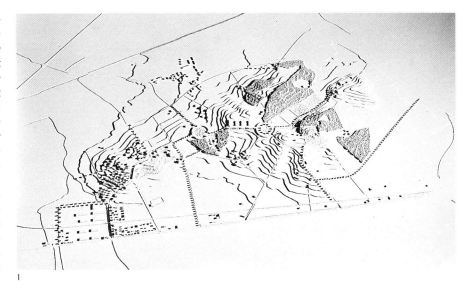

1

Study for installation   1. View of model
on Ceciliano hill   2. General plan

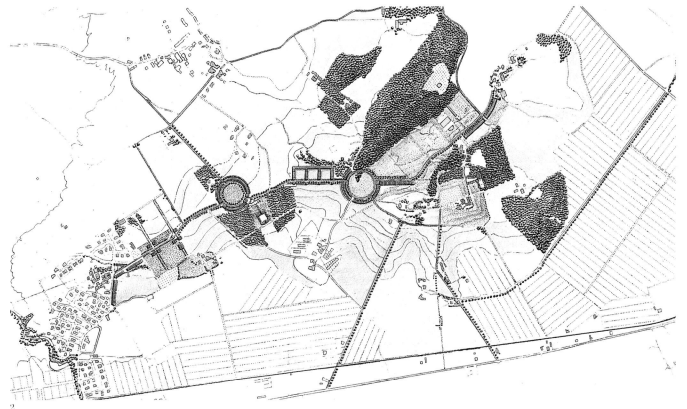

2

Central Park
and Conference Center

Darfo-Boario Terme, Brescia 1987–92

The projects for the central park and the new conference center are part of the urban revitalization projected by the new regulatory city plan.

Situated in a bend in the Oglio River and in a central position with respect to the "basin" that defines the Darfo installation, stretches the vast area upon which is planned the large new park. Here, on the greenery, are placed athletic facilities and new commercial and residential functions that will transform the unused industrial area into a central place, representative of the city, and at the junction of the relationships among the numerous little towns spread throughout the municipal territory.

The conference center is located in the area once occupied by the industrial complex of the Manifattura Olcese, which, through this project, contributes to the process of redefining and reaggregating the Darfo's polycentric installation system.

The building project, winner of the project competition, includes a center for public facilities and private services with a surface of approximately 20,000 square meters.

The articulation of the complex becomes the occasion for a formal solution where architecture and landscape enter into a direct relationship: the large arc defined by the glass walls of the conference center defines a fifth morphologically continuous building with respect to the main scenic element, the "Castellino."

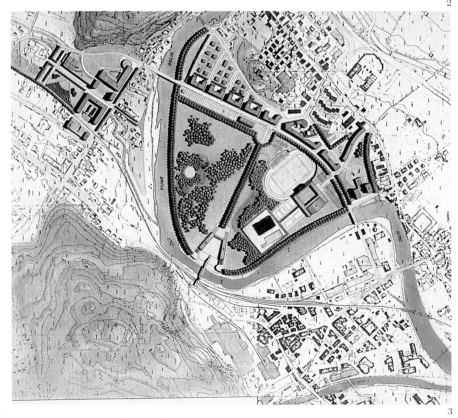

1. View of model
of conference center
2. Central Park:
perspective drawing

3. General plan

124

The Central "Spina"

Turin 1987–94

Central "Spina."
Detailed plan
of "Spina" 2, 1990
1. General view
of model for central
"Spina." Precincts
1 and 2

2. Covering of the
railroad lines: garden
of Largo Orbassano
and Viale della Spina
3. Section of Porta
Susa Station

1

The presence of a consistent quantity of unused areas along the nineteenth-century railway track and the concomitant plan. along the same track. for a railway connection and of the strengthening of the northern road penetration have formed the premise upon which to plan the transformation of these same areas into a sequence of new urban spaces that. in the city. define a central "Spina" (spine) of public service functions.

Coordinating urban and transportation needs. the project study proposed within the sphere of the new town planning envisions the covering of the railway line and the subsequent realization of the roadway project as an important axis carrying the strong streams of slow city traffic. but also as a strategic artery for the connection between the different interventions planned along its way. whose architectural image recalls the Turin tradition of the tree-lined boulevard.

If the strip of unused areas (from the former steel mill in the north. to the prisons.

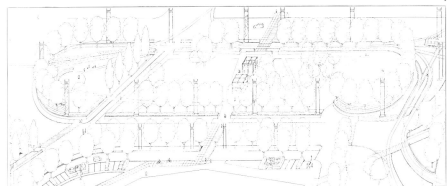

2

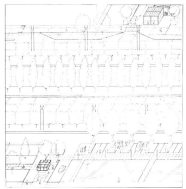

3

125

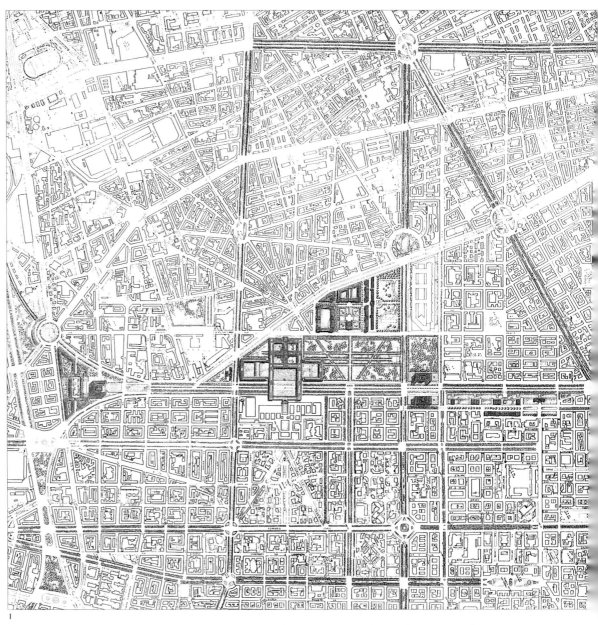

to the FF.SS. workshops up to the railway junction) has formed caesura in the city, its transformation restores that connective hinge to the city: central city parks, new public facilities—from the law courts to the expansion of the Polytechnic, to offices of public administration—are the descriptive functions of the Spina project, to which can be integrated other collective facilities (culture, exhibition, reception), administrative and residential. The "Unified Study of Four Precincts" confirms the installation of administrative functions—

public and private—of general interest and also coordinates the plans for the four precincts in relation to the increased number of residences.

Precinct 1 defines the south terminal head of the so-called spine in the tower placed on axis to the avenue and intended for urban functions. The connection with the urban fabric, behind this tower, follows the particular triangular shape defined by the location of the railway station. To the west a crescent shape ends the perspective

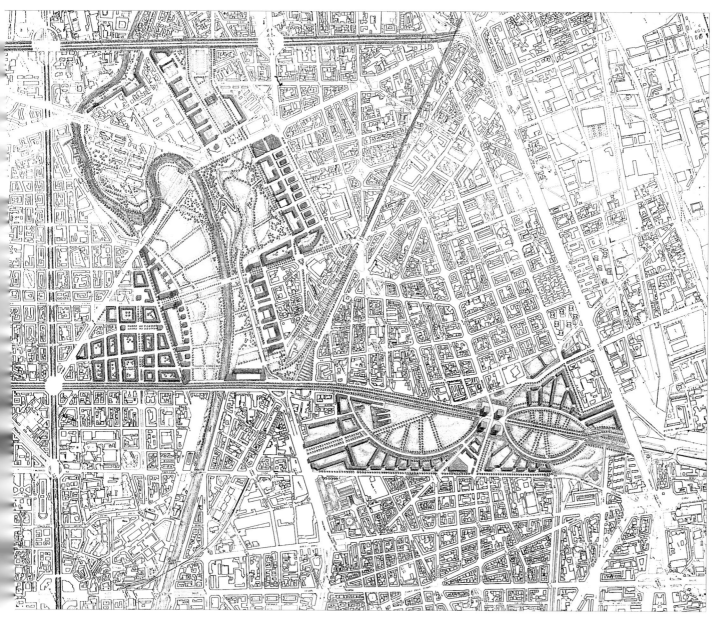

view on one side of the circular road inter-section and faces onto the new Ruffini-Rosselli Park. To the east the new park on the hill is being developed, defined by the covering of the railway connection at the Zappata crossroads.

The main public functions are located in Precinct 2, along the wide tree-lined avenue produced by the railway covering. The new branch of the Polytechnic dou-bles its size and links the buildings via a "bridge" over the "Spina." The city park

Susa relates the downtown and suburbs, historically separated by the railway.

Precinct 3 restores to the central circuit of the "Spina" a portion of outlying ter-ritory that offers the opportunity for vast renovation through the node of the reshaped Dora Station and the new road organization. On one bank of the new river-park Dora, residential functions are centered, on the other, Eurotorino exhi-bition facilities and new services for the enterprises.

Precinct 4 contains four administrative towers, constructed around Rebaudengo Station; their position is on the matrix of a double helix, which regulates the design of the park, crossed centrally by the "Spina" road, here grafted directly onto the urban link to the Milan–Turin highway.

On the green halo of the park stretch new residential structures that introduce mor-phological variables to the blocks typical of Turin and its suburbs.

The New Polytechnic

Turin 1992–93

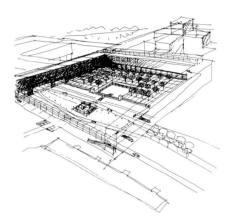
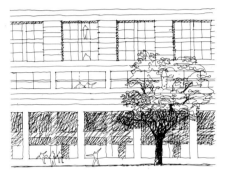
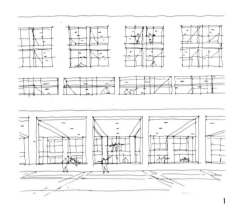

Among the transformations connected with covering the railroad lines and defined by the new regulatory plan in specific studies of important public functions for the new central spine, there is the construction of a new seat for the Polytechnic. The project for the expansion of the university on the area of the former railway offices envisions building a complex of 160,000 square meters on the existing location, inside the new urban order of this Spine precinct: the formation of the Susa Park and of the residential and administrative district here that would face and be related to the re-formed Susa Station.

Two bridgelike structures connect the extension with the existing seat and define an arcaded public piazza that demarcates the functional and symbolic center of the university branch open to the city. The interior articulation utilizes several types of functionally flexible spaces, collected in blocks that are executable in successive stages. Among the endowments planned is a technology library, also open for public use. Classrooms, laboratories, area libraries, departmental activities, and offices are arranged around a system of closed and open courtyards. A cross-shaped gallery entirely in glass connects the didactic areas to the public areas—such as cafeterias and restaurants, the large main library, and commercial establishments— so as to divide roads and crossings into a sequence of public and private spaces, fit for exchanges and connections between the different activities and the city itself.

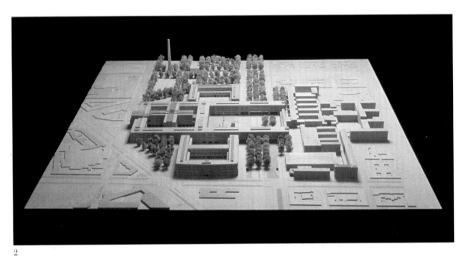

Turin Polytechnic.
Campus extension
1. Studies for central courtyard
2. View of model from southwest
3. General plan

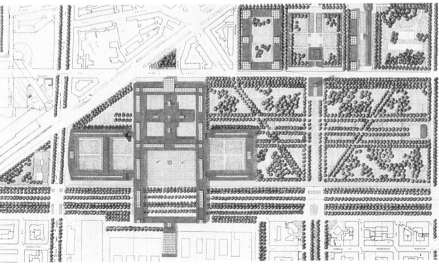

Covering for the Railroad Line

Turin 1993–95

1. Perspective drawing toward Largo Orbassano hill
2. Largo Orbassano-Corso Turati tract: view of model

The covering for the railroad line is one of the first works that will be executed under the specifications of the new general town plan. It contributes to defining the new public image of the city envisioned by the plan, beginning the formation of new wide street axes that will characterize the main urban renovations: tree-lined boulevards with new public spaces enhanced by works of art by Turinese artists and with places representative of the modernization of the city. The project marks out the configuration of covering the line in the tract from Corso Castelfidardo to Largo Orbassano up to Via Turati.

While the project for the rectilinear tract along the axis of the central "Spina" has deepened and indications already partly delineated in the "Unified Study" have been detailed, new planning proposals were put forth for the Orbassano-Turati inroad that integrate and develop the general provisions of the plan on the covering of the railroad line. Two artificial hills with a double closure of the longitudinal perspective axis are delineated as poles emerging on a graded slope to define the extended space of the area. Inside then are planned public and service activities (a covered market, underground parking). The Zappata Station stop of the line is located in a central position under Viale De Nicola, signaled on the surface by a covered piazza onto which small commercial buildings face.

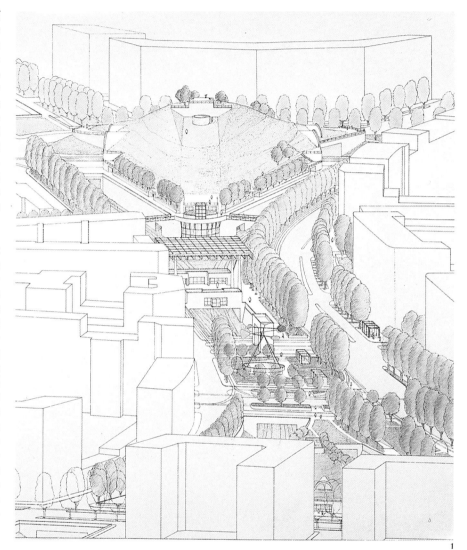

1

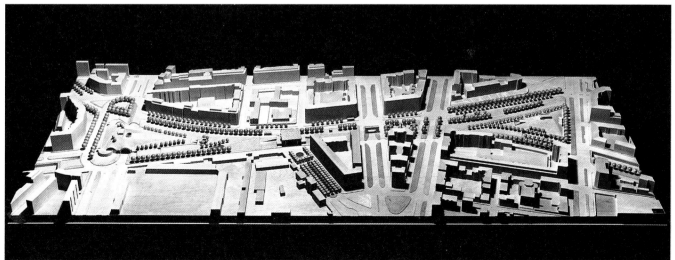

2

Riverside Park on the Banks
of the Po

Turin 1987–94

The Po Valley, which stretches within the city limits for more than 15 kilometers, is used to advantage as a forest ambiance. It makes up an extraordinary "green architecture" able to converse with the built city. The project, proposed as part of the new general city plan, envisions environmental renewal precisely within the forested regions. The villages of Madonna del Pilone and Ponte Trombetta find new faces on the river through a reconfiguration of architectural facades; the new Antonelli bridge-island increases the city's facilities for leisure time; the reopening of the Michelotti Canal allows for the renovation of the park and the transformation of the former zoo into cultural exhibition spaces. At Parco Regio is planned the substitution of some productive structures with a new complex of public structures, reception buildings, and a fully equipped park. In Borgata Sassi, a new structure with access to the city (covered parking, offices, hotel, trade, residence) is planned, integrated into the network of public transportation (steamers, Superga rack-railway, autolines for the hill). The urban axis of Via Po extends beyond the river with the renovation of the hill road for Villa della Regina. The construction of an underpass to Piazza della Gran Madre may allow for "pedestrianization" there, reestablishing the continuity of the public space with the Piazza Vittorio Veneto and the bank of the Murazzi.

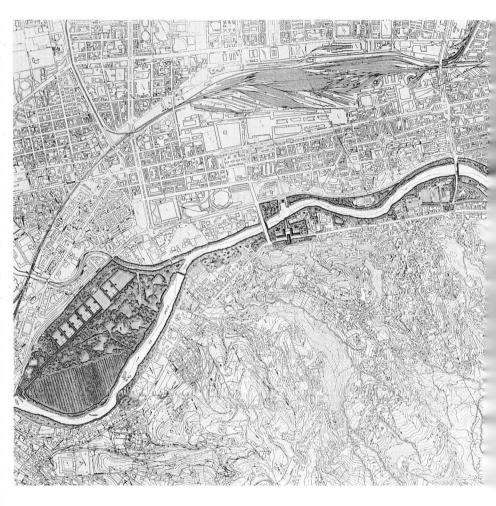

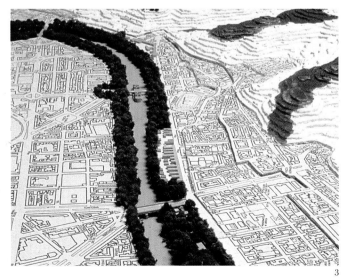

2

3

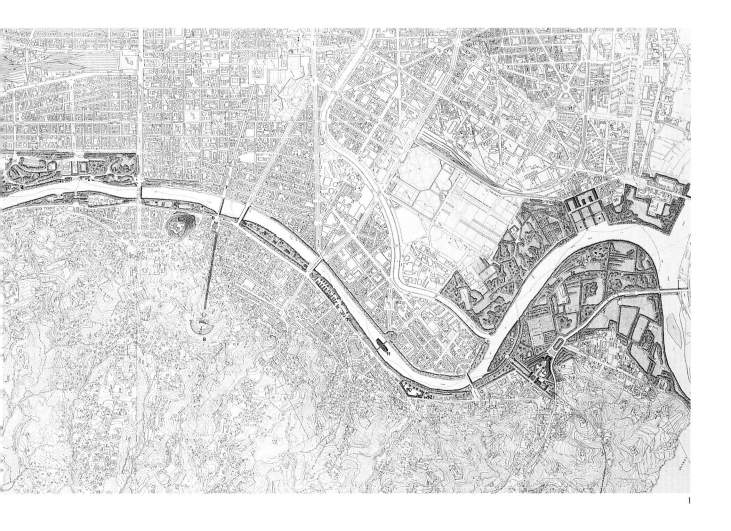

1

1. General plan
2. View of model
toward area of Regio
Parco-Borgata Sassi
3. View of model
toward Antonelli Island
4. View of model
toward the Gran Madre
in the area of Murazzi-
Borgo Po

4

Seaport

Livorno 1991–95

Study for Mediceo-
Bellana Variant
Seaport
1. Drawing
2. View of model
from south

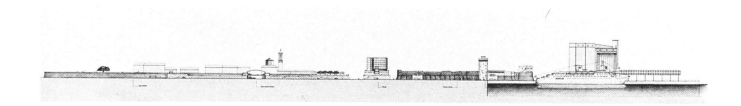

1

The Mediceo-Bellana Variant, drawn up in anticipation of the general town plan, proposes a redefinition of the harbor area that, starting from the reorganization of the shipyards around the Morosini Stocks, offers a different order within the sector's activities and a more integrated relationship between city and port. The systemization of Mediceo Port and of the Bellana Sea Front in planning proposals responds to the need to adjust the city's structural elements to the evolution of usage of the city itself. A center of reference, toward the sea, is to be established for nautical, administrative, touristic, and bathing functions, and the historic Mediceo Port finds new opportunities in the replacement of the fortress within the structure of the Livorno city walls. The proposed changes presuppose the realization of an urban addition: a piazza open to the sea onto which face a nautical hall and a new hotel. The new marine station, placed outside the walls and joined to the highway clearances, completes and improves the requisites of a modern harbor economy.

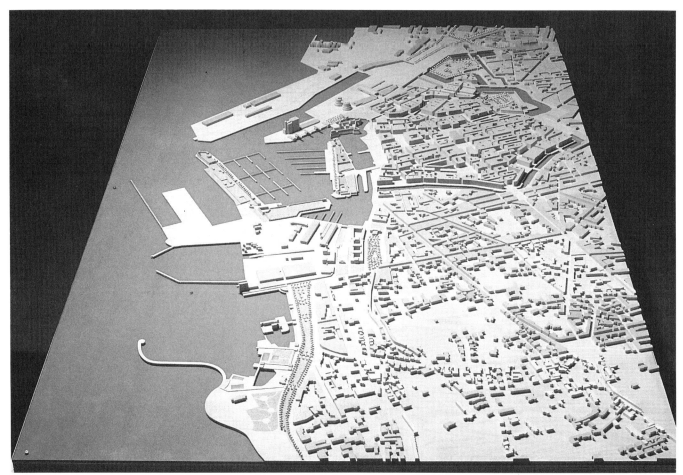

2

Land Port

Study for the
Directional Variant
Land Port
1. View of model
from north
2. Drawing

The project, drawn up within the sphere of studies for the new Livorno general city plan, concerns a vast area placed on the shoulders of the city between the railway line and the variant to the state road Aurelia. It forms a new port of entry to the city, the land port, physically recognizable and geographically opposed to the port, the traditional path of communication and entry.

The installation form of the planned buildings, the order of the roads, and the systemization of the open spaces (greenery and parking) define a complex strongly characterized in the urban sense. The two consecutive hemicycles, emphasized by the design of the parking area, redefine the limit of the Livornese constructed space for those driving along the Aurelia variant. The two exits from the latter toward the city rest on two brick structures, resembling two large entrance towers. The longitudinal avenue, an important axis of the installa-

tion, is designed like a wide tree-lined city boulevard. The functional connection with the city center is finally ensured by an underpass across the railroad tracks.

The renovation encompasses the installation of a shopping center, exhibition and reception structures, residences, and offices, as well as the completion and reconfiguration of the existing athletic facilities, both public and private.

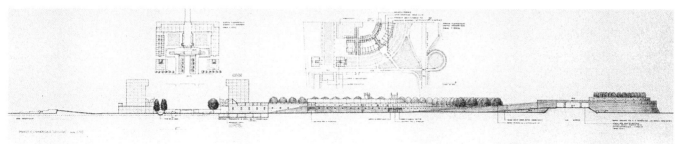

2

133

Proposal for Urban Renewal

Invited international competition
Prague 1992

New perspectives for the city take into
consideration both the geographic and the
cultural site as the center of gravity open
to East and West. The city's potential is
reinforced in a renovation and functional
reorganization of the urban structure so
as to strengthen economic, cultural, and
environmental resources.

Technologically advanced industry that is
correlated to research, direction and quality of services offered: these are the control-
ling factors of structural evolution on
which the urban project is modeled. Beginning with the protection of the old city,
administrative, commercial, exhibition,
and reception functions are made possible
in the central area. A scientific park enriches the university and cultural endowments.
The reformation of structures for sports
and shows increases the facilities for the
city's use. The potential transportation system multiplies the connections. The parks
along the Moldau will be enlarged, and a
system of city-park reunites the fortified
city with the external poles, where the residential expansions are specified.

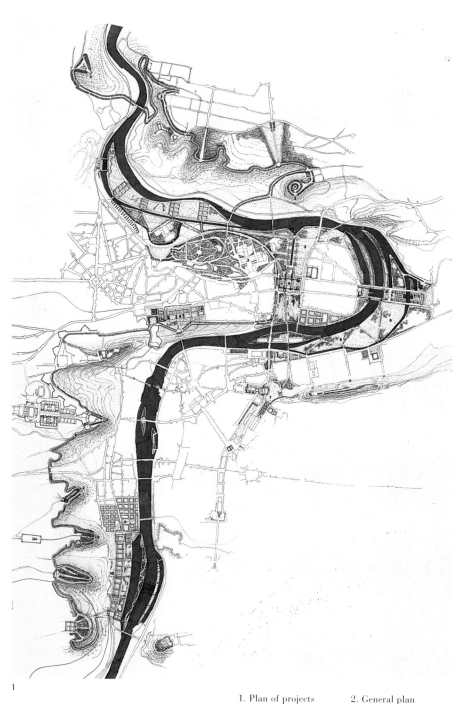

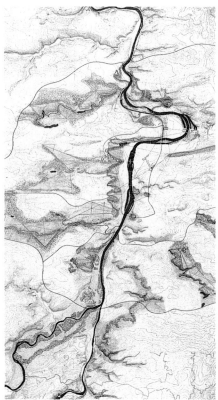

1. Plan of projects
in central area

2. General plan
of system of projects
along the Moldau

Gargano Park

National competition of ideas
Foggia 1991–92

The project won the national competition of ideas for the institution of Gargano Park; it defines an ensemble of operative schemes on which to proceed. Different levels of protection are determined based on the specification of particular qualities and protections; the expansion is directed by the definition of places for possible development; pedestrian usage of space within the territory is increased through requisite examinations of the system of accessibility.

The regime of safeguard then becomes, in the project proposal, a chance to define the directed development of an ecosystem of exceptional character such as that of Gargano.

1. General plan

Portofino Mountain Park

Portofino, Genoa 1991–93

Starting from objectives such as control of the urbanized order, improvement of different and sometimes conflicting conditions of life and of use of the park itself, and use of the historical evidence, the plan of the park is configured as a body of bonding instruments, rules of change, and organizational and management criteria of an exceptional place: the promontory with its system of landscapes. Vegetation patrimony and agricultural regime, like a constructed patrimony and residential regime, permanent and tourist, are the resources that the plan mobilizes within an extended notion of park that stretches to the littoral and the hinterland, to be the witness of active protection of a typical and varied landscape-culture in Liguria.

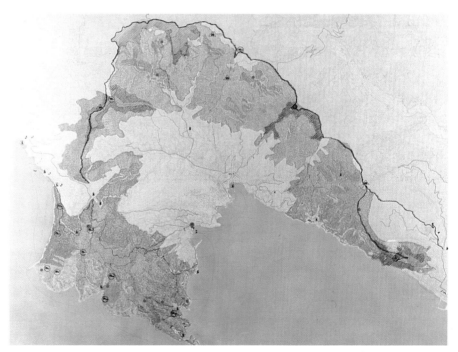

1. General plan

Park for Land Brandenburg

Potsdam 1991–93

The project for *Land Brandenburg* analyzes two possible forms of development for Berlin in 2010. The first is produced from undifferentiated expansion, indifferent to the resources of the particular places, following the megametropolis model. The second perspective examines the alternative potentialities of a concept of polycentric development that identifies a territorial system of city functionally integrated among the different centers, with also a suitable of communications infrastructure. Each one among them would be recognizable for specific historical, morphological, or scenic characteristics: a "polycentric Berlin" reconfigured in the landscape, where three railway rings allow a different connection between the limits of living, working, and leisure, through a more articulated declination of the relationships between variable "space" and "time"; where the places of anthropization and the places of nature find different forms of reciprocal relationship and precise usage.

Forests, meadows, pastures, lakes, and rivers return as first features of a strengthened landscape: signs and places of a rural regime become permanencies from which to move to a different metropolitan regime.

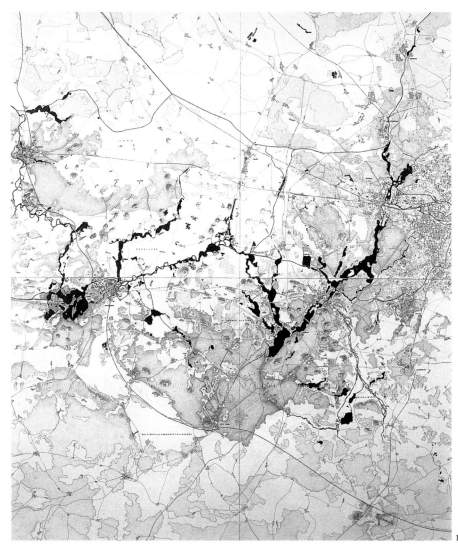

1

1. General plan
2. View of project inserted into painting by F. Frégevice, *Potsdam from Peacock Island*, 1820

2

136

Urban Design of the Suburbs

It is necessary to make the effort to reestablish a level of thought that concerns our discipline, starting a little more from its internal questions of artistic practice that works with empirical conditions as unremovable material of its action. This implies a conception of the project as dialogue with such conditions that reveal themselves to our tools of the discipline first as forms of the things, of contextual systems, of their installation principles, and as reasons that preside over those forms. Yet, even if the planning dialogue with such contextual systems starts from an awareness of the existence of the other, it is not on that account an automatic legitimization of its reasons. It has nothing to do with assimilation and reconciliation, nor, obviously, can the construction of the project be deduced from the contextual conditions. On the contrary, the project is presented from this point of view as reading and establishing the critical distance that separates us from the context: the architectural winner of that distance is the quality of the architectural project. The establishment of such quality is put in motion, not to be forgotten, by new collective necessities—true or fantastic though they may be, frequently completely extraneous to the specific case—whose compatibility we must ascertain by means of the project.

Such quality is therefore the form of the new context, that is, the mode of being of a new dialogue. Notions like those of position and relation, and the specific aspects of design that are derived from them, assume particularly relevant values, while the limited and specific truth of the case provides at least the concrete ground for the foundation of the project, even if not the foundation itself. It should never be forgotten that the city is presented above all to us as stratification and accumulation of historical materials upon which to work readings and choices. That which history and tradition have built has, in the city's reality, concrete context and a special presence. It is the field, or if you like, the "text" with which we are compared, from which we draw a large part of

our material, in which more precisely each transformation works. It is for us what was the classical language for architecture until the end of the 18th century: a corpus formed through the succession of its reinterpretations, with its own diachronic and structural installation rules. In relation to such text the innovation is practiced, rather it is that very thing that should allow and form the critical distance, that which I define as "the non-ostentatious transgression."

Finally, several reflections must be made on the value of the coherence of the relationship between the overall urban design of one part of the city like this one and the qualitative characteristics of the buildings that comprise it. The suburbs of today teach us that there is more to fear from excessive competitive confusion between the languages of different architectural objects than from the discipline, legibility, and hierarchy among the parts in the construction of a whole. Many things whimsically different, it is known, produce the faint sound of uniformity: articulation and necessary exceptions are founded instead (it is obvious to say it, much less to practice it) on the clarity of the installation rule with respect to which the same interpretative differences are measured. Such an installation rule must be projected also in the choice of several common compositional elements: the general plan, the alignments, the design of crowns and porticos, the selection of materials within oscillations between their compatibilities, and in general a strategy in which the value of the relationship among the building elements would be an important fact for the very design of the building.

The rule is therefore the opposite of uniformity. It is that which allows rhythm, sequences, variety to establish itself; it is that which makes visible the identity of the site. To construct simple, livable architecture, without seeking praise—that is what we are trying to do in the delicate passage from principles to construction.

Residential District
for 20,000 Inhabitants (Zen)

Partners: F. Amoroso, S. Bisogni, H. Matsui,
F. Purini
Invited competition
Palermo 1969–73

The district is placed on the continuation of the eighteenth-century axis of Via Maqueda. The intervention is regulated by a compact geometric grid that becomes an element of reference and measurement of the surrounding territory, restoring and reinterpreting the traces of the enclosure system dividing the land. The fabric of the 18 *insulae* arranged in three rows, from which the district is formed, recalls the typological articulation and the density of Palermo's old city, with a series of ambiguities deriving from a comparison with the tradition of Middle European rationalist neighborhoods. Thus the models of the houses are approached and hybridized—tall, low, or with a balcony—with the constant presence of wide porticos on the ground floor intended to house small commercial and artisan businesses. The main services—schools, athletic structures, the center for community services, and spaces for small productive activities—are arranged orthogonally, in three parallel bands, two external and one internal.

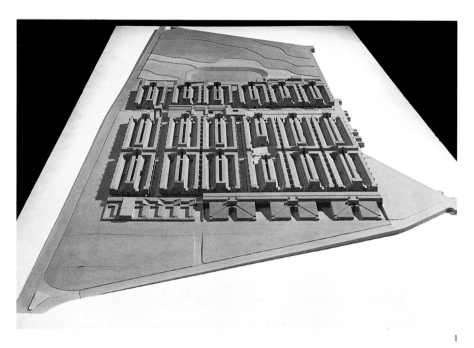

1

2

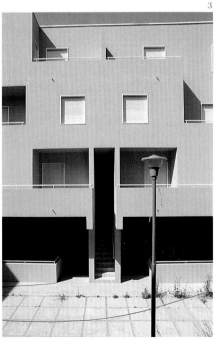

1. View of model
from west
2. View of project
toward northwest
during construction

3. Detail of a side
4. Perspective drawing
of central piazza
5. Detail of interior
courtyard

World Exposition of 1989

Paris 1982–83

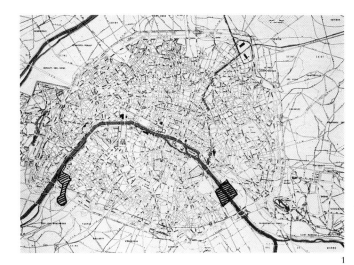

1

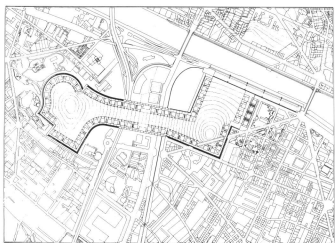

2

Divided into two large exhibition sectors facing onto the Seine and dedicated to the general theme of "The Paths of Freedom," the World Exposition, organized by the French government to celebrate the hundred years since the first Exposition and two hundred since the Revolution, is located in downtown Paris. The installation entrusts to the river the role of main connecting element between the two sectors: the valley, the west sector, developed linearly from the Champ de Mars to the Parc de la Place d'Issy; and the mount, the east sector, stretching on the left bank of the Île Saint Louis and continuing on the right bank at the height of the Tolbiac station, until Bercy. In the eastern sector the project involves the construction of a large "enclosure" spanning the Seine, defined by an inhabited bridge. On it face an entrance hall to services, a square, a covered arcade, a museum, and the pavilions of the industrial enterprises. In the western sector, from the Champ de Mars, a floating island forms a boulevard, 1200 meters long, that leads to the international pavilions. Here the shape of the former Citroèn industrial area is regulated by the use of land as material—a wide open space left green, its variable heights functioning as a needed underpass and defining the relationships with the urban fabric. On the highest point of the elevation, which allows continuity with the bank of the Seine, various pavilions are placed.

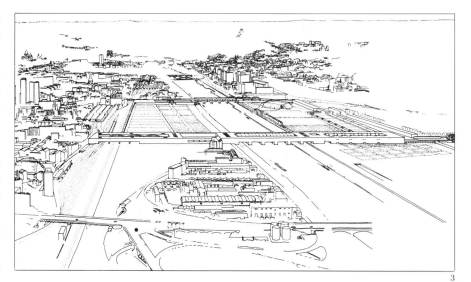

3

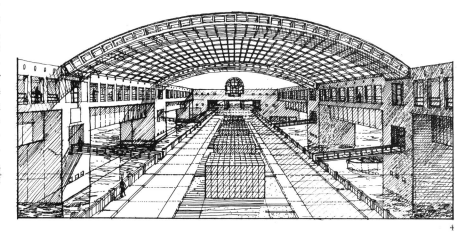

4

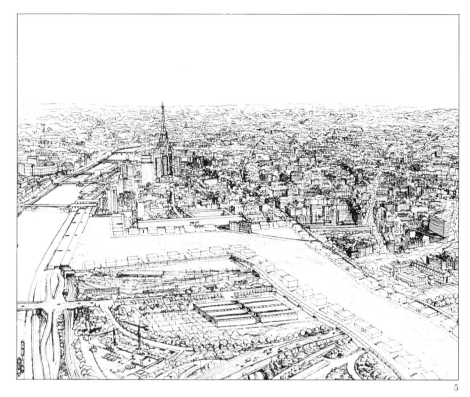

6

5

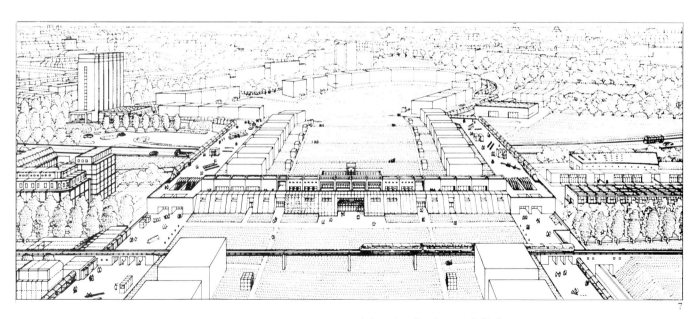

7

1. Location of project
2. Plan of west sector
3. Perspective from
south of inhabited
bridge
+. Perspective sketch
of interior of bridge

5. Bird's-eye
perspective toward
center city of west
sector
6. Entrance pavilion
7. Bird's-eye
perspective toward
the southwest

Detailed Plan
of the Corassori Area

Partners: T. Lugli, with M. Calzolari, Italprogetti
Modena 1983–84

For the renewal of the area of the motor racing track, the project proposes an articulated strategy that starts from indications on the detailed plan and includes reorganization of the general road conditions, redesign of the park, and rearrangement of the heterogeneous and fragmented building fabric.

The project envisions the realization of two large structures placed on a north–south axis. The first, 450 meters long, contains the complex of state offices arranged on three courtyards, completed by a colonnaded commercial piazza, located at the end of the elevated road that connects the installation to the sports center and the theater tent, placed at the head toward the park. The second building structure, 800 meters in length, makes up the large-scale unified element that reorganizes the whole area, shaping itself as a solid front toward the park, the strengthening element of the fragmented suburban fabric—both sign and connecting structure between the divided city parts. The new building takes on urban characteristics, arranging within its perimeter a sequence of five piazzas characterized by a high variety of building spaces and intended uses. The first square is accessed through a commercial gallery placed between the residential buildings and the public and private administrative facilities. In the second, that includes an existing school building, a series of athletic and recreational services are placed, while the next, open onto a park characterized by a large shopping center, is described as a point of interchange between the lines of public city and out-of-city transportation. A hotel also faces onto this last piazza, while the latter's interior space is articulated by the volumes of a civic center and a religious chapel.

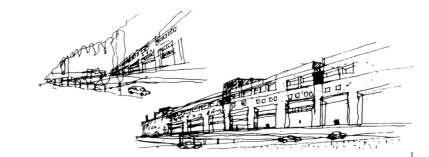

1

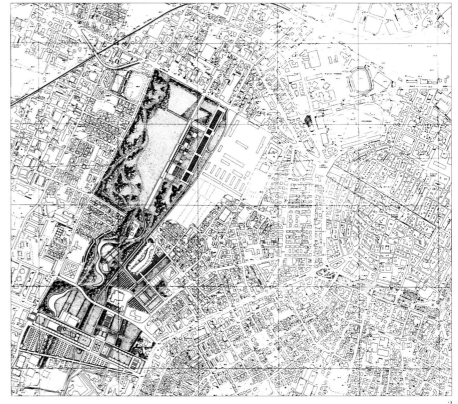

2

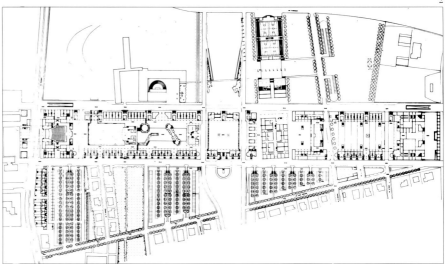

3

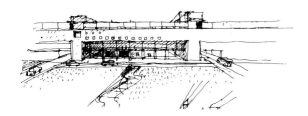

4

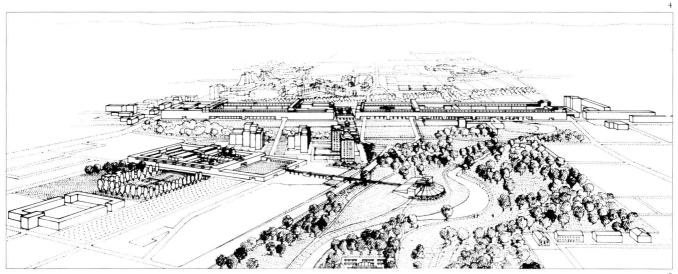

5

1. Study sketches
2. General plan
3. Ground-floor plan
4. Study sketch
5. Perspective view

Bicocca Project

Invited international competition
Milan 1986–95

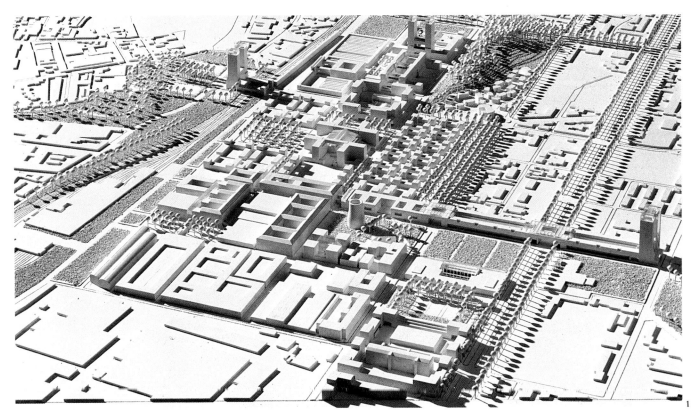

North of Milan, in an area of approximately 70 hectares and in a position to take on the strategic function of new center for the entire metropolitan system, the project for an advanced technological pole on the site of the Pirelli factories is an articulated architectural system whose characteristics of integration and multifunctionality make it potentially a new part of the city.

Confirming the existing division of the land, a sequence of four large building blocks makes up the central spine of the intervention. Inside them, an articulated sequence of roads and public spaces redesigns the urban complexity, with particular attention to the design of the land, an instrument of control able to establish overall relationships and capable of integrating precise architectural variations. The first block, to the north, displays traits of collective service, with residences, commerce, and small professional businesses facing onto a large, two-leveled, covered pedestrian piazza.

To the north the block is set in relation to a tree-lined piazza onto which face the research laboratories and the new office of the Pirelli Group, housed in the adjoining and transformed cooling tower, and the new seat of the Milanese university, placed in several existing industrial buildings, suitably restructured. The second block, crossed by Via Emanueli and by the quick surface transportation, and connected with the new Greco station, is arranged around a pedestrian piazza and will house several university faculties. To

1. View toward south
of model of first project
of competition
2. Study sketch for
comprehensive profile

3. Bird's-eye view
toward north
5. General plan
of realization stage

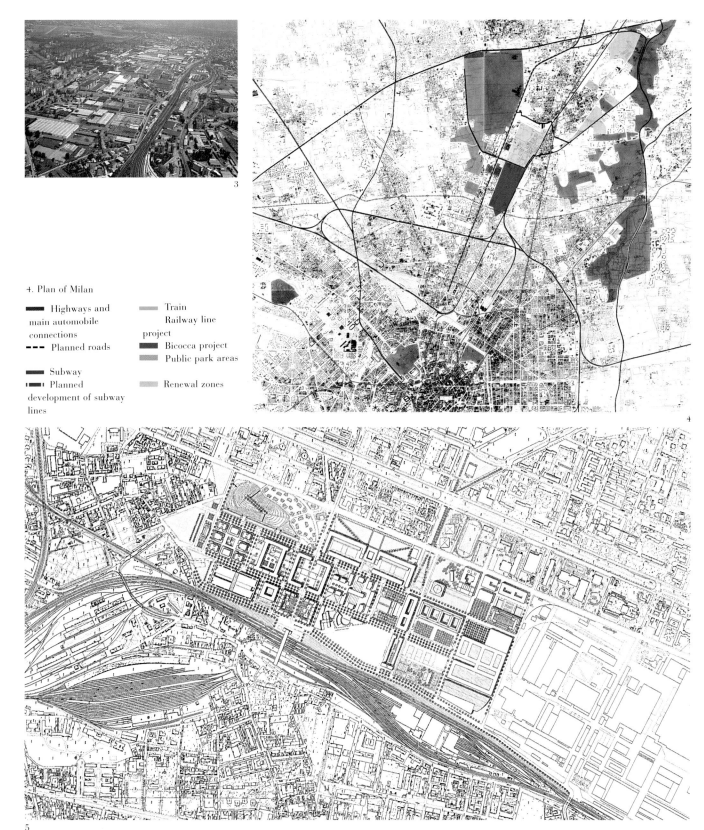

3

4. Plan of Milan

▰▰▰ Highways and
main automobile
connections
--- Planned roads

▰▰▰ Subway
▰▰▰ Planned
development of subway
lines

▰▰▰ Train
Railway line
project
▰▰▰ Bicocca project
▰▰▰ Public park areas

▰▰▰ Renewal zones

4

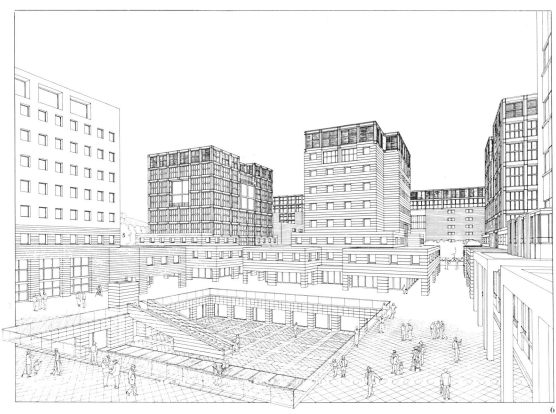

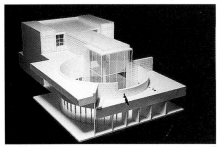

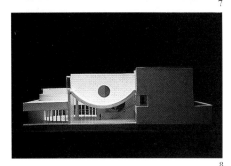

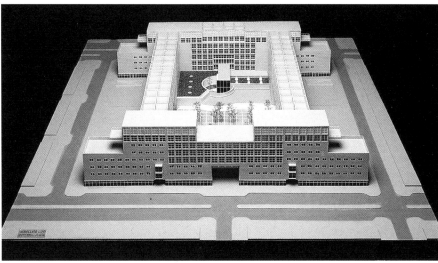

6. Foreshortened view
onto piazza of
administrative portion
7. 8. Views of study
model for spatial
representation of new
Siemens group office
9. View of model of
new Siemens group
office

10. Foreshortened view
of sunken courtyard
of new Environmental
Sciences building at the
Università degli Studi
11. 12. View of side
and transverse section
of Aem-Ansaldo fuel
cell experimental
power station

10

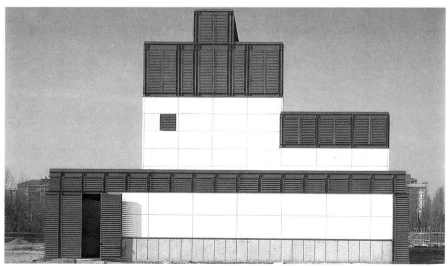

11

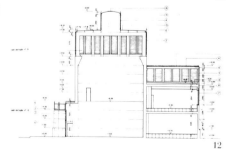

12

13

14

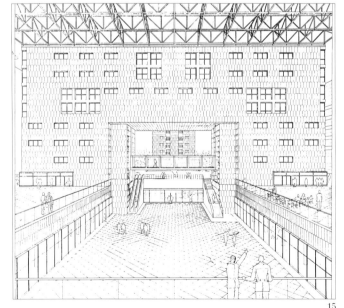

15

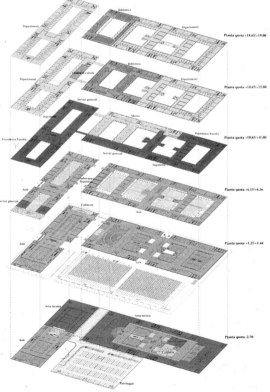

13. 14. Details of new
Environmental Sciences
building at the
Università degli Studi
15. Perspective view
of sunken pedestrian
piazza in residential
section
16. Axonometric plan
of new pole of the
Università degli Studi

16

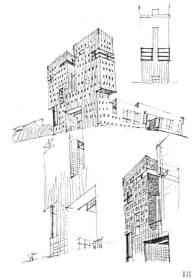

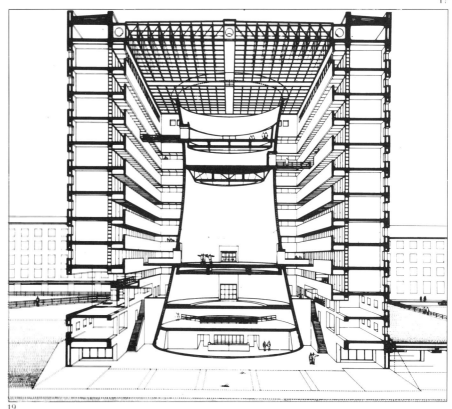

17. National Research
Council office
18. Study sketches
for a residential section

19. Perspective section
of new Pirelli Group
office

the south the third block is arranged around a central pedestrian courtyard-piazza, densely planted and articulated by the spaces representing the new office of the Siemens Group. Eight towers, intended for research and offices, arranged around a sunken central piazza, define the fourth block. An area intended for public parks, containing a hill achieved through excavation and demolition, redefines the edge of the Pirelli village, mediating the relationship with the high-speed roadway, while farther north a sloped green plain connects with double system of residences and services. A pedestrian and bicycle route, placed on the high greenery embankment, passes over the main access roads into the Lombardy capital, forming a system of portals and connecting the area with Bresso park and the adjacent athletic areas.

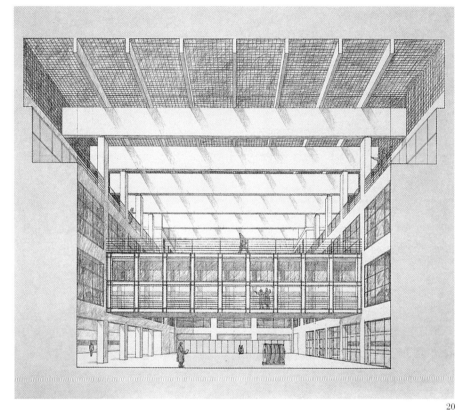

20

21

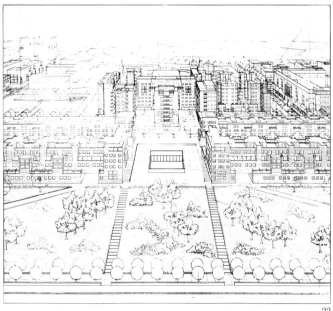

22

20. Perspective section of main hall of Pirelli research laboratories
21. Foreshortened view

of model of new Pirelli research laboratories
22. Bird's-eye perspective from west

150

Detailed Plan for the Area of the Former Sugar Refinery

Cesena 1991

The area of the former sugar refinery, approximately 220,000 square meters, is located northwest of the old city. To the north it is defined by the railway route, to the west by the Savio River, while to the south it stretches beyond the Via Zuccherificio (Sugar Refinery Road) to touch the first band of urban expansion beyond the old city. The entire area is characterized by a height difference of 6 meters between the eastern border and the embankment of the Savio River. The reconversion of the unused area lays out an urban design coherent with its context; its objective is the formation of a pivotal area between the renovated construction and the large park area that extends to the northwest to the railway line. Interpreting the particular location of the area next to the river and taking advantage of natural differences in height, the relationship between city and waterway is resolved with an artificial embankment forming the main public pedestrian space of the system and the border of the new river park. The installation, maintaining a relationship with its surroundings, is placed

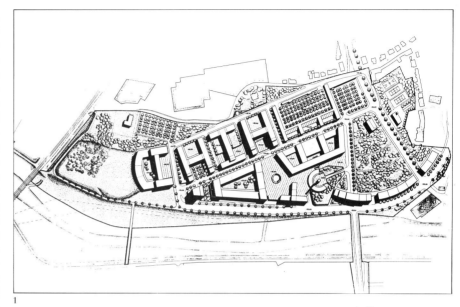

1

1. Plan
2. View of model from south

2

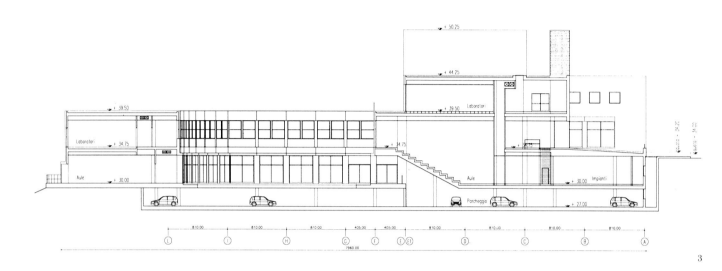

3

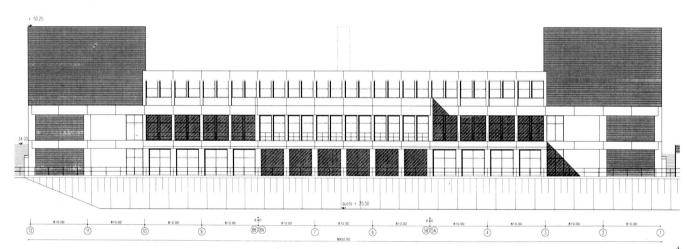

4

The new seat of the
university
3. Transverse section
4. South facade
5. Plan
6. 7. 8. Perspective
views onto pedestrian
piazzas

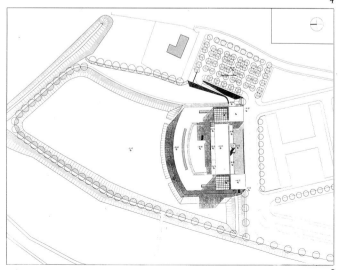

5

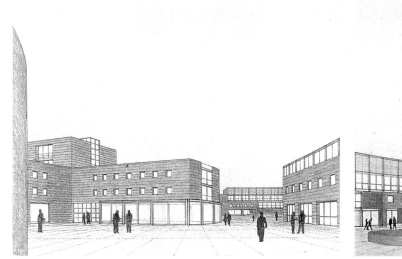

6

7

as a recognizable element inside the overall urban structure; the unified, homogeneous design makes it a built "wedge" inserted into the greenery. Starting from a central avenue, a street connects to the new bridge on the river. Due to the heavy traffic flow on Via Zuccherificio, its edges are planned as parks. Along the south side the existing row of plane trees is maintained, while a new park, located on the opposite side, extends up to the street connecting to the new bridge. In the eastern part, defined by the street and the main avenue, are located a large shopping center, equipped with a planted parking garage, and three blocks of affordable public housing. Between the main avenue and the street along the embankment, public buildings and a block of private residential buildings are projected. The offices of the administrative center, a university building, and private housing face the large piazza. A hotel encircles the old smokestack, the only evidence of the industrial past. To the south a series of houses arranged in a crescent formation act as a continuation of the existing building, while to the north the second edifice of the university heads the system toward the park. A footbridge connected to a bicycle path joins the area to the west with the racetrack park.

8

Proposal for the Development
of the Former Redaelli Area

Invited international consultation
Milan-Rogoredo 1994

The project tackles the reorganization of a nearby suburb of a large city, a place that offers limited areas on which to place new installation systems. The choice was for the establishment of urban sequences intended as large raised spaces capable of coherent control of the architecture, elevating the horizon of the landscape. The project institutes a continuity between the lengthening of Corso Lodi and the new axis on which the installation near the main hill is placed, with a bend at the railway station. A commercial system, developed around a new triangular piazza on two levels, continues along a tunnel that connects to existing public transportation. On the surface the triangular piazza, strongly characterized by administrative buildings, allows Rogoredo to join with the new installation, which presents buildings of heights consistent with the context. The most important part of the housing system is arranged in three blocks of four towers each, developed for the maximum height allowed and characterized by a high basement, that strengthens its identity.

A multilevel parking garage is located between the piazza and the system of towers. It is placed in a strategic position with respect to the expected public functions on the side, market and cultural facilities, in their turn endowed with parking lots. The system of three residential blocks, in whose basements private parking is located, is flanked by a series of athletic facilities for the housing system.

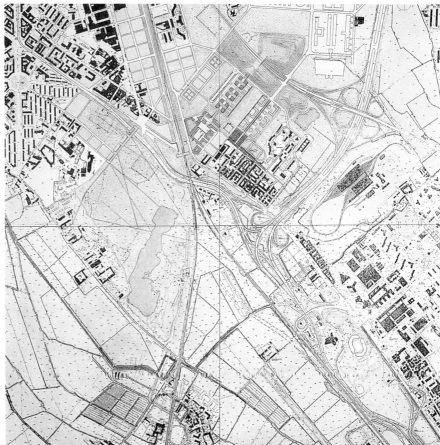

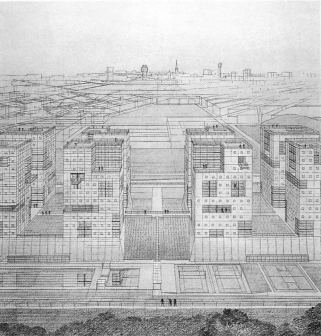

1. View of model
2. General plan
3. Perspective view toward north of residential blocks

Modifying the Existing City

There is no doubt that there is no new architecture without modifying existing architecture, but the interest that for some years has surrounded the idea of modification is not based on an overly obvious consideration, if by modification what it is intended is to become conscious of the importance of the existent—as structural material and not simply as background—within the planning process.

The project as modification tells us also that each case offers a specific truth to research and reveal, whether as essence of the goal or as a truth of the site and its geography, with regard to the physical manner of its own history. Thus, whether the concept of modification must be considered the most continuous and structural element, even if interpreted very differently, of the shifts that are verified in the theory of architectural planning of the last thirty years.

It may be asked if a language of modification were not describable, or a body of languages of modification, like the series of new languages that existed in the avant-garde years.

In the case of the architectural avant-garde, the new is pursued as value, special ties promoted with the notion of producing buildings of which architecture becomes the imitation; instead the notion of competence articulates interest in the history of the continuity of the discipline, in the idea of place as identity but also as raw material. It develops transverse relationships for which the planning process is, in the first place, a modification process that drags and organizes the area's waste contents which construct its asymmetry, its different density, and its values of diversification.

There are two methods with which the project acts in confronting the theme of the specific context. For one of these the answer is mimetic, stylistic, looks for reconciliation, recovers motifs and symbols. With the other method there is no reconciliation or apparent assimilation but the transformation of the relationships: the comparison takes on itself the value of language or, better still, of tension toward the constitution of languages. If, therefore, the quality of putting into action is that which is born from the tension between the specific case as essence of the specific goal and the truth of the site, not only the differences are values, but designing then also means modification of the very rules of our competence.

It seems that we are overturning here the famous Beaux-Arts debate between *parti* as model, *rendu* as expression, where the latter, as interpretation of the specific case, becomes structural for the formation of the former.

The project must also recognize today the impossibility of every natural coincidence with the site. The nature of architecture is first of all the nature of that non-coincidence.

There is no doubt that with the concept of modification as foundation of the project, I am also trying to describe a strategy directed especially to minimize errors and to avoid obstacles. We are dealing with a strategy that is a good distance from the risky generosities of the masters of the modern and that likewise present worrying similarities with the uncertain notion of change that crosses the indefinite and adaptable politics of our time.

With the idea of modification there is no hope therefore of definitively liberating gestures, of global reconciliations, of perfect consistencies, of definitive utopias. The context always constitutes an indirect material for the assurance of an architecture of place. That which is in a position to offer the architecture of modification is the description of the tension toward these unreachable values, certainly not the acceptance of their dissolution into environmental decoration.

From Vittorio Gregotti, *Dentro architettura* (Turin: Bollati Boringhieri, 1991)

Residences for Employees
of the Bossi Textile Industry

Partners: L. Meneghetti, G. Stoppino
Cameri, Novara 1961

The building is made up of two joined blocks, slightly offset in design, in which spaces are united by a stairway covered by a skylight.

The arrangement of the accommodations on different levels, shown by the discontinuity of the windows and by the alternating of the balconies, stresses the plasticity of the building. The choice of dark, exposed sand-blasted bricks for the perimeter walls shows clearly the unification of the installation.

1

2

1. 2. Views of building
3. First-floor plan

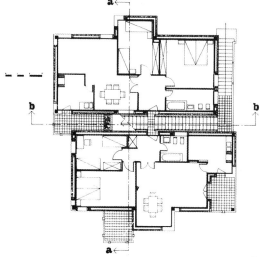

3

156

Cooperative Housing

Via Palmanova. Via L. Montegani.
Via D. da Settignano
Partners: L. Meneghetti. G. Stoppino
Milan 1962–64

The edifices on Via Palmanova are divided in two buildings of five stories each. Against the fringes of the surrounding suburb. the project sets the two residences. which reflect each other in every respect through a strict design. accented by grooved panels of hammered gritstone. The project for Via Montegani is divided into three buildings. of six stories each. whose fronts are modulated by a series of deep recesses and strong overhangs. The exposed supporting frameworks accent the fronts, which are covered in modular prefabricated slabs; the stair-elevator groups are included in cylindrical cement towers. The main entrances. the cellars. the power installations. and the garages are located in the basement. which is half underground. The facade Via Desiderio da Settignano varies the unified and typologically undifferentiated curtain wall in which is located by incorporating the plastic relief of small. prismatic bow-windows and through the chromatic use of partitions made of vertical panels of prefabricated brown gritstone. alternating with bands of white window frames.

Complex on
Via Palmanova
Detail of facade
and foreshortened
view from street

1

2

Complex on Via
L. Montegani
View of residential
complex

Building on Via
D. de Settignano
View of street
facade

Cadorna Project

Partners: G14 Progettazione,
Studio GPI, A. Calvesi
Milan 1984

Defining the edge of Parco Sempione and at the seam of the fracture represented by the band of tracks of the North Railway, the project places a large structure, 800 meters long, on the railway site. A continuous portico faces the area while the height of the park is raised in such a way as to join with the new building, which is identified as a border between the park and construction. Strongly connected to the surroundings, as a whole, the intervention is sensitive to the large variations in the urban morphology. The central part of the system, formed by two glass pavilions, contains athletic and recreational buildings and the bus station, and defines a new piazza that establishes a more open and articulated relationship with the park.

The head of the large Piazzale Cadorna resolves the complex problems of interchange among railway, streetcar and automobile lines with a large glass atrium placed over the present facade and connected to the longitudinal commercial gallery, which is entirely in glass and at triple height. Near the piazza, the glass atrium connects to a low platform that reconfigures the irregularities of the actual widening. At the opposite end the large installation is finished by a hotel, articulated in open courtyards with large portals, and buildings intended for administration, all of which face onto the park.

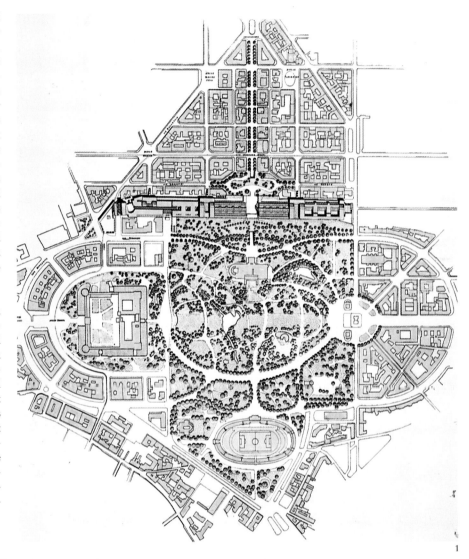

1

2

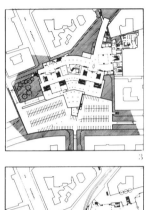

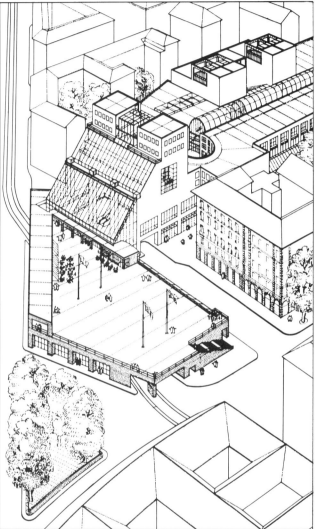

1. Plan
2. Perspective view onto
Piazza Curie toward
Palazzo della Triennale

Piazzale Cadorna
3. 4. 5. Plans of three
levels of platform
6. Axonometric drawing
7. Perspective section
of shopping arcade
8. Plan of first level

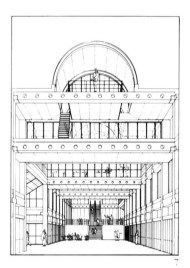

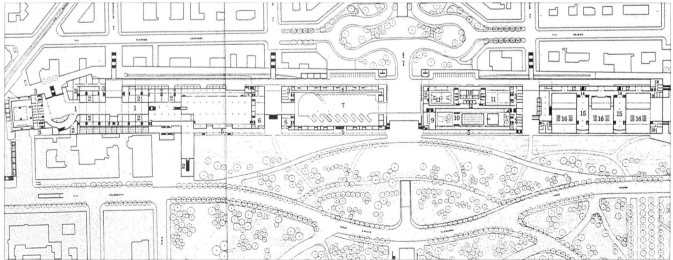

Sextius Mirabeau

Invited international competition
Aix-en-Provence 1990

The project deals with the subject of urban design, the very notion of a city and its expansion, inside a large empty space with fragmented edges but surrounded by consolidated historical areas. Starting from the axis of the wide Baroque avenue, the Cours Mirabeau, which structures the whole seventeenth-century quarter and connects it to the medieval center, the project envisions doubling it beyond the large piazza located at the border of the area, assigning it the role of new central spine for future urbanization. A series of blocks, for commercial and residential use, of different sizes and shapes, are arranged in continuity with the existing ones, recreating the missing urban fabric. It is proposed to recapture the heights of the historical buildings, restoring the alignments and several typological and morphological characteristics, such as the large courtyards filled with greenery, the layered roofs, and the strong overhangs of the roof on the line of the facade. A large piazza closes the avenue, describing itself as new central place, delimited by the special functions required in the competition: the new train station, a large hotel with casino, an opera house. The plans of these buildings, all isolated one from the other and placed slightly radially, bestow a clear legibility to the avenue on the border, placed on the layout of the ancient walls. The natural differences in ground height are utilized through the insertion of a large public parking area and a subway that crosses the whole area. Similarly, the whole railway line and the access and service roads for the new auto station, planned in connection with the train terminal, are dug out or underground, so as to save as much as possible of the area for pedestrian use.

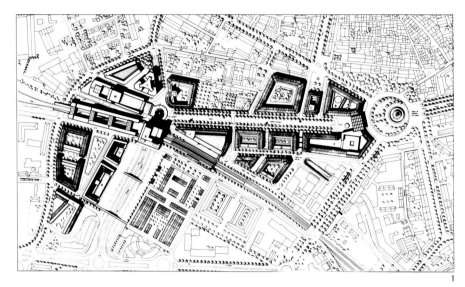

1

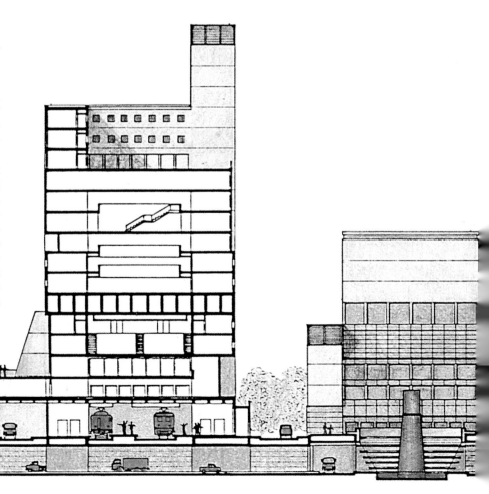

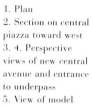

1. Plan
2. Section on central piazza toward west
3. 4. Perspective views of new central avenue and entrance to underpass
5. View of model from east

3

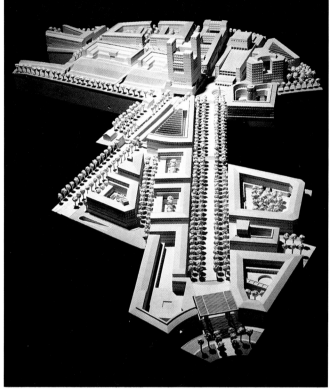

5

4

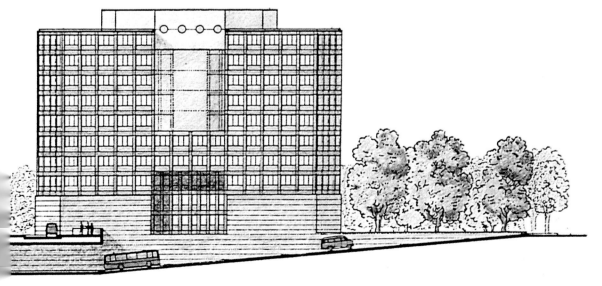

2

Place de l'Etoile

Invited international competition
Strasbourg 1991

This project, the winner of an international competition, occupies an area of 14 hectares that is currently a large empty space between the city's historic center and an outlying smaller, residential suburb. The project deals with the themes of planning on an urban scale; the area must serve the double function of port of entry to the city and to the transitional sites, as well as to provide the connecting link between these two parts. Assuming as a given that the road system is too far advanced in its construction to be modified, the arrangement would be an articulated series of buildings that follow two orthogonal axes between them, upon which lie the main pedestrian connecting roads, completely separate from vehicular traffic. The apparent rigidity of the plan is negated by the articulation of the proposed volumes and by the richness of the projected functions: a large pedestrian piazza to the north, joined along the canal, leads to a pedestrian road covered by a transparent curtain which occasions the creation of a shopping arcade. From this, access to the south leads to an international administrative center, crossed by a system of inclined piazzas; here are activities of public interest: restaurants, small stores, an athletic center, an auditorium, a small exhibition center. The system of rampways allows traffic to go beyond the

1

southern part of the rotary without the danger caused by the intense traffic for the nearby highway exit. Beyond it opens a round piazza of a more intimate nature, tied to the reduced scale of the surrounding buildings. The piazza is bounded by a residential building, characterized by a ramp that restores the natural height of the ground at the beginning of the main street of the suburb. In an east–west direction a system of footbridges connects the existing seat of municipal administrative offices, through the shopping arcade, to a public parklike terrace, open on the canal at the point of

arrival of the tourist ferry-boats. A motor-coach terminal and a series of hotel businesses complete this area. A system of inclined planes of greenery and a scenic landscape create a major connection with the canal, offering the chance to redesign the suburb's waterfront. A careful study has been directed to problems of vehicular traffic, of car parking (underground on two levels), and of the treatment of street sections: wide sidewalks, rows of trees and bicycle paths transform the area, presently an automobile clearance, in a part of the city with a strong urban character.

1. View of model
from east
2. View of head
toward south
3. Plan of project

2

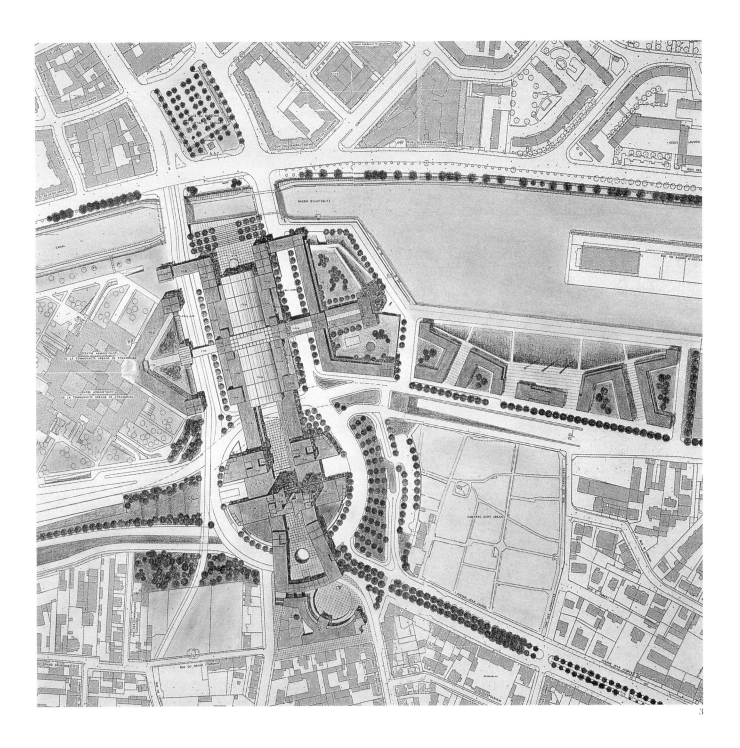

3

New Office
of the Public Services
Municipal Agency

Partners: F. Mascellani, M. Felisatti
Parma 1987–93

The intervention is placed in direct confrontation with a wide parcel of land of primarily agricultural use. In the interest of architectural interpretation of the environmental context, a study has been completed on the local rural structures. The body of the agency is made up of discrete buildings, distanced from the access roads which are considered service elements, finding their installation logic in specific reciprocal relationships and, on the whole, in the scale of the landscape. The buildings join around a triple system of empty spaces: the first such space, proceeding from the main entrance, is defined by the office building, the garage for light transport vehicles, and the staff dressing room; the second, the main space for light vehicle movement, is included between the building for laboratories and workshops, with the main warehouse and the fronts of the garage for heavy and light transport vehicles; the third, to the east, is included between the office building, the dressing room building, and the head of the service spine of the recreation center.

1. View of entrance to workshops
2. Overall view of surrounding territory
3. Foreshortened view of first piazza
4. Detail of portico that encircles laboratories
5. Plan

1

2

3

4

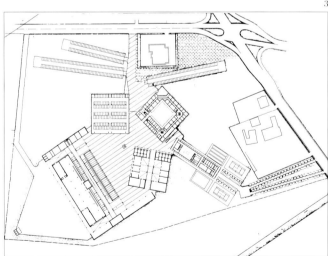

5

6

7

6. View of second
piazza
7. View of interior
of garage

Development Proposal
for the Motta Area

Milan 1988–93

The intervention area, approximately 35,000 square meters, is occupied by an unused industrial complex made up of sheds and office buildings of poor quality. The project will restore the entire district by means of comprehensive restructuring. Therefore an increase of uncovered surface and the creation of a large public park have been planned. The project envisions residential, administrative, and commercial buildings, a seniors' residence, a public building for cultural activities, and an underground parking garage. Along Viale Campania, a large portal connects the street with an interior piazza, around which buildings are ranged, intended for commercial and residential use. A strong overhang element, placed on the line of the buildings' eaves, strengthens the sense of space enclosed by the courtyard and protects the fronts from solar radiation. An inhabited tower closes the piazza, acting also as a hinge between the geometrically closed space of the courtyard and the empty space behind, transformed into a park. Two pedestrian passageways pass under the tower, establishing another permeable point in the system. The residences, arranged on the edge of the park, draw their shape from their location—in close proximity to the greenery: a series of loggias, balconies, and terraces articulate the facades, multiplying the fronts onto the park. The construction of a building for cultural and neighborhood activities is also projected.

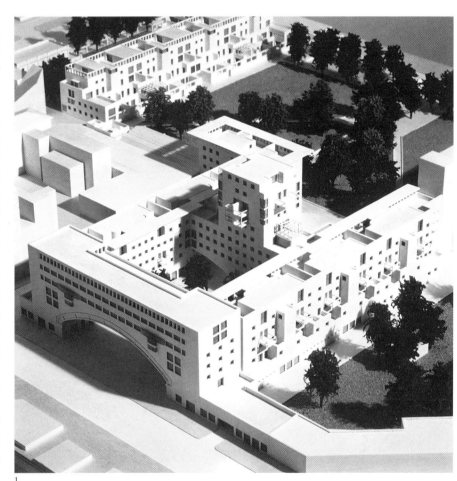

1

1. View of model from southeast

2. Perspective view of interior court

3. Bird's-eye view

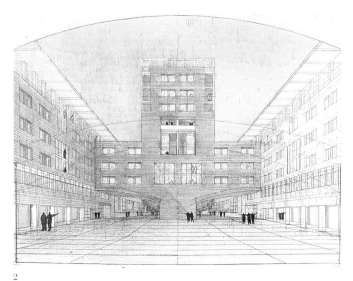

2

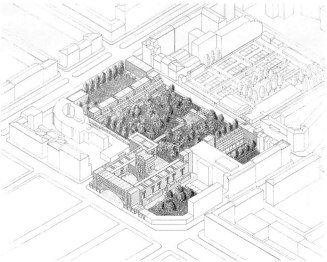

3

Building on the Goerdelerring

Invited international competition
Leipzig 1994

The project poses the problem of relating the theme of the skyscraper to the identity of the fortified old city. The area, northwest of the Ring, in close relation to the Marktplatz main station, is a place wherein different urban fabrics have historically entered into conflict, and it is still marked by the destructions of war and ensuing reconstructions. The project proposes an edifice 99 meters high, characterized by a double structure: a system of two towers, one for administrative purposes and the other residential. Such an arrangement allows the large required space, more than 40,000 square meters, to be broken up into elements more suitable in scale and continuity to the existing one. The two towers, one rotated in relation to the other, "react" to the curved progression of the Ring and offer a variable perception of the building on the urban panorama.

The plan also includes a reorganization of the public and private roads, and the elimination of the footbridge that passes over the Ring; the reconstruction of borders through the extension of the park strip along the Ring, with particular attention to the maintenance of the character of the equipped garden; the redefinition of Richard-Wagner-Platz through the addition of a semicircular structure; the enlargement of the Museum of Natural History with a new wing, symmetrical to the existing one; and the construction of a new street-car station, which, in its glassed space, appears almost as the "ghost" of the old Stadttheater, which until the war stood on this site.

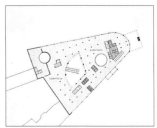

1. Foreshortening
of the Goerdelerring
(photomontage)
2. Overall perspective
view
3. Plan of ground level
4. View of model
5. Plan
6. Plan of basement
level
7. Standard floor plan
of towers

4

5

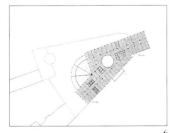

6

7

Three Towers at Danube City

Invited international competition
Vienna 1993

The project confronts the problem of the lack of a recognizable installation principle that would be capable of structuring this new part of the Viennese urban area. Seizing the particularly strategic position of the area and the possibility of developing the project in height, the project creates a very tall element that can dialogue at a distance with the consolidated fabric of the old city—a central place with which the surrounding fabric will have to compare itself.

The center of the proposed system is a circular piazza, excavated out of a platform that ends the road parallel to the river near Danube Park, crossing the whole new building area. The platform becomes an essential element of the system, establishing the front toward the canal. In the platform are incised several passageways to access the upper level of the piazza, onto which are placed the metallic structures of the towers. Double and triple heights of these armatures cross the interior spaces of the towers. The triangular form of the base is articulated in such a way as to analyze the potentials in vertical and horizontal section, the possibilities of extension and variation and therefore of identity on every level, the identification of the orientations and of the relative positions of each observer for a deepening of the theme of the tower.

The two towers near the canal are symmetrical: according to available information, one contains a hotel that uses the possibilities offered by the structure of a large, central, empty space like a hall, and the other, apartments on the top eight floors. The third tower, for offices, is rotated with respect to the first two: such a rotation is functional especially for the perception of what joins the complex from the bridge-subway system, besides being an essential variation to the overall orientation of the system.

1. Plan
2. Facades along the Danube
3. 4. Views of model from south
5. Transverse section

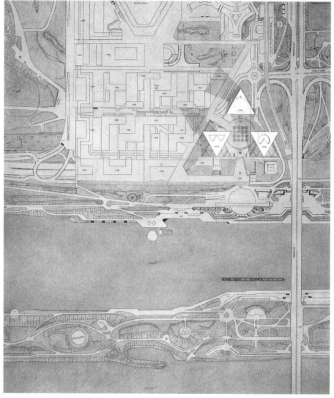

1

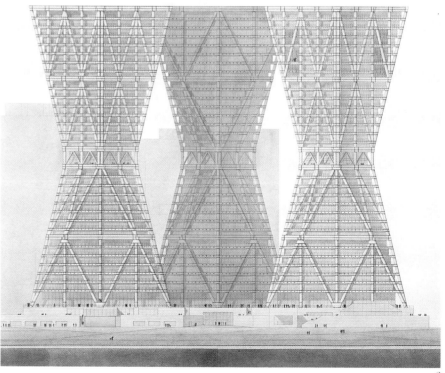

2

3

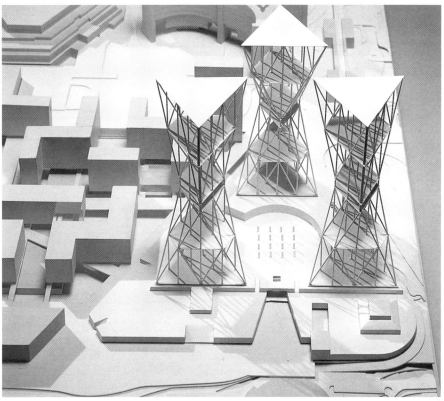

4

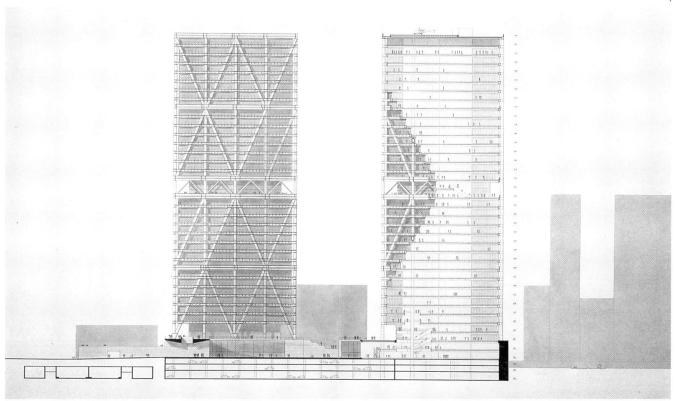

5

Building Complex along
the Holzhafen

Invited international competition
Altona. Hamburg 1993–94

The three buildings to the east of the basin, formally independent between them, are placed as a element of mediation between the urban fabric and the large harbor structures. From the volumetric relation, the diversified public spaces are defined. Linked between them, they maintain open ends from the city toward the basin. The continuous basement, which houses the parking lots, raises the public height beyond the maximum tide level and, at the same time, links the three spaces, provides a strong visual continuity underscored by the progress of the platform along the Elbe. At the scale of individual buildings, the large holes form exceptions with respect to the homogeneity of the facade. The building to the west of the Holzhafen is characterized by two structures perpendicular to the river that, setting back, reach a height of nine stories. In such a way the view from the city toward the port is kept open without putting the buildings on the back of the Elbstrasse on the second level. A three-floored building located on the edge of the basin connects the two tall structures, defining a double system of squares of different heights that relate the street to the river through a large opening at the center of the low building. The two tall buildings are connected with the edifice behind by two bridgelike structures that pass over the Elbstrasse, defining a promenade continuous in height.

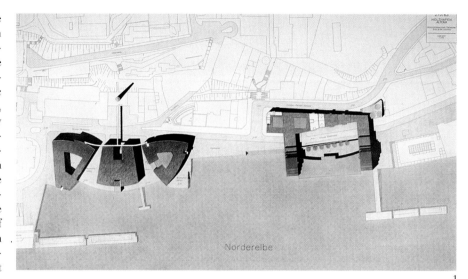

1

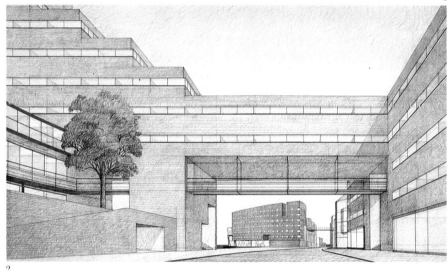

2

1. Plan
2. Foreshortened view toward west along Elbstrasse
3. Perspective view from river

3

Architecture of the Interior
and Settings

In the great tradition of the past, the architecture of the interior did not belong to any separate specialization. It was simply the result of an overall conception of the organism or the metaphor of the same architecture without any adjective. In the tradition of the modern, it has been the occasion for experiments that have formed historical turning points. In recent times temporality and impatience have made architecture of the interior slide toward the transitory nature of fashion, the constructed stage set as a function of photographic service, of image market.

It would be, I believe, necessary to return the instruments to the proper ends and to imagine to be able to restore to the interior all the coherence with respect to the organism when it may be architecturally complete, when it has to do with, for example, a large public structure upon which it acts at all levels, or, as in the case of the cruise ships, where it becomes a system of objects.

Yet, on many occasions, at least in the last century, the interior often assumes its own autonomy, for long and short periods, sometimes of the spatial microexperiment of subjects and relations, other times of the formation of the image, of atmosphere, sometimes still of the interior destined to communicate an autonomous message of stability and duration.

In the setting born as such, then, it is difficult to solve the dialectic between the aggression of the image of the setting itself and what is to be displayed. Sometimes, that is, it is the setting itself that is needed in order to communicate, other times it has the duty to disappear with discretion.

Tadini and Lambertenghi Shop

Partners: L. Meneghetti, G. Stoppino
Novara 1955

The store is organized on three levels, the ground floor, first underground floor, and a large mezzanine floor, in a building designed by Giovanni Muzio, in the town center. The plan sought to respect as much as possible the open space projected by Muzio, stressing the transparency toward the exterior and between the various levels with large glass windows: in the room on the ground floor the sales areas are distinguished from the passageways by means of flooring design in large wooden hexagons, set into the marble floor. A wide winding staircase rises to the mezzanine level. Each stair is supported by a metal tube that, from the floor, bends to carry the stair and rises again to the ceiling, producing a cage effect around the stairway. A spiral tube wraps around the cage and serves as a handrail, finished by slats of wood and bronze that form the true balustrade. All the furniture was specially designed, for example, the lamps hanging from the ceiling in two-colored glass, light green and opal white, created for this purpose by Venini.

1

1. View of ground floor
2. Foreshortened view
of mezzanine
3. Metal staircase

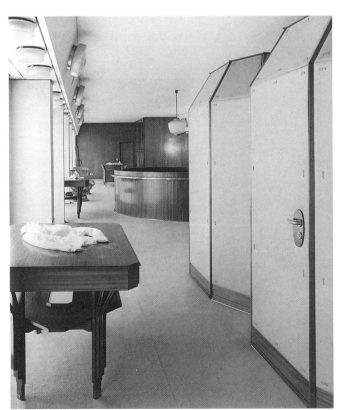

2

3

Tadini and Lambertenghi Shop

Partners: L. Meneghetti, G. Stoppino
Casale Monferrato, Alessandria 1961

The project redefines an existing sales space in a building in the old city. The shop is located under the porticoes that line the main street. The existing structures, formed by large bearing walls that are not at right angles, pose serious constraints. A series of demolitions have freed the space as much as possible, allowing for the introduction of a mezzanine level facing onto a double height parallel to the porticoed front. The interior space is unified and kept consistent by the mahogany revetment that forms the doors, shelves, closets, dressing rooms, and all the balustrades of the stairs and mezzanine. The only different elements are the panels of white stretched canvas that make up the backgrounds of the showcases, the mirrors in dark green shiny stucco on the portions of original walls not integrable in the furnishings, and the continuous bronze chrome grills that hide the radiators. The monochromatic predominance of the dark mahogany above contrasts with the light pavements—white marble on the ground floor and gray moquette in the mezzanine. The furnishings recall those designed for other sales locations of the same chain, but these were created expressly for this purpose in dark mahogany.

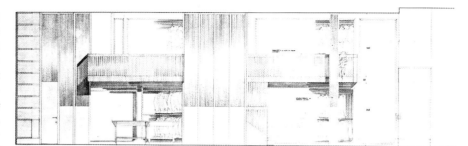

1

2

1. Longitudinal section
2. Foreshortened view
of ground floor
3. Detail of wooden
staircase

3

Apartment U.C.

Partners: L. Meneghetti, G. Stoppino
Novara 1964

The apartment is located on the top floor of a condominium and is characterized by the great freedom in design of the spaces and by the transparency between interior and exterior, achieved through the redesign of windows looking out onto a large terrace. The different heights of the ceiling, "broken down" to make the installation of skylights possible, and the large glass wall toward the terrace, reshaped to create a sunroom that penetrates into the living room, characterize the general installation of the apartment. The positioning of the day zone is unified, with a library that can be isolated by a sliding wall. The floors and revetments are matched in two tones of color: gray for the Bardiglio marble slabs, alternated with staggered slabs of pure white, and warm tones for the revetment parts in Mansonia walnut and brown cloth.

1. View toward open-sky sunroom
2. Detail of entrance
3. View of library

Apartment G.A.

Milan 1976

The design project was executed in a recently constructed building, characterized by large openings in the facade. A system of multiple screens, in uniform square modules of iron and glass, permits the fractionalization of the interior spaces of the apartment without losing the overall dimension, emphasizing the effect of brightness and filter between the interior and exterior spaces. All the floors are in rough slabs of black slate, a material chosen to accentuate the contrast with the brightness and the regularity of the glass screens.

1. Foreshortened view of hallway
2. View of living room

1

2

Missoni Boutique

Milan 1976

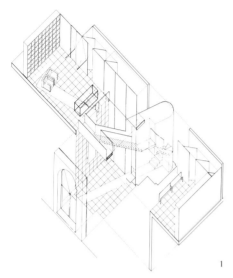

The small space on Via Montenapoleone is characterized by the black shape that diagonally crosses the double height; it contains the rectilinear tract of stairs that lead to the upper level.

A track on the floor indicates the role of the transverse element suspended in the void, transgression of the rule of the orthogonal latticework and the specularity and symmetry that define the interior space.

The floor and walls are made of slabs of serena stone, while the stairway passage and furnishings are in black-colored wood. The ceiling is covered in stretched canvas, turned again on the walls.

1. Axonometric view
2. Store-front window

Italian Autobody

Turin 1977

Realized inside the Promotion of Fine
Arts Building and dedicated to the relationship between the culture of design
and the project in the history of the automobile from the beginning of the century
until today, the exhibit hinges on the contrast between the automobiles, exhibited
as sculptures on pedestals, and the large
white rooms, between the modularity of
the reference grids and the forms of the
automobile bodies, between their smooth
surface and the natural material of the
wooden structures, tinted white.

Design Furniture from Italy

Tokyo 1983

The setting of an anthological exhibit on
Italian design takes advantage, in the
entrance space of the Sogetsu Kaikan, of
the exceptional presence of an important
contemporary work of art: the large
square by Isamu Noguchi. This work is
comprised of a sequence of levels placed
at different heights and joined by flights
of stairs of varying lengths. The Italian
objects are exhibited within containers of
white stretched canvas, each object separate, without compromising the continuity of the installation. On the upper floors
the installation is divided by a white continuous trellis-work that divides, unites,
or puts in relief the exhibited works
through use of white canvas and special
lighting.

Manhattan Apartment

New York 1984

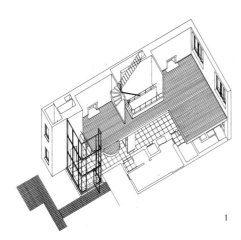

1

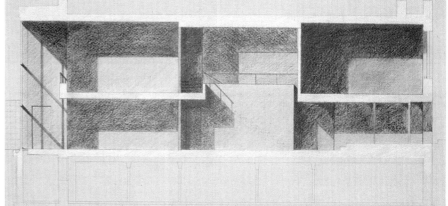

2

Intervening in the interior of an existing building, a brownstone whose first two floors and interior garden are being restored, the project tries to overcome the dichotomy between private interior and public interior, emphasizing the spatial articulation and ensuring at the same time a character of domesticity to a dwelling that houses a collection of contemporary art worthy of a public institution. Thanks to a large bow-window installed at double height and a vertical empty space corresponding with the entrance, a widened perception of the interior space and a new relationship with the garden are achieved, together with a simultaneous readability of the dimensions of the building shell. So as not to compete with the works of art housed in the apartment, the materials chosen are shown in their material state: the floors are of smooth Lara stone and natural Anjccio parquet, the walls of glazed rustic stucco and raw silk.

3

4

1. Axonometric view
2. Longitudinal section
3. View of window
toward interior garden
4. View of entrance
5. 6. 7. Details
of interior finishings

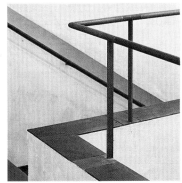

5

6

7

Bardelli Cashmere
Cotton & Silk Shop

Milan 1985–86

The theme of this project, for a store selling clothing and objects, is the spatial reordering of an unusual environment, an old carriageway and an interior courtyard, marked by countless changes and layerings undergone over time.

A cylindrical area, paved with slabs of gray trachyte and entirely faced covered in rose-colored pear wood, is inserted between the irregular progression of the courtyard walls, adapting a hall to a central plan on two levels: the first, of a lower height, is defined by a polygonal perimeter of containers, above which a circular-shaped mezzanine juts out; this is accessed by a stairway excavated in the thickness of the walls. In the resulting spaces between the precise geometric insertion and the preexisting space, the sales areas are created.

A small gallery, on the site of the carriageway, becomes the exhibition space onto which the windows face. It is conceived as a continuous front with a polygonal plan; it also acts as an interior street that assumes the role of relational element between the public road and the circular space.

1. Foreshortened view of entrance gallery
2. Longitudinal section of entrance
3. 4. Plans for both levels

1

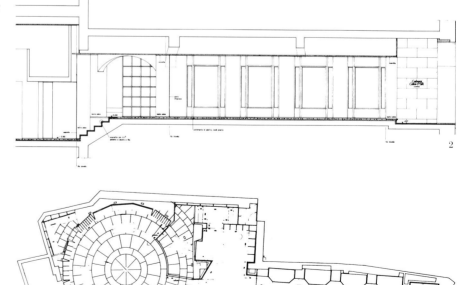

2

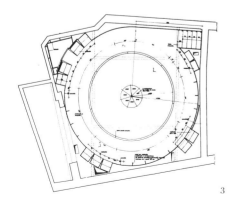

3

4

5. 6. 7. Views and
details of interior

5

6

7

Marisa Boutique

Milan 1978–88

The project for the first Marisa sales space in the old city redefines the available space, without changing the overall dimensions. A metal screen, in square modules, widens the perception of the surroundings, which reflect on the mirrored surfaces and generate a complex image despite the simple elements put into play.

Ten years later, the plan for a second boutique, facing onto the same street, confronts the theme of renewal of a space lacking particular qualities. Inside the space is inserted a large skylight that allows the height of the place not to be forfeited, masking the necessary installations and assuming the traits of a lighted ceiling. At the center, an entirely covered pillar becomes an element that reproportions the space and virtually separates the space. The furnishing is intentionally minimal: the interior surfaces are covered in slabs of Vicenza stone, dressed on the floor and sanded on the walls. Following the acquisition of the adjacent space two years later, it was necessary to reexamine the whole layout. The project develops a new "L" plan, emphasizing the hinge point through a large winding staircase in metal and pear wood, that leads to the underground floor. Refusing the traditional shop window/sales area relationship, the fronts near the street are defined by hanging panels of silkscreened glass that act as semitransparent screens. The floors are made of speckled Candoglia marble, while the walls are stucco.

1. 2. View and detail of first boutique 3. View of second boutique, no longer in existence

4. 5. 6. Views of interior
of new boutique

B & B Stand

Milan 1988

The setting for the Salone del Mobile is finalized at the exhibition for the company's technological and production history, through objects that have characterized its image.

On large inclined wooden planes an oneiric passage is set where technological elements and the objects in their final forms are compared. The systematic displacement is reinforced by large mirrored surfaces that multiply the space and by videos that project images in a continuous cycle.

Davide Cenci Store

Milan 1990

The store is located in a recently restructured building in the old city. The available surface was characterized by its unfolding on several floors but with little depth on each level. Not being able then to enlarge the space in the plan, the project fashions a large central space for the entire height; this relates the different levels to each other, connected them by a winding stairway and by platforms. For the finishing touches, a selection of traditional materials is preferred: cream-colored shiny stucco for the walls and speckled in two tones of color for the floors, with the insertion of pieces of Candoglia marble in a regular pattern and Honduras mahogany for all the furnishings, specially designed.

1. The winding staircase
2. 3. View and detail
of interior

Fila Store

New York 1991

The store is characterized from the outside by the facade in convex aluminum, almost like a part of a ship with a large porthole that, from the inside, frames a segment of Madison Avenue life and, from the outside, is a bright window clock: through it shines the rosewood that is the main revetment in the store. The two levels were designed as bridges placed over a boat, connected between them by a bright spiral stairway, finished in encaustic blue. The floors and display cases are in natural wood; the false ceiling, in punctured aluminum sheets, diffuses the light through many small points.

1

1. View of entrance on Madison Avenue
2. Ground-floor and first-floor plans

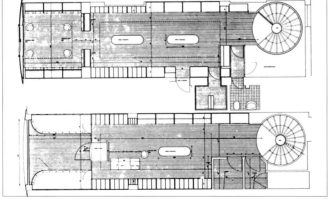

2

Os Filling Station

1992

1. 2. View of model
of typical station
3. View of filling
station on the outskirts
of Seville

1

The station located in the outskirts of Seville is the first creation of a series of sales points of the Saroil company's Os gasoline for Spain. The project focuses on the strong and immediate recognizability of the service area thanks to the extreme simplicity of the formal elements that define the spaces, the architectonic value of the letters that form the signage, the characterization of the space, and the stylistic homogeneity that distinguishes the architectural components as well as the installation components. There are three colors at play: blue, red, and yellow. Blue was used for the aluminum panels that cover the iron structure of the shelter and for the roof under which the functional elements of the station (the pumps, the store-bar) are located. The red and the yellow, the colors of Spain, distinguish the Os signage.

2

3

191

'61–'91 Italian Furniture.
The Different Ages
of Languages

Milan 1992

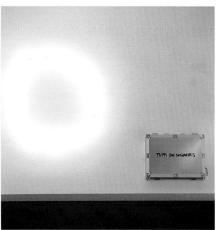

The exhibit gathers the best of the production of Italian design from 1961 to 1991. The setting is divided into three main sectors, each one intended to illustrate the production of a decade. The sectors devoted to the sixties and seventies are characterized by white rugs on multiple levels, on which the objects are exhibited, with apparent randomness.

The background is created by photos and illustrations relevant to the years of production of the exhibited materials. The products of the Eighties are instead set in small, thematic environments that face onto a central gallery. A white arcaded screen, enlivened by colored neon, separates the exhibit spaces from the public access.

Civilization of Machines

Turin 1990–93

A large exhibition system was placed within the space of the Lingotto di Torino in order to illustrate the world of Italian industry.

Technical, technological, and cultural results are gathered in a space designed with walls of sinusoidal progression. A "gallery of materials" was also created, setting in sequence four environments, entirely made in glass, steel, aluminum, and copper.

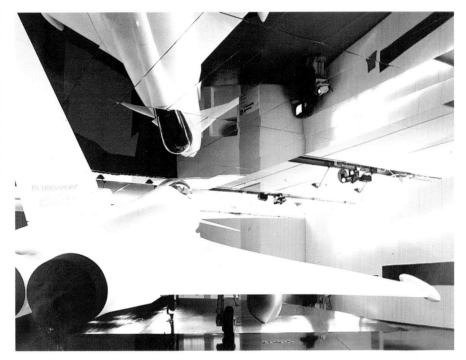

Costa Lines Cruise Ships   *Costa Classica*

1990–94

The Costa cruise ships, *Classica* and *Romantica* are conceived as large buildings, with floors-decks variously articulated, which culminate at 35 meters in height with a circular glass space that allows a 360-degree view. The project does not try to recapture the style typical of transatlantic liners but searches for an architectural consistency that fully reveals the naval machine. On one hand, the quality of spaces, furnishings, and finishings restores the image of the tradition of Italian design, which has as its

1

1. Side view   main access hall   on upper deck
2. View of space   3. Upper deck with   of bow
with metal stair   pool   5. Second open deck
suspended above   4. View of gym,   with fountain

2

3

4

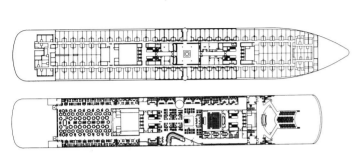

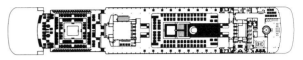

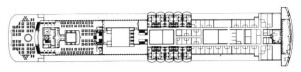

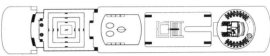

6. Plans of a cabin deck and of public decks

7. View toward buffet room at stern

8. Foreshortened view of restaurant

9. Foreshortened view of single cabin

10. View of main entrance hall with sculpture by Arnaldo Pomodoro

6

7

8

9

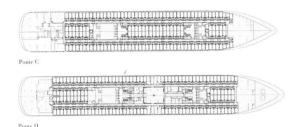

Ponte C

Ponte D

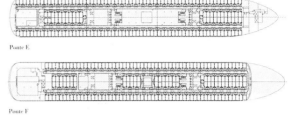

Ponte E

Ponte F

1

points of reference the large ships built between the two wars. On the other hand, a series of relationships and spatial complexities are conceived that do not grant anything to the market of scenographic camouflage. The finishing materials recapture the tradition of natural materials: woodwork of different kinds, marbles and stones lightened thanks to new technical processes, Venetian plasters, and decorated fabrics. The cabins transform themselves from large sitting rooms into comfortable bedrooms. In both ships, the entrance hall cuts through five decks, which open onto the hall through balustrades, emphasizing the effect of transparency and spatial enlargement. A series of works by contemporary artists enrich several preferred spaces: sculptures in the entrance hall by Arnaldo Pomodoro and Shingu, decorated panels by Emilio Tadini in the 700-seat auditorium on the *Costa Classica*, or mosaics in a design by Sambonet that cover the walls of the casino, and the kinetic installation of Shingu moved by the wind on the deck with the pool on the *Costa Romantica*. Bars, restaurants, shopping centers, conference and multi-purpose rooms, gyms and pools complete the project, for a total of 20,000 square meters in each ship—space intended for the sojourn of passengers.

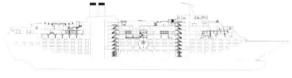

2

3

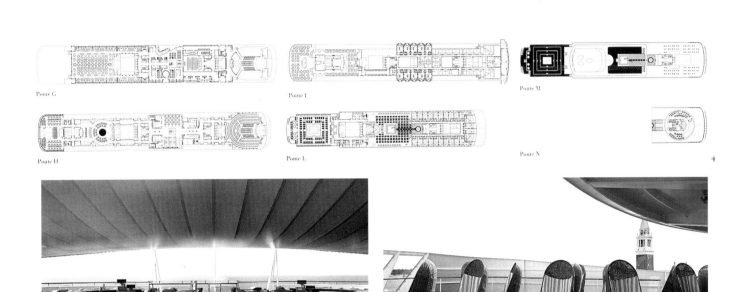

Ponte G

Ponte I

Ponte M

Ponte H

Ponte L

Ponte N

4

5

6

1. Plans of cabin decks
2. Longitudinal section
3. View of deck with pool and sculpture *Wind Message* by Susumu

Shingu
4. Plans of public decks
5. Foreshortened view toward bar on exterior stern deck

6. Foreshortened view of upper deck with rotating armchairs having wicker protection against

the wind
7. Discothèque in circular space above decks

7

8

8. View of stairway suspended over entrance hall
9. 10. Restaurant
11. View of one of ship's lounges
12. View of double suite
13. Outer balcony of a suite
14. 15. Amphitheater (Deck G/H at bow)

11

12

13

14

15

The project does not stray from the guiding criteria of the previous two. It is the largest cruise ship intended for the European market and will become the new flagship of the Costa Cruise fleet. With a tonnage of 74.000 tons and a length of 251 meters, it is capable of accommodating 3.000 passengers, including 800 crew members. The areas for the passengers, between the cabins and the common spaces, are 40.000 square meters. The interior spaces are divided around a large entrance hall that cuts through 7 of the 14 decks and culminates in a large skylight at a height of 19 meters. An installation by Gianfranco Pardi will be positioned at the center of the hall. The ship will hold 964 cabins, 14 mini-suites, and 6 passenger suites. Also planned are athletic facilities, a gym with a covered pool, a tennis court, an outdoor jogging track and two outdoor pools, a theater with 1000 seats, a library, several meeting and conference rooms, besides the restaurants, bars, discothèque, casino and games room, children's rooms, and shopping areas.

Costa Victoria

1

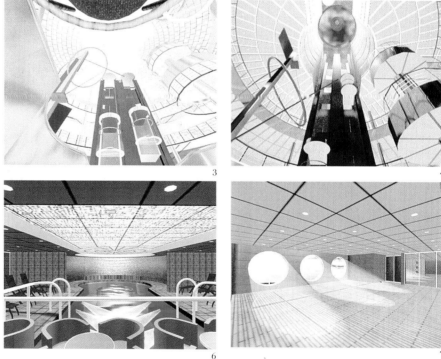

2

3

4

5

6

7

1. View of model
2. 3. 4. Simulations
of entrance hall

5. 6. 7. Simulations
of several rooms
8. Profile

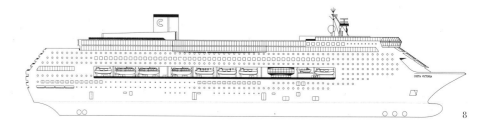

8

Exhibition System for Alenia

1993

View of model and detail of structural joint of horizontal beams

The particular productive sector, the aerospace industry, and the need to plan a flexible exhibition system able to adapt itself to various exhibition contexts, have entailed the planning of a modular system based on a structure of beams and pillars in aluminum. Beside the models, components and preparations from microchips to air-traffic control consoles are exhibited. A *Wunderkammer* was also created for the exhibition of satellite models. This space, defined by semireflective crystals that produce a refractive play of light between the floor and the ceiling, lets the spectator move around among satellites in scale, floating among stars in motion, designed by a laser installation.

Setting for Unifor

1992–95

1. Orgatec, Cologne
1992
2. Eimu, Milan 1995
3. Orgatec, Cologne
1995
4. Orgatec, Cologne
1992

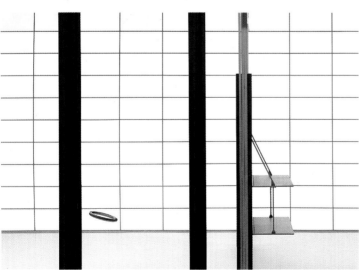

3

4

Interior Design
for a Yacht

1994

The interiors of the yacht *Blue Velvet* are distinguished by a particular attention to materials and mounting systems: the yacht had to be light in weight in order to reach the desired speed of 44 knots.

The floors, the ceilings, and the walls of the living quarters are all covered in natural leather, applied on a special support of aluminum sockets. Nothing has been screwed down: all the panels have been attached, thanks to a new system of velcro, and fixed on aluminum frames, which, in their turn, were mounted on the structure of the yacht without rigid connections, using a system of vibrostops. For the service areas, sanitary places, and

1

2

kitchen, in which the floors have a particular nonslip texture, a covering in natural aluminum was chosen. The mirrors are made of a composite formed by steel laminate, perfectly reflective, on a sheet of plastic material.

So as not to exceed the total weight fixed for the hull, the exterior decks in aluminum were exclusively treated non-slip and not with the traditional teak finish.

The terrace of the stern houses an outside dining area. On the top deck in the sunbathing area, a system of adjustable cushions and seats allow them to be changed in arrangement and use.

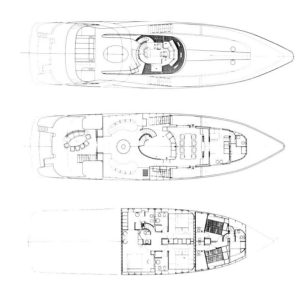

3

1. View of yacht
2. Foreshortened view of living room
3. General plans
4. Upper deck
5. Stairway connecting to cabin deck

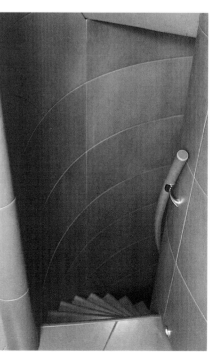

+

5

6. Owner's cabin
7. Bridge
8. Dining room

6

7

8

The identification of an image of production sites as a condenser of the social encounter, of activity for the common good, seems to be irreparably in decline.

The victorious world, quantitatively significant, seems to be that of administration and of the marketing of things and information. Or better, the places of production of manufactured things are located so far away geographically as to become, for now, not architecturally significant. Nothing excludes the possibility that these, starting from their new peripheral sites, can again become culturally and politically central. In the meantime it is those very places of the production of immaterial goods that search for their own identity, often with a self-mimicking effort.

In our case the process of the architectural identification of research typologies, of learning and of production passes through the notion of work, coincides with it, without other adjectival distinctions. For us not only an important part of the principle of responsibility in its confrontations with the collective is centered in the idea of work, but above all the subject's way of accessing the world, of knowing how to change it. Therefore, assimilated into the idea of the work site are also spaces for university education; an interpretation in which it is the actual continuous learning (knowledge moved by interest) that becomes a model of every activity: utopia of every activity as creative activity, that is, daily necessity.

For this we ascribe a special importance to architecture of the work place as the monument to the modern. And in this sense we have always tried to design them, to have them assume a role in the very development of the work.

New Departments of Science
at the Università degli Studi
at Parco d'Orléans

Partner: Gino Pollini
Palermo 1969–90

The complex rises to the north of the old city, next to the already existing university buildings that were constructed after the First World War. The intervention arranges three large enclosures on the slight slope, ordering in a unified plan the urban and territorial signs of the depression of an ancient stream. The external double image conforms in its dimensions and scale to the landscape elements and articulates its own figure through the hierarchy of constructed parts and the evidence of the roads. The project is organized around three pedestrian piazzas, which follow the successive levels of the terrain. The first, with a ramp leading to it, has the function of entrance and exchange with the collective services. The second, joined to the previous through the outdoor theater, which bridges the differences in land level, is characterized as a hanging garden; the third piazza includes a large reflecting pool, of the same dimensions as the air intakes for a service underpass, which guarantees automobile access to the whole system without damaging the existing park. Each department is developed around an interior courtyard with a height of two stories excluding the underground, used entirely for parking. The interior layout is comprised of large halls of double height. Placed on a module of 7.20 × 7.20 meters, the structural elements create an antiseismic system, which allows at the same time the accommodation of the necessary installations.

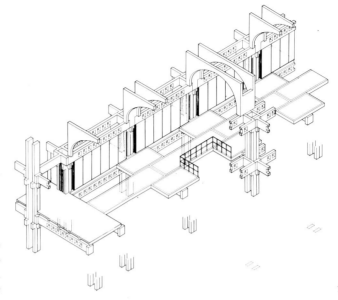

1. Axonometric exploded view of the construction system of hall
2. General plan
3. View of model from east
4. View of outdoor theater
5. Longitudinal profile

1

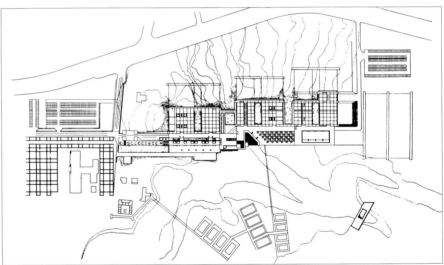

2

3

4

5

6. View of internal
walkway
7. Detail of exterior
8. Connecting stairway
between first and
second pedestrian
piazzas
9. 10. Detail of west
facade during
construction and
as finished product

6

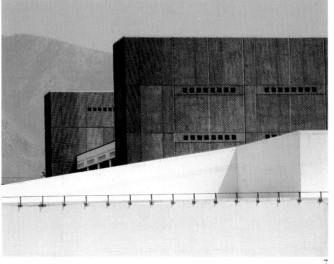

7

8

9

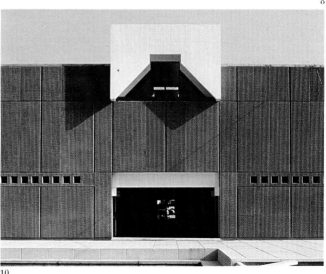

10

New Seat for the Università degli Studi

Partners: E. Detti, F. Barbagli, E. Battisti,
P. Calza, G. F. Dall'Erba, G. F. Di Pietro,
G. Fanelli, T. Gobbo, R. Innocenti, M. Massa,
H. Matsui, M. Mocchi, F. Neves, F. Purini,
P. Sica, B. Viganò, M. Zoppi
Invited competition
Florence 1971

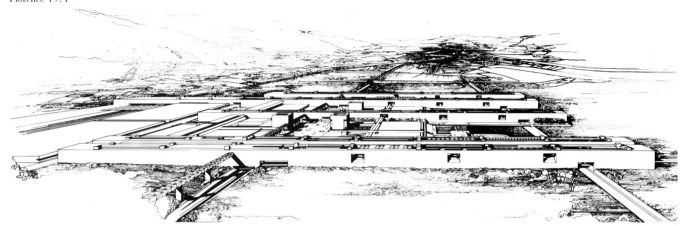

Taking into account the morphology of the Florentine plain, stretched between Mount Morello and the hills south of the Arno, the project correlates the levels of intervention of a territorial design to those of an architectural project. The installation regains the plan of a local installation development and, taking into account the agricultural-geographical references, redefines the outlying area. The intervention, located on the Florence-Sesto Fiorentino road, is emphasized by "spines of functional restructuring" arranged transversally in such a way as to establish a rhythmic measuring of the space. Thanks to the large permeable screens, which mark the intersecting points of the axis equipped with the main north–south crossings, the definition of the areas of the university, the administration center, the commercial pole, and the park is delineated. In spite of the stereometrical rigidity of the spaces, the five parallel structures, intended to house the teaching and research facilities, are differently spaced so as to achieve high typological-functional flexibility.

The buildings are characterized by a standard section, composed of double walls, to which is anchored a predominantly metal construction system that allows a suitable internal articulation.

Complementary slabs and towers with square plans integrate the linear blocks, following the reticular arrangement.

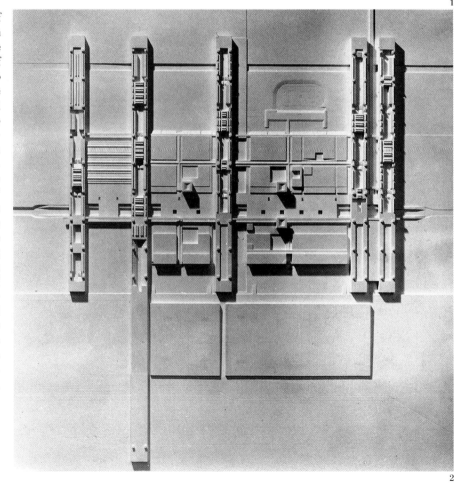

1. Bird's-eye view
2. Zenith view of model

3. Foreshortened view of body of new office building
4. Comprehensive plan of area
   (1) Employee housing 1954
   (2) Employee housing 1961
   (3) Mill 1968
   (4) New offices 1980
5. View of meeting room
6. View of interior
7. 8. Perspective and view of west facade
9. Foreshortened side view
10. Transverse section

6

7

9

8

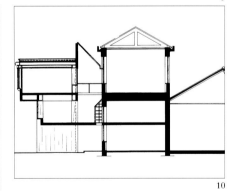

10

Factory and Offices for the Gabel Textile Industry

Rovellasca, Como 1972–86

The construction, intended to house the offices and warehouses of a textile industry, is characterized by square plan, crossed by a higher bridging structure, covered in barrel-shaped metal sheets. This element, an independent structure made of concrete partitions, contains the commercial spaces, the administrative offices, and the exhibition rooms, emerging on the main front as a special element. The first and last spans of the partitions that make up the warehouse form two service areas, intended for loading and unloading merchandise. The load-bearing structure is in exposed reinforced concrete, with an interaxial of 10 × 10 meters. The beams are placed diagonally on the orthogonal weave, so as to allow the insertion of skylights corresponding with the pillars at the intersection of the beams themselves. Recently a new warehouse was built, entirely mechanized, as well as an extension of the offices and a new installation corresponding with the entrance to the complex.

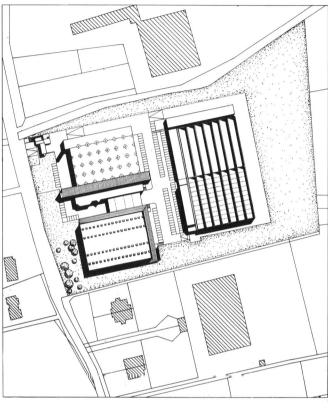

1. Plan
2. Foreshortened view of main facade
3. View of west side
4. South and east views
5. Transverse section
6. Detail of south facade

1

2

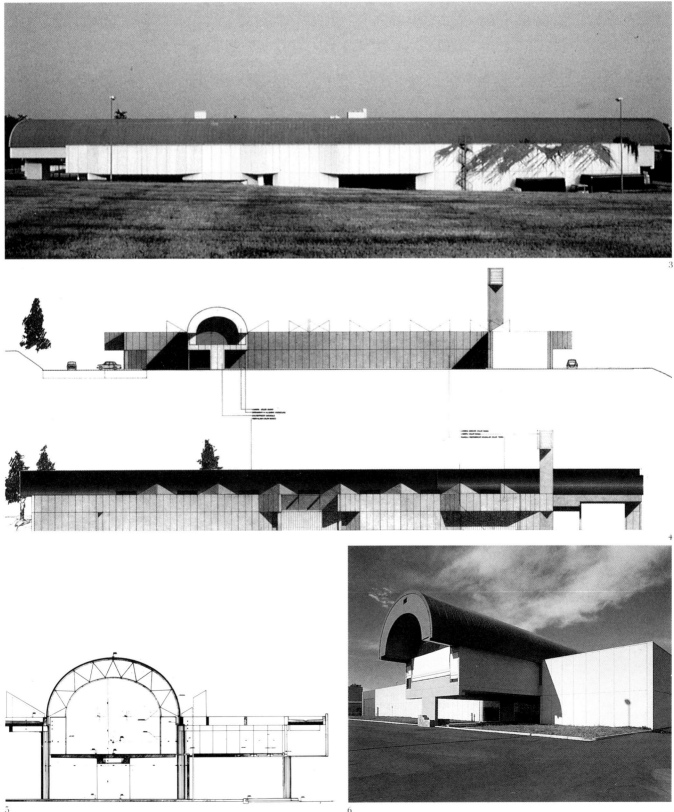

3

4

5

6

Ivi Chemical Research Center

Quattordio, Alessandria 1981

The building for the research laboratories of a chemical industry are connected closely to the hilly landscape from which it rises; it can be seen as an element of measure and connection between the two levels, which have a difference in height of 11 meters. Also on the hillside are the access road and the existing service piazza for the establishment.

Articulated longitudinal and transverse sections correspond with the compact external image, which results from the functional needs of the building.

Three bands, two of outside laboratories and one for the interior service areas, are arranged off two stair-hallways lit from above that cross the entire length of the building and allow a view of the natural terrain.

Beneath the pedestrian walkway there is a connection for the heavy loads, while the towers for the ventilation of the laboratories rise in correspondence with the stairs that connect the levels.

The ends of the building contain the offices, the technical installations, and the experiment rooms. The structure in reinforced compact cement is faced in exposed brick, while the window frames and metal walls are painted white.

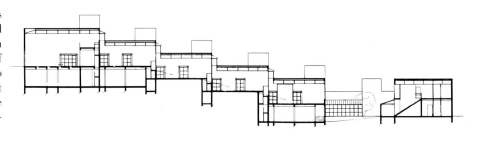

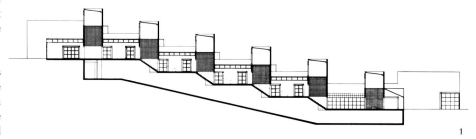

1

2

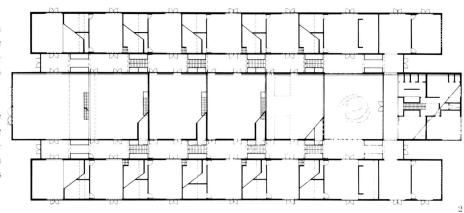

1. Longitudinal section of laboratories and hallways
2. Plan of complex
3. View of model
4. Detail of side
5. View of indoor patio
6. View of interior hallway

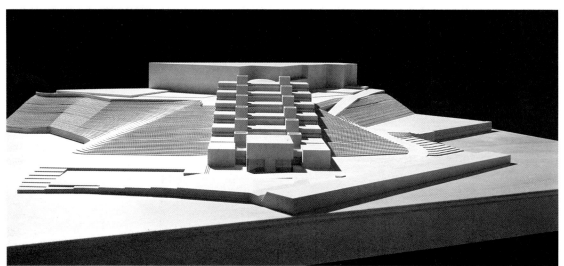

3

4

5

6

Montedipe Research Center

Portici, Naples 1978–86

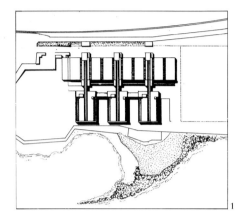

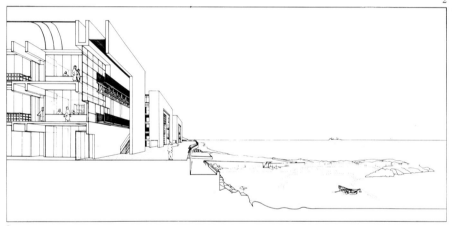

The conformation of the area, extending between the mountain railway and the front directly facing the sea, defines the development of the research center. A series of tall portals facing onto the Gulf of Naples introduces a reference to the chaotic surrounding buildings, underscoring at the same time the signaling function of the sequence of large portals on the sea. The technological sheds, the scientific laboratory-office blocks, and the research spaces are joined longitudinally by bridgelike structures, in which the libraries and the common facilities are located. The collective areas face directly onto the sea through the large portals, in whose double-thickness walls the security stairs are placed. The structures perpendicular to the sea are endowed with the double front that supports the security footbridges and serves as protection from the sun.

1. Plan of portal at the sea
2. View of complex from sea (photomontage)
3. Perspective section
4. Overall view
5. Inside service road for laboratories

6

6. Detail of joint
of connecting footbridge
to testing rooms
7. Interior hallway
of laboratories
8. Perspective section
of laboratories

7

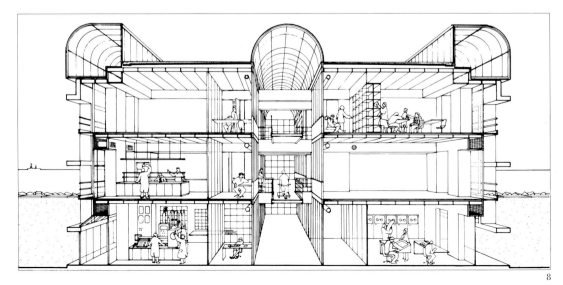

8

Heating Power Station

Sampierdarena, Genoa 1988

The theme of the project rests on replicating the typology of the power station in a different context, preserving a series of morphological, functional, and environmental features. In response to this condition of delocalization, the project aims for a sufficiently described image, not based on an imitation of technical contents, but without renouncing the possibilities and exceptionalities of form that these contents concretely suggest.

The power station is clearly divided into two parts: the first is a base in painted reinforced concrete that includes the service elements emphasizing the theme of attachment to the ground—for which there are various possible solutions; the second is the metal encasement of the main machine, shaped to follow its encumbrances, and visible in the large pyramidal form that covers the main boiler and chimney. The surface of the metal encasement rises from the base to underline the character of the revetment, while the whole system of size relationships between the parts, together with the dimension itself of the construction—which reaches a height of 40 meters—is intentionally directed to achieve an effect of proportional displacement. Particular attention has been placed on the problem of noise pollution, resolved by sophisticated soundproofing systems.

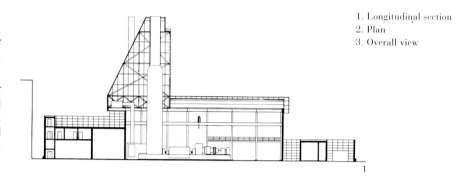

1. Longitudinal section
2. Plan
3. Overall view

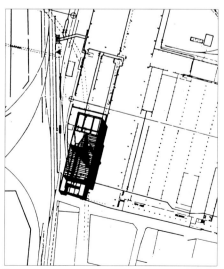

2

3

223

ENEA Research Center

Casaccia, Rome 1985–88

The building houses the reliability test laboratories and the information research laboratories of the Ente Nazionale delle Energie Alternative (National Organization of Alternative Energies). A large solid form, scanned by a network of prefabricated iron-gray panels in reinforced concrete (measuring 3.20 × 3.20 meters, marked by a module of 80 × 80 cm), is an image that makes its material figuration out of its functional content—research laboratories closed to the public.

The high technical content of the interior installations is belied on the outside in an image of austere simplicity, where there is no technological emphasis nor any domestic softening, but only the peremptory silence of the tectonic rules. Precise and closed like a fortress solidly anchored to the ground, the edifice makes an instrument of proportional displacement out of the modular scansion of the facades: the partition of the fronts and the unusual size of the windows (160 × 160 cm), like the total absence of reference details, allow for the verification of the real dimensions of the building only in direct perception. The building is arranged around two large halls for mechanical and technical tests, separated by a glass hallway for control. The laboratories and offices are located on the perimeter, laid out on a series of galleries, separated from the hall by zenith-lit transverse cuts. Through the main entrance door at the level of the hall, placed as a large exception at the center of the west facade and marked by a space covered in metal, it is possible to measure the interior of the large central rooms and to access the laboratories on the upper floors through a metal staircase at the center of a room lit from above. The marked depth of the outside wall (approximately 70 cm), which contains the circle of all the installations, allows the placement of the window frames in an interior row, marking again the effect of depth and of mass with electric blue metallic panels that constitute the transverse finishings corresponding to the windows.

1

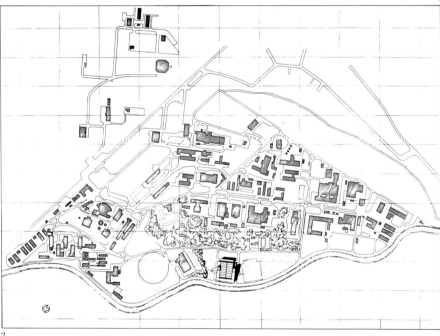

2

1. Overall view
2. Plan
3. Foreshortened view of south facade

224

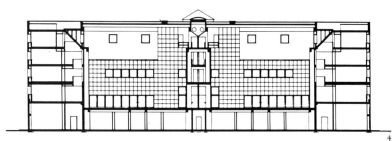

4

5

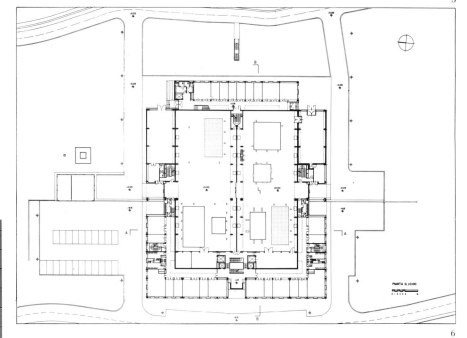

6

7

4. Transverse section
5. View of complex from southwest
6. Ground-floor plan
7. Detail of main entrance
8. View of side car entrance

9. Stairway in main entrance hall
10. Test room for reliability
11. View of side pedestrian entrance

8

9

10

11

Technological and Scientific Park

Pula, Cagliari 1994

The scientific and technological park of Sardinia is located in an area of 160 hectares, approximately 30 km from Cagliari, inside the natural Sulcis Park. The plan involves the installation of such functions as seats of innovative production enterprises, services, and offices for the formation and continuation of scientific research. The installation system is based on the construction of a large park around which are located the new offices. carefully positioned in relation to the morphology of the land and mountains. Each building is designed as an independent architectural event related to the other buildings through the internal distribution road and the pedestrian walkway along the external perimeter of the area. The environmental compatibility of the intervention is guaranteed by rigorous geological controls, as well as by careful rules for the construction of the buildings (maximum of two stories, level roofings. whitewashing of the facades, use of local stone materials).

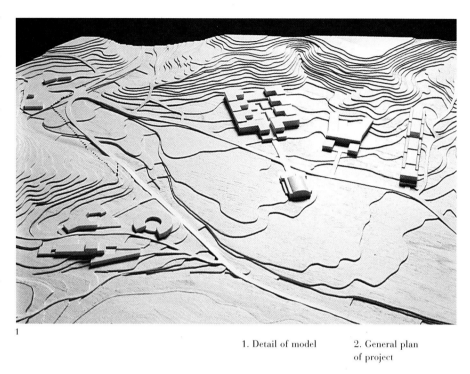

1

1. Detail of model

2. General plan of project

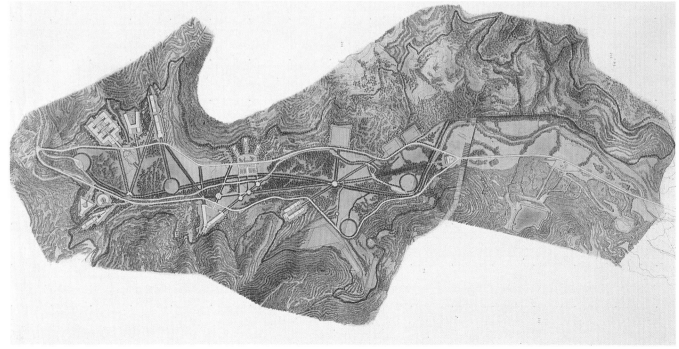

2

Exhibiting Works of Art

In the same way in which in the sixties and seventies the university seemed to have assumed, in the heart of architects and in the mind of the community, the particular significance of the sign of the condition of the advancement of an entire society, also of imitations of the future society of intelligence and reward, there is no doubt that in the seventies and eighties it was the museum that assumed the symbolic significance of index of the maturity of a social group.

Naturally this choice belongs to the wider phenomenon of the influence of the American model, which, among others enjoyed, with respect to museum institutions, legislative conditions at that time special with respect to Europe. It is not for nothing that West Germany, the European nation most influenced by the American model, gave the impulse and developed the construction of the new museums. The reasons of these social choices are complex but certainly not inexplicable: certainly they are also connected to the wider availability of free time and to the discovery of "culture" as suited to fill it partially, but also to the development of mass communications and to the "star" regard for culture as spectacle.

It is not by chance that the museum of the masses, the museum-supermarket, is in this way overbearingly placed—whether it is submerging the principles of the active museum, a place of production and discussion predicated by the avant-garde, or whether it is opposing the nineteenth-century tradition of the "museum of rooms," responding to precise principles of sacralization that certainly represented a vision socially quite different from that of the collection which had dominated art collecting for centuries. Today a new sacredness is opposed to the museum-supermarket of interchangability, of "cultural production," of flexibility. Architects actually strain to attribute this sacredness to this typology: as a way to measure with art as subject and content of the work of architects, with the art that remains, in the middle of each secularization, a world of values for excellence. It can also be said that Italy is in large part left out of this dialectic.

In these last twenty years there were simply no new museums constructed (the few exceptions were certainly not successful), and the number of reorganizations is not high if compared with a patrimony among the most important in the world with regard to ancient art. If this fact is combined with the great availability of antique monuments, whose more natural refunctionalization was the very intended purpose of museum use, the response, albeit partial, is achieved of establishing in Italy a very special conception of the museum.

Such a tradition is founded on a strong selection of the exhibited works and on a very tight solidarity between environment and work and therefore between arrangement and setting, a setting that is not only the restoration of the ancient building, even if it moves from it, but a new reading of the monument, a confrontation between it and the result of modern culture and its figurativeness. It is evident that consequences of this attitude are the explicitly contemporaneous reading of the ancient work of art and a strong fixedness of the museum, which responds however to the closed collections and to the poor dynamic of new acquisitions in Italian museums.

I spoke of setting not by chance, because in the ways to build, from the interior of the new museum, this conception owes much to the tradition of establishing temporary environments in order to exhibit, a tradition that includes renowned examples in Italy since the thirties; these were often the most important experimental terrain for the construction of modern architecture in Italy.

The tradition of the setting has the advantage of being able to force, protected by its temporary nature, the imaginative aspect of the environment and the drawback, or at least the risk, of projecting often on the same plane materials of often markedly different qualities and values. This brings us back again to a conception of art as commodity and of the museum as supermarket or means of transferring its sacredness to the setting, which becomes the true thing to exhibit.

Giovan Battista Crespi
called il Cerano

Partners: L. Meneghetti, G. Stoppino
Novara 1964

The impressive character of the great medieval court of Broletto, with the eighteenth-century loggia and the Arengario hall, rich with composite presences, is contrasted with a setting in which preponderant value is given to unity and balance, all the while not renouncing, at intervals, the dialogue with the historical surface.

The visual path is foreshadowed in the outside extension of the setting, which relates to the surrounding architectural environment. According to the preceptive necessities of the individual works, the project arranges a series of environments of different dimensions and characteristics. For the smaller-sized works, a series of screens in natural-colored and orange jute create more intimate environments, characterized by ceilings with wooden frames and white stretched canvas, made uniformly bright by the neon from above. For the large altar-pieces a more "dramatic" setting is created. Directly hung on the beams of the hall, the works stand out in the almost total darkness, lit individually by projectors that accentuate their plasticity.

1

1. View of Broletto courtyard

2. 3. Views of several exhibition rooms

2

3

Venice '79. Photography

Venice 1979

Housed in the ancient salt warehouses at the Customs Point, the setting accentuates the perspective depth of the large spans, developing lengthwise. In the first hall the exhibition panels are suspended by means of thin metal tie-beams, shown clearly by grazing bands of light. In contrast, the second hall is characterized by a large inclined panel in wood, whose upper border has different heights, according to the materials exhibited.

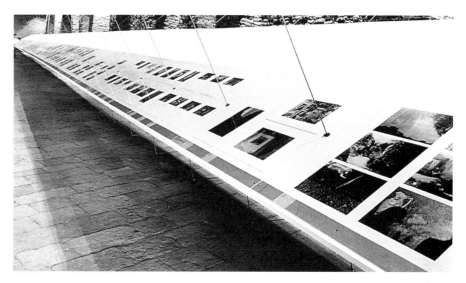

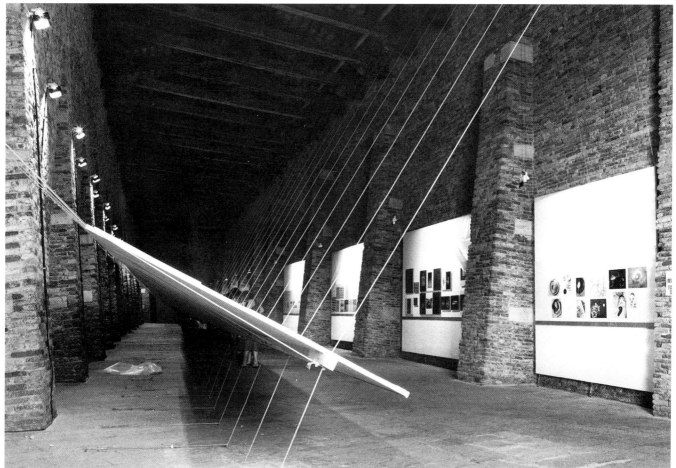

Identité Italienne.
L'art en Italie depuis 1959
(Italian Identity.
Art in Italy since 1959)

Paris 1981

The arrangement of this show, inside the spaces of the Pompidou Center in Paris, includes the exhibition of the works of eighteen Italian artists. The organization of the space was set through a grid, rotated 45 degrees with respect to the perimeter walls, upon which are placed several wooden panels, painted white. In this way a division of the exhibition space into triangular and square areas was achieved. This division organizes the space into more intimate areas and still permits a view of the whole, characterized by angles that emphasize the perspective effect.

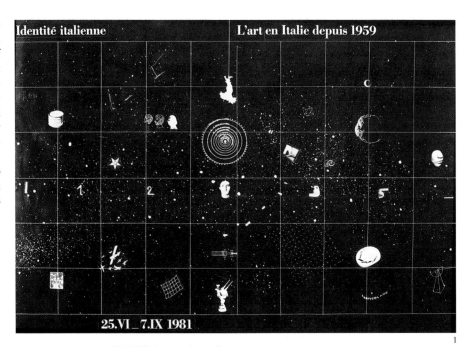

1

2

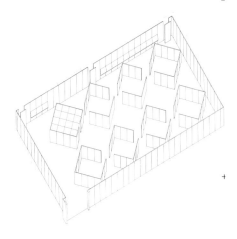

3

4

1. Poster for exhibit
2. 3. View of layout
4. Axonometric
drawing of layout

Arnaldo Pomodoro
at the Belvedere Fortress

Florence 1984

The exceptional geographical and historical nature of the Belvedere Fortress has
directed the project for the layout of the
show toward calibrated and minimal
choices that favor the direct relationship
among sculptural work, dimension, and
surrounding space. The sculptures are
exhibited with apparent randomness on
the green bastions of the fortress.

Their relationship with the building and
the city behind carries the visitor's sight-
line beyond the physical dimensions of
the place, merging Pomodoro's sculpture
with the panoramic view of Florence.

Foreshortened views of
installation on bastion
of Fortress

Brera Picture Gallery
Raphael Room

Partner: A. Citterio
Milan 1983

The restructuring of the Raphael room, with the subsequent placement of the most famous works of the Brera Picture Gallery—Raphael's *Marriage of the Virgin* and Piero della Francesca's *Sacred Conversation*, to which director Carlo Bertelli wanted to add the rebuilt banner of Luca Signorelli—departs from an analysis on the current meaning of museum and, in particular, tends to show the relationship between work of art and surrounding environment. The project establishes a mutual glorification between monument, respectfully modified, and work of art according to mutual environmental relationships. The three rooms designed by Portaluppi in 1925 are reunited in a single large space, reopening the door-window that leads to the open gallery, restoring the unity between courtyard and interior, at one time denied. Through a cut in the entire length of the false ceiling, the natural indirect light descends skimming the walls, touching the works that reacquire, in their altered position, an intensity and a strength previously canceled by the rigid frontal positioning. The light becomes the catalyst, spreading "discreetly," thanks to the use of natural and opaque materials: the stone floors worked to a smooth finish; the inert sand-colored walls made of cold-polished plaster; the iron baseboards and doorframes painted with metal spray.

1

1. 2. View and transverse section of room

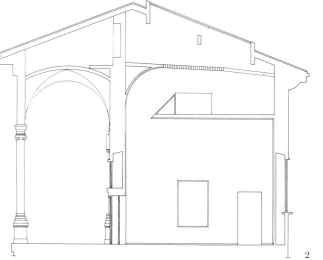

1   2

Restructuring of the
Brera Picture Gallery

Milan 1983–94

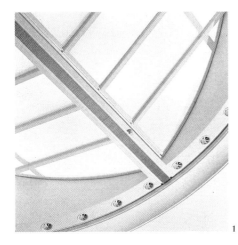

The project confronts the total reorganization of the exhibition spaces as well as the relative support services for the whole picture gallery. The amount set apart has until now allowed the construction of an important part of the necessary installations for climatization, the restoration of the Napoleonic rooms with the insertion of new velaria and the restructuring of a room that will serve as a model for future interventions in the remaining part of the exhibition floor. The use of diffused zenith light is reconfirmed through the redesign of the velaria, employed also as elements for spreading the treated air. The exhibition spaces are standardized to the greatest extent possible, eliminating the variations in color, style, and materials that have overlapped over the years, following the partial renovations. The existing safeguards are kept for the floors, while the walls are finished with glazing superimposed with color on a base of plastic whitewash.

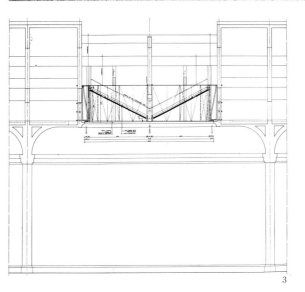

1. Detail of skylight
in a Napoleonic room
2. View of an exhibition
room
3. Transverse section
of new skylights
in Napoleonic rooms

Accademia Carrara, Gallery of Modern and Contemporary Art

Bergamo 1987–95

The project confronts the problem of the reuse of a building whose condition results from a complex historical stratification and heavy recent structural changes. The complex will house the modern art section and the service structures of the Accademia Carrara. The facade that is aligned with the road possesses the element of greatest clarity and morphological uniformity, while toward the interior it reveals the formation for successive groupings. Using the project indications for the creation of a pedestrian walkway to connect Via S. Tommaso and the Parco Suardi to the south, the interior space has been conceived as a public piazza, onto which the entrances of the different functions open. In the internal piazza the stretch of transverse structure toward the mountain is recovered (today destroyed) with a jump in height that defines the park entrance and allows for the completion of the new wing, which constitutes the most highly valued building of the entire complex. A circular space completes the transverse structure, while the entrance to the museum is created along the new facade, at the closure of the opening left by the recent transformations. For the interiors a neutral tone is preferred, not conflicting with the exhibited works: the walls are treated in a respectable colored plaster, while the floors are oak parquet with borders of plastered and dressed basalt; where possible the wooden beamed ceilings were preserved.

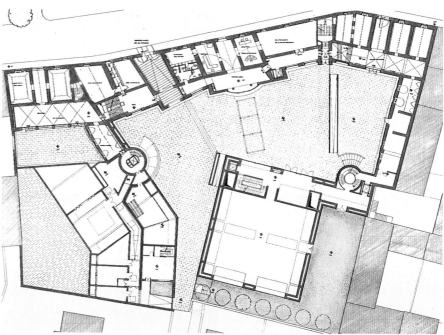

1. General plan
2. Ground-floor plan
3. Foreshortened view of a room

4

4. Street front
5. View of a room

5

Le Corbusier

Paris 1987

The installation of the large exhibit on Le Corbusier at the Pompidou Center in Paris responds to the needs of an exhibit arranged by thematic groups of different genres of work of the Swiss master, in which, among the period maquettes, drawings, and photographs, more than four hundred works were exhibited. In the available space on the fifth floor, left entirely in view in its simple conformation, a series of low transverse "walls" were installed, used as supporting structures for the drawings as well as containers for objects and documents, while the pictorial works were placed on the side walls. The magnificent view of Paris from the large exposed glass wall to the north creates a counterpoint to the works of Le Corbusier dedicated to the city.

1. View of entrance space
2. Perspective of installation

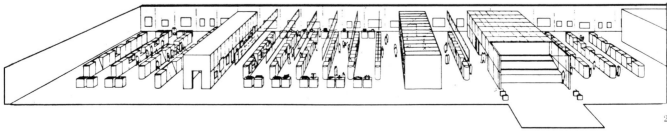

Marcel Duchamp
The Bride and the Readymade

Milan 1988

The characteristic details of Marcel Duchamp's work suggested an installation that favors a mutable and variegated perception. Five screens, placed transversally in the room, were used to exhibit the material and to define perspective axes, which find their point of departure in separate sculptural objects. The white of the finishings shows off the objects, otherwise exhibited to advantage through the technical illuminations of the project.

1

1. 2. Foreshortened views of installation

3. Comprehensive plan

2

3

Photography

Milan 1988

The arrangement for a room in the Palazzo della Triennale defines a space triangular in section, which allows at the same time a particular perspective effect without giving up space necessary for the show. Visitors find themselves in a sort of telescope, which invites them to look toward the large monitors placed at the end, transmitting images in a continuous cycle. Other material is exhibited on wooden lecterns, which decontextualize and isolate the individual photographs, allowing a more concentrated and silent viewing.

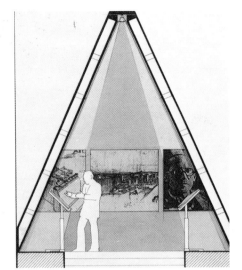

1. Cross section
2. View of the room

1

2

Las Formas de la Industria
(Forms of Industry)

Madrid 1987–88

The project is confronted with the problems dictated by the available space, a wide portico of significant depth, and by the large variety of objects to exhibit: drawings, prototypes, models, and all that concerns visual communication linked to Fiat products. The space is organized according to a module of 120 × 120 cm, which, widening, creates and defines the pure spaces of the exhibition supports in negative and positive: platforms, inclined planes, scooped-out areas, pillars. The exhibited objects, thus separated from one another, are, however, reunited by the containing space, readable in its totality and unified by the white finishing of all the surfaces.

Views of entrance and interior installation

The Ferrari Idea

Florence 1989

The exceptional geographical and historical nature of the place, the Belvedere
Fortress, has directed the project for the
installation of the exhibit toward calibrated and minimal choices that favor the
direct relationship among exhibits,
objects, and surrounding space. Large
cubes, finished in pear wood, white marble, or corten steel, and simple platforms
of marble or *pietra serena* are placed
directly in contact with the bastions of the
fortress in a relationship of apparent randomness. Forcing the characteristics of
monumental objects out of scale, ideal
connections are established between the
cube-exhibits, the building, and the city
below, forming an ideal relationship that
goes beyond the physical dimensions of
the place, using to advantage a reading on
a territorial scale.

Views of the installation
on the bastion of the
fortress

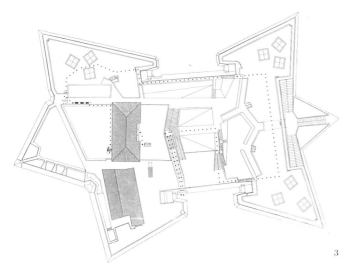

1. 2. Views of outside installation
3. Comprehensive plan of installation on bastion

4. View of an inside room
5. Perspective drawings of several rooms

4

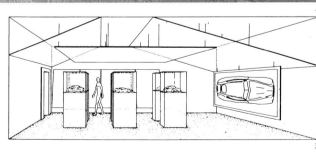

5

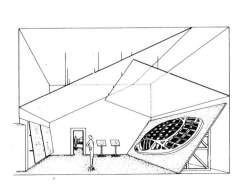

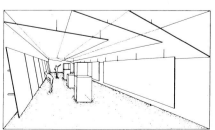

Louvre Museum
Proposal for the Redesign
of the Salle des Etats

Invited international competition
Paris 1990–91

The interior space of the room responds to the need to restore the original space to public view, reopening the apertures toward the short sides and showing clearly the great iron-and-glass vault, as well as responding to the possibility of having more exhibit surfaces on which to relocate 72 paintings in a single row (today in superimposed registers). Six areas of continuous perimeter are formed that, in addition to the central room, permit a clearer arrangement of the works. In the central space are works of exceptional character, including *The Marriage at Cana* by Paolo Veronese and, in a single showcase, all the museum's paintings by Leonardo. The division of galleries on the perimeter from the interior space is underscored by the proposed finishings: semigloss Venetian stucco on the outside and opaque on the inside, floors in stone in the perimeter areas and parquet in the central space.

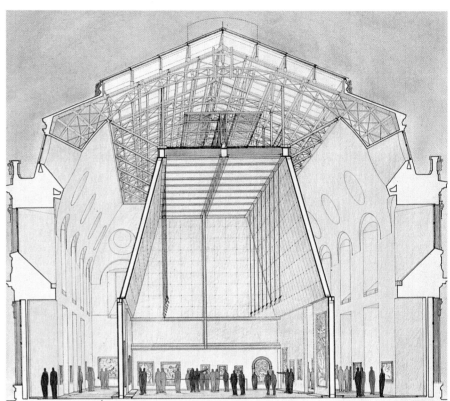

1

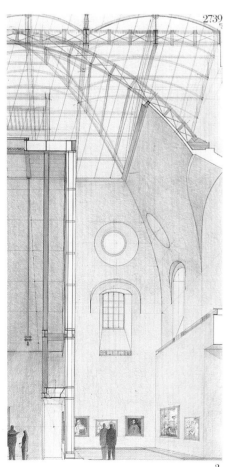

2

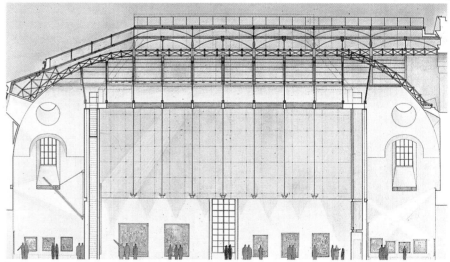

3

1. Perspective transverse section
2. Perspective section of showcase with

paintings of Leonardo
3. Longitudinal section of room

Central America
Art Treasures
of Pre-Columbian Civilization

Milan 1990

The exhibit for pre-Columbian art was planned pursuing "denial," in a sense canceling itself in order to exalt the exhibited works of art.

Dark gray exhibition cases and walls disappear in the half light, while a lighting system shows only the large stone sculptures. Blue Indian raw silk was used as a background for the jewelry.

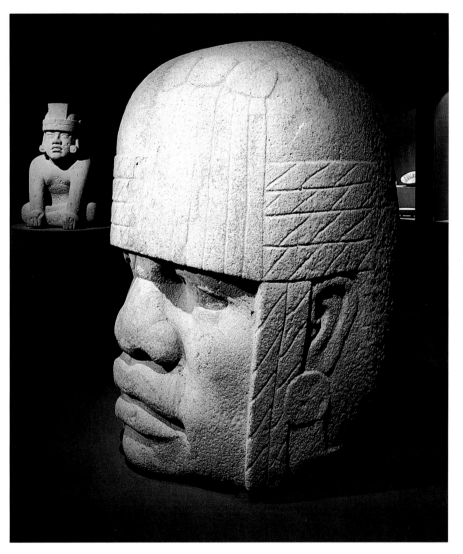

Erdsicht-Jorden

Bonn and Stockholm 1991–93

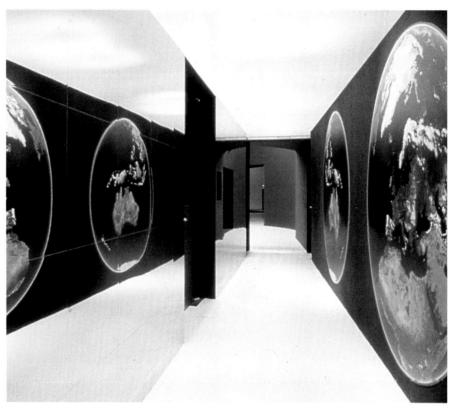

The exhibit, an investigation of the state of planet Earth with satellite views, was first housed at the Kunst-und Ausstellungshalle in Bonn and later at the Moderna Museet of Stockholm. It marries scientific and popularized aspects with artistic approaches to these themes, reproposing the art-science relationship. As buildings within a building, the exhibition structures wind along a road described by simple spaces in which scientific experiences dominate through their strong emotional impact, alternating with artistic productions created for the occasion.

Views of the installation in Bonn

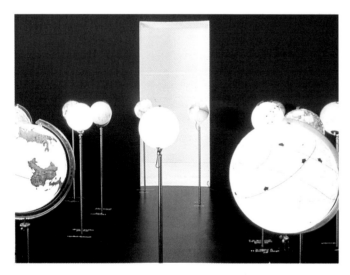

Views of the installation
in Stockholm

The Ferrari Idea

Berlin 1994

The installation for the exhibit "L'Idea Ferrari," housed at the Nationalgalerie designed by Mies van der Rohe, is declaredly simple and strict, so as not to contrast with the prestigious building that houses it.

A gallery, in which the design drawings are set up, leads to a second space, where the cars, engines, and models for the wind tunnel are exhibited.

City Project

The project on an urban scale, the moment of reflection on an entire urban installation, has become increasingly rare with the shifting of attention away from the need to plan a new city toward the need to take care of the existing city. The passage has been particularly significant in our country [Italy], where the focus of the urban theme is already the restructuring of the existing. Occasions of intervention in the existing city are precise, sporadic, problematically connectable with the entire evolving course of the city. Such relationships with context become privileged because intervention often is limited to a reconnection of road networks or a repetition of morphological links.

Very rarely in this end-of-the-century Europe are sociopolitical conditions produced in which the study of a new city is proposed. It may occur, after environmental catastrophes (new city in Ukraine–Antichernobyl) that demand large movements of population, or after destructive wars or political revolutions like the fall of the Berlin Wall (studies for the area of Potsdam-Land Brandenburg and studies for Prague). In these cases, the landscape and the socialist city are put back into the discussion on the theory of improving the urban condition without causing decline in the remaining positive environmental conditions. It may happen that designs for new urban environments can become city prototypes or paradigms, when new aggregations, like the technological parks, assume large-scale proportions (Pole Technologique de l'Arbois) or of colonization of virgin lands (Polo Tecnologico di Pula), following a principle of a city in untouched woods.

The possibilities to reflect on the city in its totality are much broader if a strong design content is introduced in drawing up the town plans. These must concern the urban whole. In this broad field we can trace the city not to be built, where the environmental conditions must prevail, the city to be defended, to be passed on as historical testimony to the civilizations lodged in it for centuries, the city to be improved in quality, especially in the recently constructed parts, and the city to be transformed, on which to graft the principles of large- and small-scale innovation capable of modifying the urban structure or only the way of life. Working on the totality of these conditions, a design can be produced that takes the entire city into consideration, plans the immediate opportunities, and suggests those in the future through a body of urban projects and rules of transformation.

Augusto Cagnardi

New General Town Plan

Scandicci, Florence 1982–87

1. Study sketches for
new city center
2. Structure plan. Detail
of new city center

Among the primary objectives of the plan is the transformation of the identity of Scandicci in order to change the critical role of Florentine suburbs. With the process of tumultuous growth completed and facing expectations that indicate population movement and industrial expansion, the plan works toward reorganizing the existing city, which seeks its renewed reidentification. The general town plan lends Scandicci the elements of urban structure able to affirm the city's autonomy and its integration on the territorial scale. With this they concur: the realization of a new urban center of high functional quality, the definition of new ways and places to live, the organization of public spaces, the promotion of the economy of the plain. The proposals of the general town plan are configured as a program of controls and interventions: controls and regulations to standardize precisely the transformations and adaptation of the existing place; plans and rules for those interventions of new construction promoted by the administration of their strategic nature. The plan, in fact, besides defining the projected zoning and standard elements projected by legislative instruments, also includes city projects. The opportunity to define these projects not only as zoning, but also as installation and building principle, springs from the inadequacy on the part of the traditional plan in reaching qualitative objectives which are precise and controllable in the urban outcome. The projects have a demonstrative content, but, at the same time, make clear the administrative picture in which the management promotes the realization. Attached to the general town plan, these do not have a limiting character but provide the references to draft current detailed plans. In this sense, they become organic to the objectives of the plan, as their location is strategic for the urban recomposition.

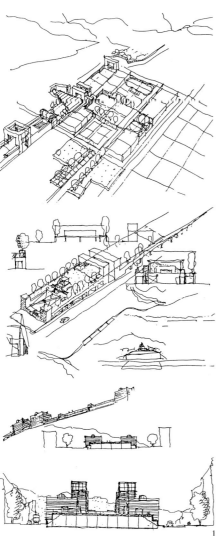

1

2

New General Town Plan

Arezzo 1984–87

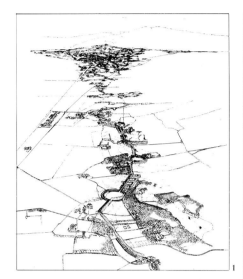

Geographic expansion and physical variety of the municipal territory are the goals of the plan. The balance between the constituent parts of the context is delicate: the general town plan seizes the integration potential, enriching the alternatives of use and development. The conception of the town plan stands in the definition of specific ecologies and of interventions divided with respect to the variety of sites and the expenditures estimate. Central to the Plan is the structural role of the large public services to be arranged in the territory. Ecology of the city: the duality between historical center and modern part is formed through interventions that exploit the walled city, opening it to the land with a new "hinge" of valued functions.

Ecology of the hill: the peripheral condition that has corrupted the ancient installation system is rectified with environmental safeguards and with a system of equipped parks that reintroduce the Etruscan hill into the city circuit. Ecology of the Apennines: the mountain range is described with the restoration of the woods and with the opportunity for recreational use. Ecology of Chiana: the street of Valdichiana finds more stable urban traits in the renewal of the public spaces and in the integration of the old nuclei through the displacement of new residential opportunities. Ecology of the Arno: the reconstitution of environmental and historical values of the valley through a system of strongholds for tourism and leisure.

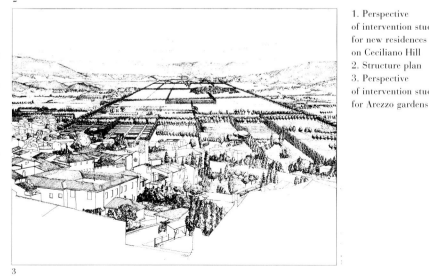

1. Perspective of intervention study for new residences on Ceciliano Hill
2. Structure plan
3. Perspective of intervention study for Arezzo gardens

New General Town Plan

Darfo-Boario Terme, Brescia 1987–92

The plan proposes policies intended to rearrange the current discontinuity along the valley, where the safeguarding of the geographic, scenic, and architectural features becomes one of the most relevant requisites for the environmental renewal. In order to place the various protected areas around the river into an urban regime, the plan proposes the consolidation of the central quadrilateral of Darfo. That renovated site would contain the central public place and spaces representative of the thermal city. In this sense the wide free area along the river at the center of the installation is reformed. There both the unused industrial areas to be renovated and the main city businesses are located, in a condition of maximum accessibility guaranteed by the main road network. The construction of the urban heart is parallel to the strengthening of the thermal economy for the city. In fact, more than for the presence of heavy industry, Darfo can establish itself as a pole of reference in the valley for specialized city activities: the economic development will have to aim at the reinforcement of the administrative sector, besides the commercial sector and the services sector, and also for tourist demand for the hot springs. The plan confirms Darfo as central administrative pole in a integrated valley system. In the "minor" old centers and in the ancient remains, the plan specifies the territorial elements to be used together with the protection of the most significant examples of local architecture, in which the historical villages become other resources to be used. The plan promotes the renovation for residential uses there and reorganizes services to strengthen the individual towns and integrate them in the overall structure. The public spaces, too, are the object of a replanning inclined towards recomposing the urban environments, through a framework of roads, gardens, and community activities able to form the main connective fabric. Finally, another objective of the plan is to take advantage of the permanence of the Camuna civilization with the development of an archeological park.

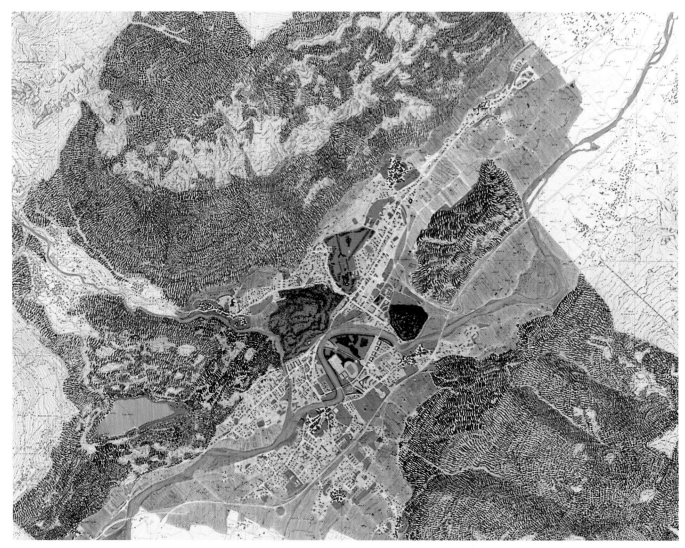

New General Town Plan

Turin 1987–95

The horizon of the metropolitan area is the installation condition not to be omitted in the definition of specific proposals on a citywide scale. In the present urbanization the categories of downtown and suburbs fade into congestion or marginality in which the values of places and functions are deadened.

The general town plan promotes new metropolitan synergies through a territorial rearticulation of the notion of center and renews the notion of city through urban reforms for parts of exceptional significance and diffuse textural transformations on a minor scale.

Three new metropolitan centers are laid out. The transformation of the unused areas along the railway line define the central spine of the public service functions. In the western outskirts the planned connecting north–south axis between tangentials becomes the junction center of metropolitan service. The urban banks of the Po are renewed as the axis of leisure and repose. The historic center in this way is unburdened of the undifferentiated concentration of administrative services, which are replaced by more appropriate functions such as culture and education; in addition, the monumental and residential values are redeemed.

Sited in locations of historical and collective (villages, gates, piazzas) significance, the new central positions of "quarter" come together with the renewal of the residential fabric and light industry to reshape the suburbs.

The river parks along the Stura and Dora, the parks in Gerbido and on the hill beyond the Po form a metropolitan system of greenery integrated with the territorial system of exceptional places singled out by the Savoyard residents.

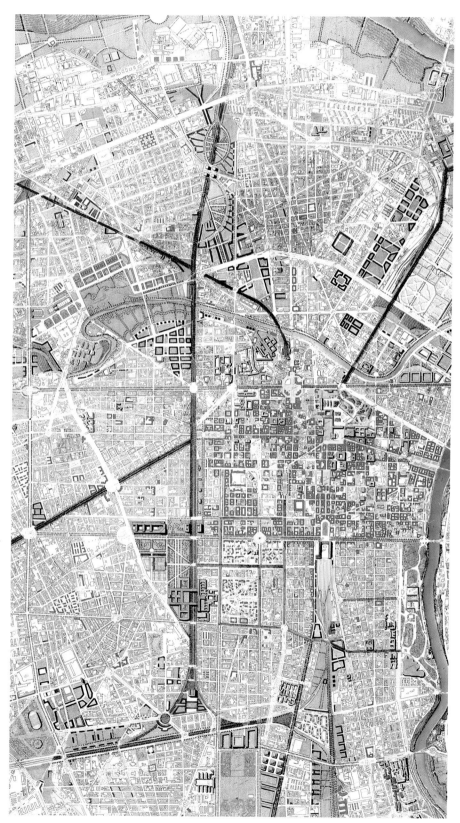

Structure plan.
Detail of area of Central
"Spina"

New General Town Plan

Sesto San Giovanni, Milan 1988–94

1. View of model
of general town plan.
Detail of new Scientific
Park of Environmental
Technologies
2. Structure plan

Sesto San Giovanni is exceptional for elevated height in an already urbanized territory, for its high building densities and for the presence, within the urban fabric, of vast unused industrial areas. The renewal of Sesto is entrusted as much to the two new parks and to the interventions of urban renewal as to small transformations in the building fabric. The restructuring of historic industrial areas modifies the urban structure: the plan rejoins them on the ring of a new tree-lined city avenue that recenters the city, connecting into one system of reference the new sites for urban functions. Besides, the Scientific Park of the Environmental Sciences, planned in the Vulcan area to the north,

and the transformation of the Breda district, to the south and contiguous to the technological pole of Bicocca in the Municipality of Milan, insert Sesto into the dynamics of the metropolitan area through the offering of qualified environments for production and research, enriching the city with public piazzas, parks, and services.

A new city center connects the present center to the south with the residential expansions of the sixties. Among wide park spaces, a school center, and a senior-citizens center, facilities for culture and leisure connect the city-garden of Bottoni with the parks of the ancient villas and with the historic city.

New General Town Plan

Cameri, Novara 1992–95

The identity of the territory of Cameri is tied chiefly to its particular geographic and environmental condition. The new plan preserves the geography of the places and contains future expansions within a controlled urban form.

A general principle of citizen equity is sanctioned in the face of the necessity to build a new house: a single territorial index is applied to all areas of new construction and is extended to areas where interventions are realized as well as to areas slated for the realization of services. New construction is planned within the area of urban reformation, in areas adjacent to those already built and urbanized with the possibility of constructing residential units with gardens that would be consistent with the fabric and consolidated building types. The new plan, however, marks a threshold beyond which, for expansion, a new strategy will be necessary. To gird the residential core a tree-lined path is proposed, a mark of delimitation of the city. Such a limit skirts the last houses, existing or planned, defines new park and athletic areas, stretches out toward the country in correspondence with the main country roads that lead to the Ticino Valley and to the main farms, connecting the significant places of the built city with those of its territory.

The plan intervenes finally to safeguard the character of the urban center, defined by the outline of the irrigation ditch. The renovation of existing residential buildings and the recovery of the rustic garrets and storehouses are planned, increasing spaces less intended for agricultural activity, but today precious in order to improve existing dwellings. Standards are being established for the protection of the urban image—whether public space or the private or semiprivate space of courtyards.

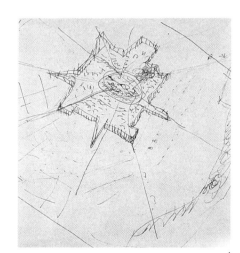

1

1. Study of urban form   2. Plan of structure.
                      Detail of urban nucleus

2

New General Town Plan

Partner: G. Ferrari
Asiago, Vicenza 1993–95

1. Plan of structure.
Detail of urban nucleus
and of the valley

The new plan intervenes to regulate territorial relationships brought on by different needs: to reside, to work—chiefly in agriculture and tourism—to protect the environmental, scenic, and historical values.

The interventions favor the residential dwellings, including the race to the most profitable building of second houses. Within the inhabited center there is in fact a pre-set quota of building reserved for the residents. The new buildings are localized in such a way as to saturate areas already partly built and to redefine the borders of the inhabited area, today in many cases frayed. The plan also envisions a circular pedestrian walkway, the *Anello delle laste*, that connects, all around the inhabited area, the pastures, the main service areas, and the various existing pedestrian walkways that innervate the valley and link the downtown to the countryside districts and these to each other. The construction tied to agriculture offers concrete development and growth opportunities to the vital farms without renouncing the suggestion of protection measures for the landscape. The new buildings are concentrated in proximity to existing buildings and centers, often inside the town districts, preserving the visual unity of the pastures.

The plan also provides rules of reference for all the planned interventions, so as to integrate the new construction within one single process of redefining the urban form and protecting environmental and scenic values. Specific measures regulate interventions in the old city, rebuilt in 1921 after its almost complete wartime destruction. The protection does not concern only individual buildings, but also the whole of the urban environment of postwar reconstruction.

The territory of Asiago hides finally a resource of extraordinary historical value, one with great tourist potential: the traces left by the Great War (trenches, military cemeteries, fortifications, etc.). The plan proposes a large War Museum: a "territorial museum" in which boundaries coincide with the true stage of the war's events.

Chronology and Bibliography

Chronology

Vittorio Gregotti,
Ernesto N. Rogers,
Giotto Stoppino

1951 Milan
**IX Triennale, Set-up
and arrangement of the
Size and Greatness of Man room**
completed

Vittorio Gregotti,
Lodovico Meneghetti,
Giotto Stoppino

1953 Novara
Fair Pavilions
completed

1953 Stradella, Pavia
Sforza House
completed

1953 Novara
Village House
completed

1954 Novara
Rosetta House

1954 Garbagna, Alessandria (1)
Large shed for farm machinery
completed

1954 Milan
**X Triennale, Standard furniture
for an Ina-Casa lodging**
completed

1954–56 Cameri, Novara
**Residences for employees
of the Bossi textile industry**
completed

1955
**Game table
in curved heavy wood**
completed

1955 Novara
Fontana House
completed

1955 Novara
Multipurpose tower building

1955 Novara
Tadini and Lambertenghi Shop
completed

1955 Vigevano, Pavia
Tadini and Lambertenghi Shop
completed

1956 Novara (2)
**Residential building
on Via Sant'Adalgiso**
completed

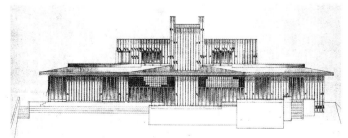

1956
Vis type bronze door handles
completed

1956 Novara
L.G. apartment
completed

1957 Milan
**Iacp. Residential building
in "Feltre" district**
completed

1957 Novara
**Buildings for residences
and offices**
completed

1958 Cameri, Novara (3)
Iacp. Residential building
completed

1958
**Disassembling bookcase
in heavy curved wood**
completed

1958 Novara
**Cooperative residential
building**
completed

1959
Cavour armchair
completed

1959 Milan
Don Lisander Restaurant

1959 Alessandria (4)
**Competition for Municipal
Theater**

1960 Bra, Cuneo
**Office of the Banca Popolare
di Novara**
completed

1960 Romagnano Sesia, Novara (5)
Mira House
completed

1960 Verbania, Novara
**Competition for the new
Justice Building**

1960 (6)
Table lamp
completed

1960 Milan
XII Triennale, Country lodging
completed

1960 Novara
Office building
completed

1960 Milan
XII Triennale. Table lamp
completed

1960 Borgomanero, Novara (1)
Iacp. Residential building
completed

1961 Casale Monferrato,
Alessandria
Tadini and Lambertenghi Shop
completed

1961 Solcio di Lesa, Novara (2)
Magni House

1961 Milan
**Wicker stool, seat, and chair
for La Rinascente**
completed

1961 Solcio di Lesa, Novara
Fregonara House
completed

1961 Portofino, Genoa
Single-family house

1961 Cameri, Novara
**Residential center
for employees
of the Bossi textile industry**
completed

1961 Omegna, Novara
**Restructuring
of the municipality**

1961 Vespolate, Novara
Enlargement of the cemetery

1961 Trecate, Novara
New office of the Council House

1961 Romagnano Sesia, Novara
**Council House, cinema,
cooperative residential
building**

1961–62 Varese (3)
Poretti House

1962 Novara
E.G. furniture
completed

1962 Novara
R.S. furniture
completed

1962–63 Milan
**Cooperative residential building
on Via Palmanova**
completed

1963 Novara
General Town Plan

1963 Novara
Plan for low-income housing

1963 Novara
**Detailed plan
for the area of the former
Perrone barracks**

1963–64 Milan
**Cooperative
residential building
on Via D. da Settignano**
completed

1963 Milan
**XIII Triennale, International
Introductory Section**
Partners: P. Brivio, U. Eco,
M. Vignelli
completed

1964 Novara
U.C. apartment
completed

1964 Novara
**Installation for the exhibit
*Giovan Battista Crespi,
detto il Cerano* at Broletto**
completed

1964 Milan
**Cooperative
residential building
on Via L. Montegani**
completed

1964
Floor lamp for Arteluce

1965 Florence
**Installation for the exhibit
*La casa abitata***
completed

1965 Milan
**Italsider Pavillion
at the Milan Trade Fair**
completed

1967 Porto Rotondo, Sassari
Layout of the main square
completed

1968 Cameri, Novara
**New mill for the Bossi
textile industry**
completed

Vittorio Gregotti

1969 Turin (4)
**New location
of the La Rinascente stores**
with P. Brivio, F. Purini

1969 Palermo (5)
**New location
of the La Rinascente stores**
with F. Purini

1969–90 Palermo
**New science departments
of the Università degli Studi**
Partner: G. Pollini
completed

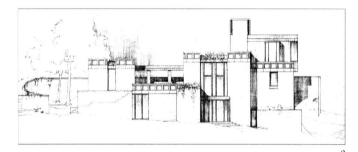

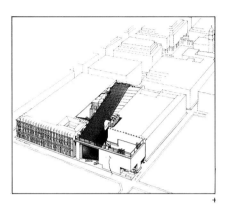

5

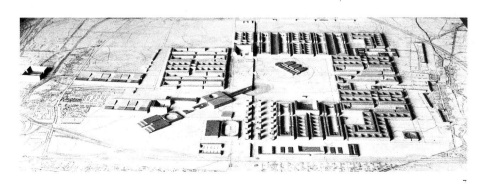

6

7

1969
**Coordinated image
and furnishings
for the Upim stores**
completed

1969 Milan (6)
**Sma Gruppo Rinascente
Supermarkets**
with P. Parmiani, B. Paulis
completed

1969–73 Palermo
**Competition for a residential
district of 20,000 inhabitants,
Zen**
Partners: F. Amoroso, S. Bisogni,
H. Matsui, F. Purini
completed

1970 Vienna (7)
**International competition
for the enlargement of the city**
Partners: E. Battisti, P. Calza,
S. Bisogni, H. Matsui

1970 Milan
**Administrative and commercial
center for the Verona paper
mills**

1970 Mortara, Pavia
**Administrative and commercial
center for the Bossi textile
industry**

1971 Gibellina, Trapani
**Plan for the buildings
of the new city center**
Partners: A. Samonà, G. Samonà,
G. Pirrone

1971 Florence
**Competition for the new location
of the Università degli Studi**
Partners: F. Barbagli, E. Battisti,
P. Calza, G. F. Dall'Erba, E. Detti,
G.F. Di Pietro, G. Fanelli, T. Gobbo,
R. Innocenti, M. Massa, H. Matsui,
M. Mocchi, F. Neves, F. Purini,
P. Sica, B. Viganò, M. Zoppi

1972 Rovellasca, Como
**Factory and offices
for the Gabel textile industry**
completed

1972 Cantù, Como
Single-family house
with B. Viganò

1973 Milan
Ricordi sales location
with R. Cecchi, P. Cerri
completed

1973 Milan
Apartment on Via Mozart
with S. Azzola
completed

1973
**Logo for *Semiotic Studies*
conference**

1973 Cosenza
**Invited international
competition for the new
location of the Università
degli Studi**
Partners: E. Battisti, H. Matsui,
P. Nicolin, F. Purini,
C. Rusconi Clerici, B. Viganò
completed

1974 Milan
**Giangiacomo Feltrinelli
Foundation**

1974 Milan (8)
Marco Bookstore
Partner: P. Cerri
completed

1974 Setubal, Portugal
**Residential district
for 12,000 inhabitants**

1974 Malaga
Tourist center
Partners: J. Martorell,
O. Bohigas, D. Mackay

8

In 1974 Gregotti Associati was founded by Pierluigi Cerri, Vittorio Gregotti, Hiromichi Matsui, Pierluigi Nicolin, and Bruno Viganò.

Bruno Viganò and Pierluigi Nicolin left the company in 1976 and 1977, respectively.

In 1981 Augusto Cagnardi joined, while the following year Hiromichi Matsui left.

In 1986 the Campo design company was founded in Venice by Augusto Cagnardi, Pierluigi Cerri, Vittorio Gregotti, and Carlo Magnani, who would leave it in 1990.

In 1990 Spartaco Azzola and Michele Reginaldi became partners.

1992 was the year of the foundation of Gregotti Associati Ricerche/Manuel Salgado, with an office in Lisbon.

1

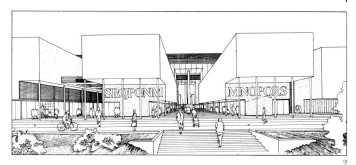

2

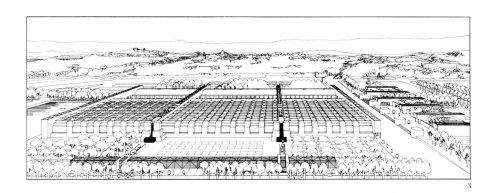

3

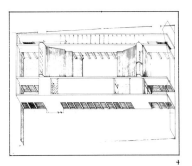

4

5

6

7

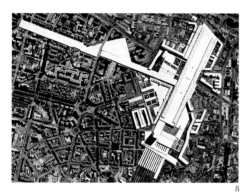
8

9

1975–82 (1)
Editorial series for Bompiani
completed

1976 Milan
G.A. apartment
completed

1976–95
Coordinated graphic image
and design of furnishing
elements for Fontana Arte
completed

1976 Venice
Coordinated graphic image
for the XXXVII Biennale
completed

1976–79 Cefalù, Palermo
Plan for low-income housing

1976
Editorial series
for Sonzogno
completed

1976 (2)
Project for the integrated
development of Adda
Partners: Cepro, Laris

1976–88
Graphic image for the Electa
publishing company
completed

1976 Laghouat, Algeria (3)
New center
of Public Administration

1977 Milan
Missoni Boutique
completed

1977 Novara (4)
Single-family house

1977–78
Ceramics design for Cedit
completed

1977–83 Oleggio, Novara (5)
Casa Beldì
completed

1977 Turin
Installation and visual
communication
for the exhibit
La Carrozzeria italiana
at the Fine Arts Promotion
Building
completed

1977 Paris (6)
Installation for the
Arnaldo Pomodoro
exhibition at the Museum
of Contemporary Art
completed

1978 Milan
Marisa Boutique
completed

1978–86 Portici, Naples
Research center
completed

1978 Milan
Coordinated graphic image
for the Salone delle Notizie
completed

1978
Project for the new Krizia
logos

1978 Jeddah, Saudi Arabia (7)
Dar al Hanan School
Girls' School
completed

1978–80
Coordinated graphic image
for the Bossi textile industry
completed

1978 Berlin
Installation for the exhibit
Peter Behrens und die Aeg
at the Industrial Design Center
completed

1978–95
Graphics project for the
journal *Rassegna*
completed

1979 Abbiategrasso, Milan
Park layout of the Fossa
Viscontea

1979 Venice
Installation for the exhibit
Venezia 79. La Fotografia
at the Salt Warehouses
of the Customs Point
Partners: D. Ferretti, N. Valle
completed

1979 Milan (8)
Consultation for the area
of the Milan administrative
center

1979 Paris (9)
Missoni Boutique
completed

1980–90
Handles for Fusital
completed

1980 Milan
Librex store
completed

1980 Venice
New shipyards for the Venice
Municipal Transportation
Company at the Giudecca

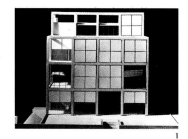

1

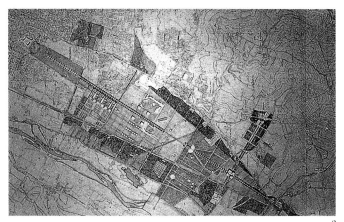

2

3

4

5

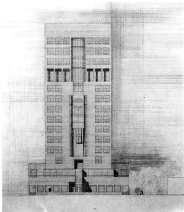

1980 Berlin
Iba, Invited international competition for the layout of the Lützowstrasse area
completed

1980–81 Paris
Ermenegildo Zegna Store
completed

1980 Cameri, Novara
New offices for the Bossi textile industry
completed

1980 Tokyo (1)
New seat of the Italian Cultural Institute

1980
Furnishings for the Ermenegildo Zegna sales locations

1980
Editorial series *Hokuspokus* for Emme Edizioni
completed

1981 Sassuolo, Modena (2)
Academic center for the senior high-school education

1981 Republic of San Marino
Tourist terminal and restructuring of the roads

1981 Quattordio, Alessandria
Chemical research center Industrie Vernici Italiane
completed

1981 Paris
Installation for the exhibit *Identité Italienne. L'art en Italie depuis 1959* at the Georges Pompidou Center
completed

1981–94 Venice
Residential quarter in the district of Cannaregio
completed

1981–88 (3)
Coordinated graphic image for Ubulibri
completed

1981 Venice
General accessibility and detailed plan of the island of Tronchetto

1981
Coordinated graphic image and design of furnishings for Casanova
completed

1981 Rome
Graphic image for the exhibit *Roland Barthes. Carte, Segni* at the Palazzo Pallavicini

1981
Trademark for the Como Textile Society

1981 Como
Parco Spina Verde

1981
Coordinated image for Xilitalia
completed

1981
Editorial series for Editori Riuniti
completed

1981
Editorial series *Laboratorio Politico* for Einaudi
completed

1981 Milan (4)
Office furniture producers stand at the XXI Salone del Mobile
completed

1981 Bulgarograsso, Como
"Monticello Ranch" residences and athletic installations

1981 Milan
Installation for the exhibition on the restoration of the altarpiece of the *Sacra Conversazione* at the Brera Picture Gallery
completed

1981–83
Coordinated graphic image for B&B Italia
completed

1981 Muggiò, Milan
Athletic center

1981 Milan
Aurora Stand at the Trade Fair
completed

1981 Milan
Neglia store

1982 Ponticelli, Naples
Consultation for the Earthquake Commission

1982 Milan (5)
Public service and office towers at QT8

1982 Turin
Iveco Regional Center

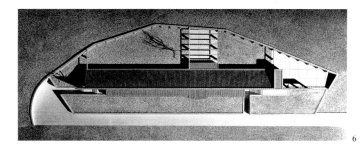

6

7

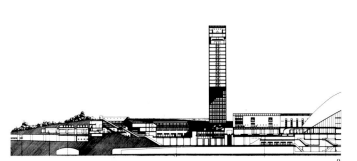

8

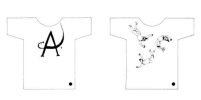
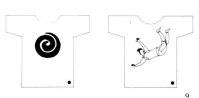

9

1982–86 Scandicci, Florence
General Town Plan
approved

1982–95
Graphic image for Unifor
completed

1982–84
**Handbook for Leca
Blocchi-Laterlite**
completed

1982
**Project for a new Zucchi
trademark**

1982–83 Coldrerio, Chiasso (6)
Single-family house

1982 Riccione, Forlì
Tourist service center
Partners: G. Franchini, M. Federico

1982 Milan (7)
IBM Stand
completed

1982–95
Graphic project for *Casabella*
completed

1982
**Editorial series
for Costa & Nolan**
completed

1982–83 Paris
1989 World Expo

1982–83 Paris (8)
**Invited international competition
for the heading of the "Défense"**

1982 Trieste
**Invited international competition
for the Scientific and
Technological Research Center**

1982 Rome
Catalogue for the exhibit
Hic sunt leones
completed

1982
O'Tool trademark
completed

1982 Cologne
**B&B Italia stand at the Salone
del Mobile**
completed

1982
Graphic image for Vistosi
completed

1982 Kortryk, Belgium
B&B Italia stand at the exhibit
Interior 82
completed

1982–83 Venice
**Sales point for the Textile
Financial Group**

1982 Milan
B&B stand at Eimu
completed

1983 Turin
**Invited international
competition** *Venti progetti
per il futuro del Lingotto*
[*Twenty projects
for the future of Lingotto*]

1983 Turin (9)
Graphic image of the
Alexander Calder
exhibit at the Palazzo a Vela
completed

1983 Cologne
**Poltrona Frau stand
at the Salone del Mobile**
completed

1983–84 Turin
Graphic image for the exhibit
*Venti progetti per il futuro
del Lingotto*

1983 Tokyo
Installation for the exhibit
Design Furniture from Italy
at Sogetsu Kaikan
completed

1983 Milan
IBM store

1983 Milan
**Castelli stand at the Salone
del Mobile**
completed

1983 Stuttgart
Installation for the exhibit
Moebel aus Italien
at Design Zentrum
completed

1983–84 Modena
**Detailed plan
of the Corassori area**

1983 Milan
**Brera Picture Gallery: Raphael
Room and Mantegna Room**
Partner: A. Citterio
completed

1983–85 Ghedi, Brescia (10)
Residential buildings
Partner: F. Maffeis
completed

1983 Rome
Poltrona Frau store

1983 Bologna
Poltrona Frau store

10

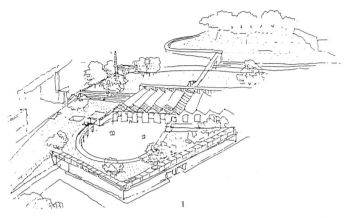

1

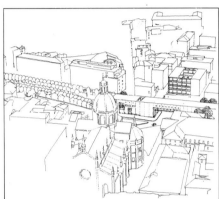

2

3

Napoli

4

1983 Milan
Studio of Arnaldo Pomodoro
completed

1983 Cologne
Casanova stand at the Salone del Mobile
completed

1983 Cologne
B&B Italia stand at the Salone del Mobile
completed

1983 Florence, Paris, Venice
Display system for the sales points of the Textile Financial Group

1983 Cameri, Novara
Expansion of the Bossi textile industry
completed

1984 Caserta
Organization and graphic image of the consultation for San Leucio

1984–95 Menfi, Agrigento
Piazza Madrice: Chiesa Madre, Torre Federiciana, Palazzo Comunale
completed

1984 San Marino
Public services building
completed

1984–85
Graphic project for *Quaderni di Casabella*
completed

1984 Florence (1)
Museum of Contemporary Art

1984–90 Arezzo
Restructuring and enlarging the Palazzo Comunale (city hall)
completed

1984
Graphic image of the XVII Triennale

1984 Milan
Graphic image for the RAI stands
completed

1984 Como (2)
North Milan Railway Terminal
Partner: Studio Quaglia

1984–87 Arezzo
General Town Plan
approved

1984 Barcelona
Invited international competition for the Olympic athletic installations
Partner: S. Zorzi

1984 Novara (3)
Il Duomo Boutique
completed

1984 Berlin
Courtyard house in Lützowstrasse

1984 Rome
Archeological park at the Imperial Forums
Partner: L. Benevolo

1984
Graphic image for the touring exhibition *Achille Castiglioni*

1984 Los Angeles
Graphic applications for Knoll International
completed

1984 New York
Manhattan apartment

1984 Milan
Cadorna Project
Partners: G14 Progettazione, Studio GPI, A. Calvesi

1984–85 Fano, Ancona
Layout of the western beach

1984 Naples (4)
Coordinated graphic image for the Fondazione Napoli 99
completed

1984 Florence
Graphic image and installation for the *Arnaldo Pomodoro* **exhibition at Belvedere Fortress**
completed

1984 Bologna
Castelli showroom
completed

1984 Rome
IBM store

1984–95
Coordinated graphic image for De Padova
completed

1984 Courmayeur, Aosta
Sergio Tacchini store
completed

1984–85 Venice
Coordinated graphic image for Palazzo Grassi

5

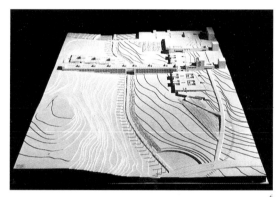

6

7

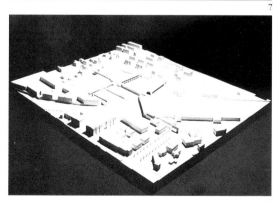

8

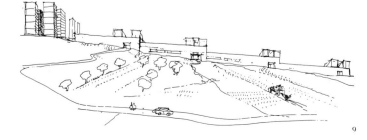

9

1984 San Polo, Brescia
New city park

1984 Milan
**Participation in the research
"Progetto finalizzato trasporti"**

1984 Milan
Ungaro showroom

1984 Milan
Sofas for Poltrona Frau
completed

1985 Milan
Unifor stand at Eimu
completed

1985 Milan
**B&B stand at the Salone
del Mobile**
completed

1985 Milan
**Invited competition
for the logo of the XVII
Triennale and its application**

1985 Milan
Marzotto showroom
completed

1985
**Graphic project
for the monograph
La Pittura in Italia, Electa**
completed

1985 Stuttgart
**Poster for the Thieme
publishing company**
completed

1985–86 Milan
**Bardelli Cashmere
Cotton & Silk salesroom**
completed

1985 Venice
**Catalogue and poster
for the performance
Il Corso del Coltello
by Claes Oldenburg, Coosje Van
Bruggen, Frank O. Gehry**
completed

1985 (5)
**Coordinated graphic image
for Molteni**
completed

1985 Marseilles (6)
**Invited international
competition for the Institut
Méditerranéen de Technologie**

1985
**Graphic project
for the monograph
La Moda italiana, Electa**
completed

1985 Cologne
**B&B Italia stand
at the Salone del Mobile**
completed

1985–86 Salemi, Trapani
**Invited international
competition for the planning
of a city park**
first prize

1985 Lodi (7)
**Invited international
competition for the seat
of the Banca Popolare di Lodi**
Partners: Intertecno, S. Zorzi

1985 Milan
Apartment on Via Brera
completed

1985
**Project for the logo
of Gruppo Finanziario Tessile**

1985–86 Como
**Athletic facilities
in the Lazzago Plain**

1985–88 Casaccia, Rome
ENEA research center
completed

1985
Page layout for Il Giornale
completed

1985
Study for L'Espresso masthead
completed

1985 Foligno, Perugia (8)
Exhibition center

1985 Milan
**Designs for monographs
for the Municipal Energy
Company**
completed

1985 Livorno (9)
**La Scopara district
Proposal of installation
for 7500 inhabitants**

1985 Milan
**Restructuring
of the Abet Spa warehouse**
completed

1985 Morciano di Romagna, Forlì
Boccioni Piazza
completed

1985 Spotorno, Savona
**Restructuring of Via Aurelia
and tourist facilities**

1985 Milan
B&B stand at Eimu
completed

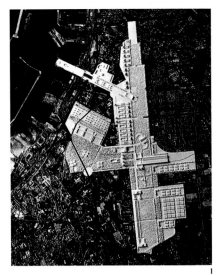

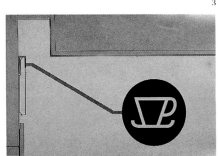

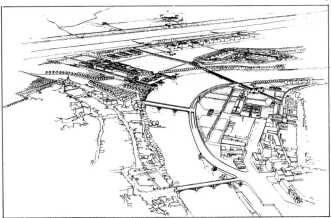

1985 Milan
Castelli stand at Eimu
completed

1985
**Graphic project for the
monograph *Rimini che torna*
for Jac Edition**
completed

1985
**Silver coffee service
for Cleto Munari**
completed

1986–88 Barcelona
Olympic Stadium
Partners: Corma (C. Buxadé,
F. Correa, J. Margarit, A. Milá)
completed

1986 Milan
**Invited international
competition for the
transformation of the Pirelli
area in Bicocca**
first prize
work in progress

1986 Milan
Apartment on Via Ciovasso
completed

1986 Naples (1)
**International consultation
for the renewal of the city**
Project for the east area

1986 Ghemme, Novara
New Ponti offices
completed

1986 Madinat Yanbu Al'Sinaiyah,
Saudi Arabia
**Invited international
competition for the planning
of a recreational coastal park**
Partners: Tekne, Politekna Harris,
Rasim Sha'ath, Noorami & Partners
nominated design

1986 Milan
**B&B stand at the Salone
del Mobile**
completed

1986 Venice (2)
**Graphic project for the exhibit
Futurismo e Futurismi
at Palazzo Grassi**
completed

1986 Frankfurt (3)
**Invited international
competition for a gymnasium
near the Südbahnhof**

1986 San Marino
**Central office of Cassa
di Risparmio of the Republic
of San Marino**

1986 Genoa
**Restructuring of the Luigi
Ferraris stadium**
completed

1986 Milan
**Graphic project for the RAI
pavilion at the Trade Fair**
completed

1986 Paris (4)
**Graphic project
for the interior sign system
of the new IBM office
Europa alla Défense**
completed

1986 Milan
**Coordinated graphic image
Società Supporti
per la Comunicazione**
completed

1986 London
**Poltrona Frau display
at Harrod's department stores**
completed

1986 Milan
**Apartment on Viale Monte
Rosa**
completed

1986 Lugano
**Installation for the exhibit
I Tesori dell'Ermitage
at Villa Favorita**
completed

1986–87 Vicenza
**Invited competition of ideas
for the rearrangement
of Piazza Matteotti**
first prize

1986 Seville (5)
**International competition
of ideas for the layout of the
area for the 1992 World Expo**
first prize

1986 Frankfurt
**Invited international
competition for the expansion
of the University of Frankfurt**
nominated design

1986
Display system for Ragazzeria
completed

1986 Rome
**Graphic project for the
Quadriennale Internazionale
d'Arte**
completed

1986 Geneva (6)
**Alfa Romeo stand
at the Salone dell'Auto**
completed

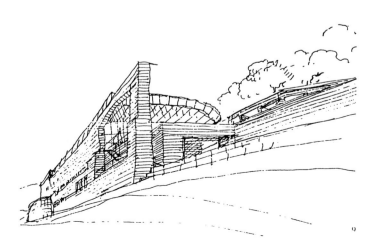

1986
**Graphic project
for the "National Conference
of Justice"**
completed

1986
Valli and Colombo handles
completed

1986
**Design of an institutional space
BTicino**
completed

1986 Arezzo (7)
Academic center
completed

1986
**Coordinated graphic image
for Molteni**
completed

1986 Nîmes
**Invited competition for a soccer
and rugby stadium**
Partners: M. Chausse, Beterem
completed

1986 Rovellasca, Como
**Enlargement of the Gabel textile
establishment**
completed

1986 Santa Palomba, Rome
IBM technology center

1986
Sofa for Poltrona Frau
completed

1986
Visual design for Molteni
completed

1986 Milan
**Graphic project
for monographs for the
Rosellina Archinto
publishing house**
completed

1987 Rome (8)
"Città di Roma" Stadium
Partners: Reconsult, A. Bernardi

1987
**Graphic project for the
monograph *Bruce Nauman*
for Rizzoli International**
completed

1987 Mira, Venice
**Organization and redesign
of public spaces**

1987 Brescia
**Reuse of the Azienda Tubi
Brescia area**
Partner: G. Lombardi

1987 Neuchâtel, Lausanne (9)
**Invited international
competition for an
archeological museum**

1987 Milan
**Interior sign system
for the Salone del Mobile**
completed

1987 Turin
**Installation for the exhibit
Civiltà delle macchine
at Lingotto**
completed

1987 Ferrara
**Proposal for several parking
areas within city limits**
Partner: N. Ventura

1987
**Aluminum chair
for B&B Italia**

1987 Paris
**Installation for the
Le Corbusier exhibition
at the Georges Pompidou
Center**
completed

1987 New York
B&B Italia showroom
completed

1987 Milan
**Report on the feasibility
of an Italian Industrial
Design Museum**

1987–93 Parma
**New location
of the Municipal
Public Service Company**
Partners: F. Mascellani,
M. Felisatti
completed

1987 Milan
**Installation for the exhibit
*Arte in Lombardia dal Gotico
al Rinascimento*
at the Brera Picture Gallery**
completed

1987 Milan
**Apartment
in Piazza Marengo**
completed

1987–95 Bergamo
**Accademia Carrara
Gallery of Modern
and Contemporary Art**
completed

1987 Frankfurt
**Alfa Romeo stand
at the Salone dell'Auto**
completed

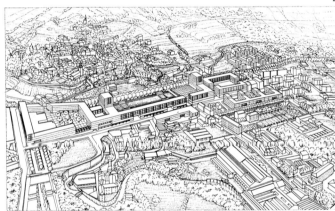

1987 Cantù, Como
Sports building
Partners: S. Cavalleri,
E. Mantero, G. Medri
work in progress

1987 Florence
**International competition
for the recovery of the Walls**
Partner: F. Landini
first prize

1987 Padua (1)
**Service center in
the San Carlo-Arcella area**
completed

1987 Venice
**Graphic project
for the exhibit
Jean Tinguely
at Palazzo Grassi**
completed

1987 Marseilles
Sergio Tacchini showroom

1987 Milan
B&B Italia stand at Eimu

1987 Ancona
**New location for the offices
of the Marche Region**
completed

1987 Istanbul
**Invited international
competition for
a new square in Scutari**
Partner: Baran Ciagà
nominated design

1987 Ferrara
**Installation for the
Arnado Pomodoro
exhibition at the Palazzo
dei Diamanti**
completed

1987–90
**Multi-fuel off-shore
power station**
Partner: Ismes

1987 Genoa
**Consultation
for a harbor town plan**

1987–88 Madrid
**Installation
for the Fiat exhibit
*Las Formas de la Industria***
completed

1987 Stockholm
Alfa Romeo stand
completed

1987 Ferrara (2)
Exhibition center
completed

1987 Ferrara
**Proposal for the areas along
the new Via Bologna**

1987 Lecco (3)
**Recovery plan of the industrial
area S.A.E.**
work in progress

1987–92 Darfo-Boario Terme,
Brescia
General Town Plan
approved

1987 Novara
Sergio Tacchini showroom

1987
**Coordinated image for the
urban spaces exhibit *Italia '90***
completed

1987 Rovereto, Trento
**Competition of ideas
for the layout of the Follone
[Fuller] area**

1987 (4)
**Editorial series
for Bollati Boringhieri**
completed

1987 Milan
**Installation for the exhibit
I Maggiolini
at the Salone del Mobile**
completed

1987 Milan
**Installation for "Forum Design"
at the Salone del Mobile**
completed

1987–95 Turin
General Town Plan
approved

1988 Venice (5)
**Graphic project for *I Fenici*
exhibition at Palazzo Grassi**
completed

1988 San Polo di Piave, Treviso
**Proposal for the use
of the central city area**
Partner: G. Trabucco

1988 Marghera, Venice
**Competition for the Montedipe
research center**

1988 Turin
**Installation for the
Le Corbusier exhibit at the Fine
Arts Promotion Building**
completed

1988 Geneva
**Alfa Romeo stand at the Salone
dell'Auto**
completed

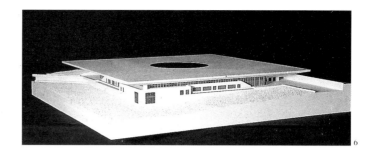

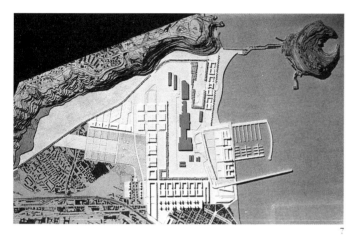

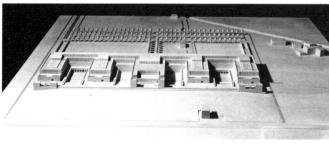

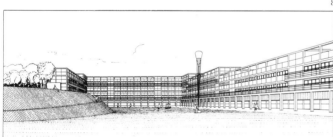

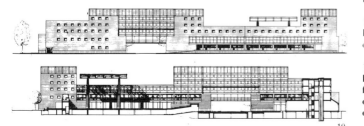

1988 Milan
I Guzzini stand at Euroluce
completed

1988 Bilbao
**Invited international
competition for the graphic
image of the city**

1988 Benidorm, Spain (6)
Sports building

1988 Turin
**Alfa Romeo stand
at the Salone dell'Auto**

1988 Amsterdam
Catalogue for the exhibit
Paolo Deganello
completed

1988 Milan
Marisa Boutique
completed

1988 Mogliano Veneto, Treviso
Renewal of the Zerman center

1988 Brescia
**Study for the layout
of the Colle Cidneo hill**
with B. Albrecht and I. Tognazzi

1988 (7)
**Recovery plan
for the Iri areas in Genoa,
Naples, Taranto and Terni**

1988 San Giovanni Valdarno,
Arezzo (8)
Valdarno Hospital
work in progress

1988 Turin
**Electa stand
at the Book Fair**
completed

1988 Siena
**Invited international
competition for the seat
of the Monte dei Paschi bank
and the Chamber of Commerce**

1988 Stockholm
**Alfa Romeo stand
at the Salone dell'Auto**
completed

1988
Fidis trademark

1988
Display system for Electa
completed

1988 Bologna (9)
**Bid competition
for the research center
of the National Council
of Research**

1988 Milan
Installation for the exhibition
La Fotografia **at the Triennale**
completed

1988 Milan
Installation for the exhibit
*Marcel Duchamp—La sposa
e il readymade* [*The Bride
and the Readymade*]
at the Brera Picture Gallery
completed

1988 La Spezia (10)
Block in the old city
work in progress

1988 London
Installation for the exhibition
The Fiat Case **at the Science
Museum**
completed

1988 Barcelona
Installation for the
Le Corbusier **exhibit
at the Fundació Juan Miró**
completed

1988
Display system for Missoni
completed

1988
**Poster for the Bicentenary
of the French Revolution**
completed

1988–93 Milan
**Proposal for the development
of the Motta area**

1988 Milan
**B&B stand at the Salone
del Mobile**
completed

1988 Milan
New Costa Cruise offices
completed

1988 Sampierdarena, Genoa
Teleheating power station
completed

1988 Venice
**Invited international
competition for the Italia
Pavillion at the Santa Elena
Gardens**

1988 Frankfurt
Electa stand at the Book Fair
completed

1988 Milan
Hotel on Via Pasubio

1988 Milan
Signs for the Salone del Mobile
completed

1

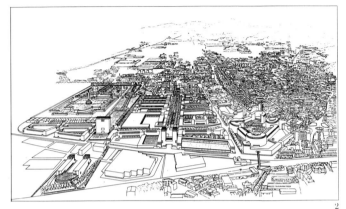

2

3

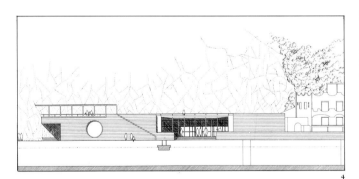

4

5

1988 Milan
**Installation for "Forum Design"
at the Salone del Mobile**
completed

1988 Milan
**Installation for the exhibit
Razionalismo Italiano
at the Salone del Mobile**
completed

1988 Milan
**Installation for the exhibit
Federchimica at the Museum
of Science and Technology**

1988
**Competition for the Credito
Industriale Sardo trademark**

1988
**Corporate Image for *Pitti
Immagine***

1988
**Graphic project
for *Leggere* magazine
for the Rosellina Archinto
publishing company**
completed

1988 (1)
**Coordinated graphic image
of Le Promeneur publishing
company**
completed

1988
**Graphic project for the
monograph *Saras*, Electa**
completed

1988
Zucchi Brochure

1988
**Graphic project for the
monograph *I Fenici*, Fabbri
Editore**
completed

1988 Brescia (2)
Reuse of steel-mill area
Partners: Lombardi Associati:
G. Lombardi. G. de Carli

1988–93 Lisbon
**Invited international
competition for the Cultural
Center of Belém**
Partner: Manuel Salgado
completed

1988–94 Sesto San Giovanni.
Milan (3)
General Town Plan
adopted

1988 Lecco
**Competition for the new
hospital**

1988
Poster for Polaroid
completed

1988 Florence
Zucchi stand at Palazzo Pitti

1988 Sant'Angelo d'Ischia,
Naples (4)
New facilities at the tourist port

1988
***Costa Classica* cruise ship**
completed

1988 Milan
Innovative transport system
Partners: Ansaldo Trasporti,
S. Zorzi

1988 Milan
**Restructuring the office
of *Corriere della Sera***

1989 Milan
**Invited competition for the
planning of the new Bayer
Italia office in Portello**

1989 New York
**Poster for the *Mario Merz*
exhibit at the Solomon
R. Guggenheim Museum**
completed

1989 Reggio Emilia (5)
**Competition for a swimming
center**
first prize

1989 Estoril, Portugal
**Invited international
competition for Conference
Center**

1989 Milan
B&B Italia showroom
completed

1989 Novara
**Installation for the *Arnaldo
Pomodoro* exhibit
at the Sala del Broletto**
completed

1989 Venice
**Installation for the exhibition
Arte Italiana 1900–1945
at Palazzo Grassi**
completed

1989 Nîmes
Sports Building
completed

1989 Milan
**Reuse of the Asea Brown
Boveri industrial areas**

1989
Cosmit trademark

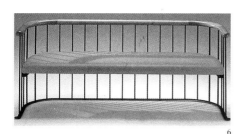

6

7

8

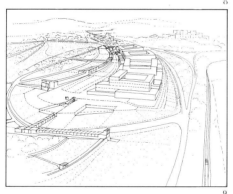

9

10

1989 Florence
Installation for the exhibit
***L'Idea Ferrari* at the Belvedere**
Fortress
completed

1989 Milan
Marisa Boutique
completed

1989 (6)
"Undula" sofa for Zanotta
completed

1989 Frankfurt
Alfa Romeo stand
at the Salone dell'Auto
completed

1989 Tokyo
Catalogue for the exhibit
Creativitalia
completed

1989 Birmingham
Invited international
competition for the Heartlands
industrial areas

1989 Marseilles
Bid competition for a concert hall

1989–91 Cesena
Detailed plan for the former
Sugar Refinery areas

1989 Nîmes (7)
Pavilion for fairs and
temporary exhibitions
completed

1990 Milan
Restructuring of the
La Rinascente Duomo stores
work in progress

1990 Iesi, Ancona
System of ascent to the old city

1990 Aix-en-Provence
Invited international
competition for the Technopole
de l'Arbois

1990 Milan
Cise laboratory and offices

1990 Nairobi (8)
Invited international competition
for the *Times* Kenya Complex

1990 Paris
Fila store
completed

1990 Milan
Installation for the exhibit
Central America. Art Treasures
of Pre-Columbian Civilization
at Palazzo Reale
completed

1990 Turin
Enlargement of the Polytechnic
work in progress

1990 Monza
Competition for the Sports
Building
first prize

1990 Milan
Davide Cenci store
completed

1990 Berlin
Invited consultation "Berlin
Morgen" for the "Frankfurter
Allgemeine"

1990 Geneva/Paris/Turin
Alfa Romeo stand
at the Salone dell'Auto
completed

1990 Stuttgart (9)
Invited international
competition for the Hewlett
Packard office

1990 Siena
Invited international
competition for the restoration
of the Santa Maria della Scala
Hospital

1990 Aix-en-Provence
Bid-competition
Sextius-Mirabeau
second prize

1990–93 Turin
Installation for the
Federmeccanica exhibit *Civiltà*
***delle Macchine* at Lingotto**
completed

1990 Venice
Reorganization of the port area
of the old city

1990 Milan
Experimental cell fuel system
for Aem, Ansaldo, Enea at
Bicocca
completed

1990–91 Paris
Invited international
competition for the
rearrangement of the Salle des
Etats and of the Denon wing
at the Louvre Museum

1991 Strasbourg
Invited international
competition for Place
de l'Etoile
first prize

1991 Cà del Bue, Verona (10)
Solid urban waste treatment
system of the District of Verona

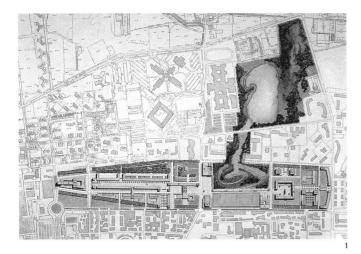

1991–93 Portofino, Genoa
Plan for Portofino mountain park

1991–93 Bonn
Graphic image of Kunst- und Ausstellungshalle
completed

1991 Treviso
Reuse of the former Garibaldi cinema
Partners: L. e M. Gemin, G. Pravato

1991 Campegine, Reggio Emilia
New Coop 7 office and factories

1991 Treviso
Recovery plan for the former Cerato area

1991 Milan
Installation for the exhibit Ori e Argenti Russi [Russian Gold and Silver] at the Fiera Contemporanea
completed

1991 Montreuil, Paris
Reuse of an industrial area along the 'Périferique'

1991 San Donato, Milan (1)
Invited competition of ideas for the multipurpose city center

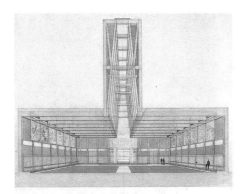

1991 Lisbon
Exhibition center near the airport
Partner: Manuel Salgado

1991
Costa Romantica cruise ship
completed

1991 New York
Fila store
completed

1991–95 Livorno
General Town Plan
work in progress

1991–93 Potenza
Reorganization of the ascent to the Old City (Portasalza and Cocuzzo districts)

1991 Prague
Invited international competition for "Workshop Praga '91"
first prize

1991–93 Potsdam, Germany
Park for Land Brandenburg

1991 Berlin
Invited international competition for the rearrangement of Potsdamer Platz and Leipziger-Strasse

1991 Montreuil, Paris
"Bas Montreuil," invited international consultation

1991 Lecco
New courthouse

1991 Turin
Graphic image of the exhibit Arte Americana at Lingotto
completed

1991 Bonn
Installation and graphic image for the Erdsicht exhibit at Kunst- und Ausstellungshalle
completed

1991 Barruccana di Seveso, Milan (2)
Church and parish buildings

1991 Gargano, Foggia
Competition for the national park of Gargano
first prize

1991 Malaga
Theatine Quarter

1992–95 Cameri, Novara
General Town Plan
adopted

1992 Madrid
Os service station
completed

1992 (3)
Display system for Lancia
completed

1992
Editorial series for Einaudi
completed

1992 Milan
Installation for the exhibit Arte Precolombiana at Palazzo Reale
completed

1992 Washington (4)
Invited competition for the new office of the Italian Embassy

1992
Display system for Alenia
completed

1992 Cadoneghe, Padua
Building for residences, offices, and shopping center
work in progress

1992 Berlin
Rummelsburgerbucht invited competition

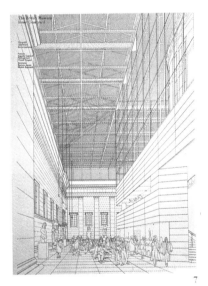

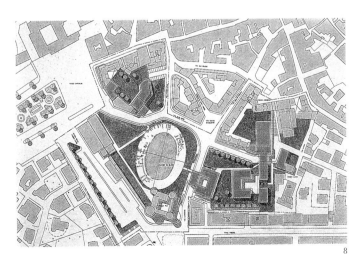

1992 Ukraine
Invited international competition for a new city on the Black Sea
first prize

1992–93 Berlin
Invited international competition for the reordering of Leipziger-Strasse
first prize

1992 Milan
Installation for the exhibit *1961–1991. Le varie età dei linguaggi* **at the Triennale**

1992 Amadora, Lisbon
Theater and Cinema School
work in progress

1992 Lisbon
Restructuring of a building in the old city
work in progress

1993 Venice
Graphic image for the exhibit *Marcel Duchamp* **at Palazzo Grassi**
completed

1993 Darfo-Boario Terme, Brescia (5)
Conference Center
completed

1993–94 Hamburg-Altona
Invited international competition for a building complex along the Holzhafen

1993 Vienna
Invited international competition for three towers at Danube City
Partner: Ove Arup Associated

1993 Dordrecht, Holland
Invited international competition for a penitentiary

1993 Sondrio
Athletic center

1993–95
Ferrari Auto corporate image
completed

1993 Milan
Unifor stand at Eimu
completed

1993
Naòs furnishing system for Unifor

1993 Pordenone
Cinema Cristallo and adjacent shopping center

1993 Berlin
Invited international competition for Aalemannkanal

1993 Treviso
Detailed plan for the Via Verdi area

1993 Lisbon
Expansion of the office of the Banco di Santo Spirito

1993–94
Display system for Alenia

1993–95 Asiago, Vicenza
General Town Plan
adopted

1993
Street lamp for I Guzzini

1993 Berlin
Invited international competition for the rearrangement of the Spreeinsel

1993–94
Graphic image for Candle
completed

1993 Milan
Installation for Euroluce public spaces at the Trade Fair
completed

1993 Milan (6)
I Guzzini stand at Euroluce
completed

1993 Stockholm
Installation for the exhibit *Jorden Global Change* **at the Moderna Museet**
completed

1993
Trademark for the Fondazione Micheli

1993 Nîmes
Invited international competition for a building at Place des Arènes
work in progress

1994 Turin
Ground plan of the layout of the railway pass

1994 Berlin
Installation for the exhibit *L'Idea Ferrari* **at the Nationalgalerie**
completed

1994 London (7)
Invited international competition for the rearrangement of the British Museum

1994 Tivoli, Rome (8)
Detailed plan for the Castello area
work in progress

1994 Lisbon
Single-family villa

1994
***Blue Velvet* yacht**
completed

1994 Berlin (1)
**Invited international
competition for the reuse
of the Treptow industrial areas**

1994 Turin
**Signs for the multipurpose
cultural center at Lingotto**
completed

1994 Rimini
**Funerary monument
to Federico Fellini**
completed

1994 Milan-Rogoredo
**Invited international
consultation for the reuse of the
former Redaelli industrial areas**

1994 Cascais, Lisbon (2)
**Invited international
competition for the redesign
of the sea front**
first prize

1994 London
**Invited international
competition for the restoration
and expansion of the South
Bank Centre**
Partner: Ove Arup Associated

1994 Berlin
**Invited international
competition for the planning
of the former military areas
in Biesdorf**
third prize

1994 Lipsia
**Invited international
competition for an office tower
on Goerdelerring**
first prize

1994 Berlin
**Invited international
competition for the
Lehrter Bahnhof area**

1994 Lisbon
Competition for the Expo area

1994
***Costa Victoria* cruise ship**
completed

1994
"EncycloMedia" trademark

1994 Pula, Cagliari
**Technological
and scientific park**

1994 Milan
**Graphic image for the
Guiseppe Verdi Symphony
Orchestra of Milan**

1994 Frankfurt
**Poster for the exhibit *Ein Stück
Großstadt als Experiment*
at the Deutches Architektur
Museum**

1994–95 Berlin-Spandau
Residential buildings
work in progress

1995 Milan
**New office of the National
Council of Research in Bicocca**
completed

1995 Milan
**Faculties and departments
of the new pole
of the Università degli Studi
di Milan in Bicocca**
work in progress

1995 Milan (3)
**New office of the Siemens
Group in Bicocca**
work in progress

1995 Pavia
New Town Plan
in the drafting process

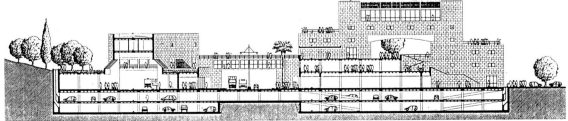

Bibliography
Gregotti Associati

The following selection of books and articles is suggested for publications dedicated to Vittorio Gregotti and Gregotti Associati's projects and products.

AA.VV. *Il progetto per l'Università delle Calabrie e altre architetture di Vittorio Gregotti*. Milan: Electa, 1979.

Francois Burkhardt. *5 Architekten weichen für Berlin: Arbeitsportraits der Architekten: Gottfried Bohm, Vittorio Gregotti, Peter Smithson, O.M. Ungers, Alvaro Siza Vieira: Ergebnisse des IDZ Sympasioms Stadtstruktur-Stadtgestalt vom Herbst 1976*. Berlin: Archibook, 1979.

Manfredo Tafuri. Vittorio Gregotti. *Progetti e architetture*. Milan: Electa, 1982.

Sergio Crotti, Vittorio Gregotti. *Progetti e architetture*. Bologne: Zanelli Editore, 1986.

Riccardo Roda. *Un progetto per Livorno: riflessioni e proposte del movimento cooperativo per una nuova qualità urbana: laboratorio di progettazione, Consorzio Cooper Toscana, Cooper Livorno, Unicoopcasa, Abitcooper aderenti all'ARCAT/Lega con Gregotti associati*. Florence: Alinea, 1986.

Exhibition catalog, Vittorio Gregotti Architecture, MA Gallery, Tokyo, October 1987, Italian Institute of Culture, Moscow, January 1988.

AA.VV. *Gregotti Associati, 1973–1988*. Milan: Electa, 1990.

Gerardo Brown-Manrique. *Architekturführer Tessin und Lombardai. Die neuen Bauten*. Stuttgart: Hatje, 1990.

AA.VV. *Progetto Bicocca. Un contributo per una Milano policentrica*, exhibition catalog for the Milan Triennale, Electa, 1995.

Major articles appearing in field-related journals and periodicals:

AA.VV. "On the XIII Triennale," in *Architectural Design*, n. 9, 1964.

Pier Carlo Santini, "Gregotti, Meneghetti, Stoppino architetti 1958–1968," in *Ottagono*, n. 13, 1969.

"Traveaux d'equipes," in *L'Architecture d'aujourd'hui*, n. 170, 1973.

Oriol Bohigas. "Gregotti o una estructura teorica desde una practica proyectual," in *Architecturas Bis*, n. 4, 1974.

"Berlin old and new," in *Lotus International*, n. 13, 1976.

AA.VV., "Vittorio Gregotti," monograph issue of the journal, *A+U*, n. 7, 1977.

Project for the development of Adda, in *Lotus International*, n. 14, 1977.

Bernard Huet. "Formalisme-Réalisme," in *L'Architecture d'aujourd'hui*, n. 190, 1977.

"Università come fabbrica e fabbrica come Università: i nuovi Dipartimenti di Scienze dell'Università di Palermo," in *Parametro*, n. 67, 1978.

"Apartment in Milan, Italy, 1975–77: Architects: Gregotti Associati," in *GA Houses*, n. 5, 1978.

"Il progetto per il Centro Ricerche Montedison a Portici," in *Domus*, n. 594, 1979.

Kenneth Frampton. "Città senza bandiere," in *Domus*, n. 609, 1980.

"Case da vendere," in *Domus*, n. 611, 1980.

"Houses for sale," in *Architecture and Urbanism*, n. 12, 1980.

Hal Foster. "Pastiche/Prototype/Purity: 'Houses for Sale', Leo Castelli Gallery, New York," in *Artforum*, n. 7, 1981.

"Variations on a grid shape: three boutiques," in *Architectural Record*, n. 6, 1981.

"L'université industrialisée: nouveaux departements de sciences, Université de Palerme, Sicile," in *Architecture d'aujourd'hui*, n. 216, 1981.

"Riti di fondazione: l'Università di Palermo," in *Domus*, n. 621, 1981.

"Université de Calabre, Cosenza, Italie," in *Techniques et architecture*, n. 339, December 1981.

"Gregotti Associati: the Geography of Architecture," in *Space Design*, n. 211, 1982.

Costantino Dardi, "Un pensiero verde in un profilo verde," in *Domus*, n. 628, 1982.

Philippe Tretiack. "Concours international de la Tête-Défense, 424 projets dans l'axe," in *Techniques et architecture*, n. 349, 1983.

Olivier Boissierre, "Parigi per Parigi," in *Domus*, n. 646, 1984.

"Bossi Factory's Extension, Novara, Italy, Design: 1980; Completion: 1983; Architects: Gregotti Associati," in *GA Houses*, n. 15, 1984.

"House in Oleggio, Italy, 1977-1983: Architects: Gregotti Associati", in *GA Houses*, n. 15, 1984.

"Begegnung mit dem Ort," in *Daidalos*, n. 12, 1984.

"Concurso de proyectos para el Anillo Olimpico de Montjuic," *Arquitectura: revista del Colegio Oficial de Arquitectos de Madrid*, n. 247, 1984.

Manolo De Giorgi e Agata Torricella, "Atlante comparato dell'architettura contemporanea: Le otto posizioni emergenti e le loro teste di serie," in *Modo*, n. 69, 1984.

"Gregotti serves as first Tange Visiting Professor of Architecture and Urban Design," in *GSD News/Harvard University Graduate School of Design*, n. 5, 1984.

"Vittorio Gregotti & Gino Pollini: Science Departments at the University of Palermo," in *Architectural Design*, n. 11–12, 1984.

AA.VV. "Gregotti Associati," monograph issue of *Process Architecture*, n. 48, 1984.

"Neubau der Università della Calabria: die Utopie des Zweifels," in *Bauwelt*, n. 46, 1985.

"Territory and architecture," in *Architectural Design*, n. 5/6, 1985.

"The University fabric. Department for the Università di Palermo," in *Lotus International*, n. 4, 1985.

"Architektur für das kollektive Gedächtnis. Universität von Palermo - neue wissenschaftliche Abteilungen am Parco d'Orléans, 1969–1984," in *Werk,-Bauen-und-Wohnen*, n. 3, 1985.

Kenneth Frampton "Edificio per abitazioni a Berlino: Gregotti Associati," in *Casabella*, n. 252, 1996.

Vittorio Magnago Lampugnani. "Università della Calabria, Cosenza," in *Domus*, n. 673, 1986.

Stefano Boeri. "Alte Architektur für neue Technologien: Wettbewerb zur Umnutzung des Pirelli-Werks Bicocca in Mailand," in *Bauwelt*, n. 46, 1986.

"Negozio di abbigliamento/Pierluigi Cerri," in *Domus*, n. 678, 1986.

Marco De Michelis "Nuovi progetti alla Giudecca: tipi di edificazione e morfologia dell'isola," in *Lotus International*, n. 51, 1986.

"Concorso a inviti progetto Bicocca Milano," in *Domus*, n. 675, 1986.

"Muri in mattoni e portali d'acciaio: Edificio per abitazioni a Berlino, Luetzowstrasse," in *Lotus International*, n. 48–49, 1986.

Mirko Tebaldi, "Siviglia—concorso di idee per l'Esposizione Universale 1992," in *Domus*, n. 677, 1986.

Vittorio Magnago Lampugnani. "Gregotti Associati. Università della Calabria, Cosenza," in *Domus*, n. 673, 1986.

Benoit Bucaille, "Barcelone 92: les J.O. au stade du projet," in *Architectes architecture*, n. 176, 1987.

"Neubau: Housing, Lützowstrasse (Southern Tiergarten) [West Berlin]," in *Architectural Review*, n. 1082, 1987.

"Quatre stades de Gregotti," in *Architecture d'aujourd'hui*, n. 250, 1987.

"Football and Rugby Stadium, Nimes, France, design: 1986," in *GA Document*, n. 18, 1987.

Ermanno Ranzani, "Gregotti Associati: Stadio 'Luigi Ferraris', Genova," in *Domus*, n. 682, 1987.

Oreste Pivetta. "Milano si rinnova," in *Arca*, n. 5, 1987.

Sebastiano Brandolini, Marja-Riitta Norri, "Ajatuksia euurooppalaisesta regionalismista: keskustelu Vittorio Gregottin Kanssa" [On

European Regionalism: Conversation with Vittorio Gregotti], in *Arkkitehti*, n. 3, 1987.

"La ville décline ses mémoires: O. Bohigas et J.A. Gotysolo à propos de Barcelone olympique," in *Techniques et architecture*, n. 373, 1987.

"Prächtiges Kaleidoskop gebauter Leidenschaften IBA Berlin -eine Bilanz," in *Art*, n. 9, 1987.

Silvano Stucchi, "Edificio per abitazioni a Berlino," in *Industria delle costruzioni*, n. 195, 1988.

Fulvio Irace, "Berlino 1988," in *Abitare*, n. 264, 1988.

"Progettare un edificio semplice è un problema: Centro di ricerche Enea alla Casaccia," in *Lotus International*, n. 57, 1988.

Hugh Aldersey-Williams, "A Designer Olympics [1992 Olympics, Barcelona, Spain]," in *Progressive Architecture*, n. 6, 1988.

Tudy Sammartini, "Agenda Veneziana: costruire dove non sono ammesse periferie," in *Parametro*, n. 167, 1988.

"Housing on Lützowstrasse, Southern Tiergarten, Berlin, 1982–86," in *GA Houses*, n. 23, 1988.

"Skylight and Clerestory Center for Energy Research, Rome," in *Progressive architecture*, n. 9, 1988.

Manolo De Giorgi, Frank Spadaro, "Gregotti Associati: appartamento a Manhattan," in *Domus*, n. 697, 1988.

Jean-Patrick Fortin, "Milan La Bicocca," in *Architecture d'aujourd'hui*, n. 259, 1988.

Ermanno ranzani, "Milano, Progetto Bicocca: risultati finali del concorso," in *Domus*, n. 698, 988.

Silvano Stucchi, "Edificio affidabilità e qualificazione dell'Enea alla Casaccia, Roma," in *Industria delle costruzioni*, n. 205, 1988.

Bernardo Secchi, "Il concorso per l'area di piazza Matteotti-la Lizza a Siena," in *Casabella*, n. 552, 1988.

Giovanni Klaus Koenig, "Che lavoro porsi in Siena!" in *Ortagono*, n. 91, 1988.

"Banlieue," in *Architecture d'aujourd'hui*, n. 259, 1988.

Sebastiano Brandolini, "Off-shore Gregotti," in *Architectural review*, n. 1105, 1989.

"Cadrages sur le ciel venitien: quartier d'habitation du Cannaregio. Venise," in *Techniques et architecture*, n. 383, 1989.

Ermanno Ranzani, "Gregotti Associati: quartiere residenziale area ex-Saffa, Venezia," in *Domus*, n. 704, 1989.

Augusto Cagandri, "Il Prg di Arezzo," in *Urbanistica*, n. 95, 1989.

Hiromichi Matsui, "International competition of invitation for new architectural solution of urbanisation at the Piazza Matteotti-La Lizza area in Siena," in *Architecture and Urbanism*, n. 6, 1989.

Walter Arno Noebel, "Stadtplan oder Projekt," in *Bauwelt*, n. 24, 1989.

Hans Michael Herzog, "Wohnquartier in Venedig-Cannaregio," in *Bauwelt*, n. 28–29, 1989.

Patrizia Catalano, "Streng: Showroom Marisa in Mailand," in *Architektur, Innenarchitektur, Technischer Ausbau*, n. 9, 1989.

Marco Frascari, "Il Particolareggiamento in the narration of architecture," in *Journal of Architectural Education*, n. 43, 1989.

"Pirelli-Gelände, 'Bicocca' in Mailand, Italien. 2. Stufe," in *Architektur + Wettbewerbe*, n. 140, 1989.

Pierluigi Nicolin, "Tessuto e monumento: due interpretazioni al concorso per il centro culturale di Belém a Lisbona," in *Lotus International*, n. 61, 1989.

"A Cannaregio," in *L'Architecture d'aujourd'hui*, n. 266, 1989.

Gernot Bayne, "Barcelano und die Olympiade 1992 - ein Zwischenbericht," *Bauwelt*, n. 4, 1990.

Silvano Stucchi, "Intervento residenziale nell'area ex- Saffa a Venezia," in *Industria delle costruzioni*, n. 221, 1990.

"Ort und Stadion: neue Fussballstadien in Italien", in *Werk, Bauen + Wohnen*, n. 9, 1990.

Bruno Fortier, "Il concorso per il quartiere Sextius-Mirabeau a Aix-en-Provence," in *Casabella*, n. 572, 1990.

"Wettbewerbsprofil des Architekten Vittorio Gregotti, Mailand I.," in *Architektur + Wettbewerbe*, n. 144, 1990.

Gerhard Ullman, "Der Glanz der Ringe. Neue Sportastdien in Barcelona," in *Werk, -Bauen-und-Wohnen*, n. 9, 1990.

Manolo De Giorgi, "Vittorio Gregotti. La fatica del distacco teorico," in *Domus*, n. 717, 1990.

Urs Graf, Werner Blaser, Gibellina Nuova, "Ein Beispiel für den Widerstand gegen den Kulturkolonialismus," in *Docu-Bulletin*, n. 4, 1990.

"Genua. Eine Baubeschreibung," in *Stadtbauwelt*, n. 106, 1990.

Nicola Di Battista, "Gregotti Associati: riorganizzazione dell'area portuale di Venezia," in *Domus*, n. 726, 1991.

Gerhard Ullmann, "Zwitter: Umbau des Montjuic-Staions in Barcelona," in *Deutsche Bauzeitung*, n. 5, 1991.

Sergio Petruccioli, "Edificio per attività di interesse pubblico nella Repubblica di San Marino," in *Industria delle costruzioni*, n. 236, 1991.

"Olympisches Stadion in Barcelona Spanien," in *Architektur + Wettbewerbe*, n. 145, 1991.

D. Mandolesi, "Berlino: idee per una metropoli," in *Industria delle costruzioni*, n. 239, 1991.

Claude Vuillermet, "Nimes," in *Abitare*, n. 300, 1991.

Christoph Stroschein, "Ein Stadt-Umland-Ideal für Berlin-Brandenburg," in *Bauwelt*, n. 48, 1991.

Mirko Zardini, "Il Corso negato: nel centro di Aix-en-Provence," in *Lotus International*, n. 70, 1991.

Oliver Hamm, Barcelona baut. "die Sportanlagen für die Olympischen Spiele 1992," in *Deutsche Bauzeitung*, n. 5, 1991.

Michael Monninger, "Berlino: progetti per il Postdamer/Leipziger Platz," in *Domus*, n. 734, 1992.

"Le renouvellement Strasbourgeois," in *Techniques et architecture*, n. 400, 1992.

"Centro Culturale di Belém, Lisbona," in *Domus*, n. 738, 1992.

"La Grande Nave: Gregotti Associati, un progetto per la Crociera/Pierluigi Cerri," in *Abitare*, n. 306, 1992.

Thomas Fischer, "Stadium in the city," in *Progressive Architecture*, n. 4, 1992.

Clemens F. Kusch, "Le Arti Industriali," in *Deutsche Bauzeitschrift*, n. 7, 1992.

"Torino: piano, struttura, progetto Contributi di Gregotti Associati Studio," in *Casabella*, n. 592, 1992.

"Stranieri in Francia," in *Abitare*, n. 309, 1992.

Alvaro Siza, "Gregotti en el estuario: Centro cultural de Belém," in *Arquitectura viva*, n. 27, 1992.

"Remodelacion del Estadio de Montjuic, Barcelona," in *ON disegno*, 1992.

Fulvio Irace, "Una porta per la città," in *Abitare*, n. 309, 1992.

Manuel Delluc, "Montreuil," in *Moniteur architecture AMC*, n. 40, 1993.

Richard Ingersoll, "Il concorso per la nuova Cancelleria dell'Ambasciata d'Italia e Washington D.C.," in *Casabella*, n. 602, 1993.

Tamara Molinari, "Nuova Architettura," in *Abitare*, n. 320, 1993.

"Experimentelles Kraftwerk in Mailand-Bicocca," in *Bauwelt*, n. 37, 1993.

Luca Gazzaniga, "Gregotti Associati: Nuova Sede della REgione Marche, Ancona," in *Domus*, n. 754, 1993.

"Neugestaltung der Piazza Madrice in Menfi,"
in *Bauwelt*, n. 47, 1993.

Linda Pollak, "The Visible City: Reflections
on a Lecture by Vittorio Gregotti," in *GSD
News/Harvard University, Graduate School
of Design*, 1994.

M. Faiferri, "La pietra mutevole," in *Industria delle
costruzioni*, n. 268, 1994.

Clemens F. Kusch, "Eine Architektur der grossen
Dimensionen: zum Werk von Vittorio Gregotti,"
in *Deutsche Bauzeitschrift*, n. 268, 1994.

Marco Romanelli, "Nave da crociera Costa
Romantica Pierluigi Cerri (Gregotti Associati),"
in *Domus*, n. 760, 1994.

"Kulturfestung: Centro Cultural de Belém,
Lissabon," in *Bauwelt*, n. 19, 1994.

"Cuatro propuestas residenciales para Teatinos,"
in *Geometria*, n. 17, 1994.

Renato Rizzi, "Vittorio Gregotti: Belém, Wien,
Kiev," in *Lotus International*, n. 83, 1994.

AA.VV., Gregotti Associati, Manuel Salgado,
"Lisbona, Centro Culturale di Belém 1988–1993,"
monograph issue of *Anfione Zeto*, il Cardo Editore,
1995.

Augusto Cagnardi

Graduated in 1962 from the Milan Polytechnic, Augusto Cagnardi spent the first period of his work (1962–67) as a researcher at the Town-Planning Institute of the Milan Polytechnic.

Subsequently (1967–73) he served as a researcher in the Milan Intertown Plan; he participated in drawing up the general plan of the area, in drafting special projects like the park system, in designing the new organization of area transportation (the Milan railway connection), maintaining the relationships between territorial planning and transportation planning as the focus of this research activity.

In his third period (1974–81) he moved toward research, studies, and projects and founded the Laris Society. Its fields of activity were defined within the sectors of transportation, environmental planning, and urban projects. Cagnardi's collaboration with Gregotti Associati began when he drafted the installation plan for the Universities of Calabria and Cosenza and the plan for the city of Adda. In 1976 the same group formed Sinco, a company active in the field of information applied to 'territorial problems. During these years, Cagnardi, continuously a member of interdisciplinary groups, participated in and won the competitions for the Bergamo railway crossing, the Florence administrative center, and the Pollino regional park.

In 1981 Cagnardi became the new partner of Gregotti Associati, bringing to the group his own specific abilities and a new interest in urban themes, the integration between town planning and architecture, between the activity of the plan and that of the architectural project.

In 1982 and 1983 he acted as consultant for the Regional Territorial Plan of Lombardy and for the landscape design for the region of Liguria. He was president of the Lombardy section of the INU (National Town-Planning Institute) from 1979 to 1985, president of AIAP (Italian Association of Landscape Architects), and president of the National Committee for Environmental and Territorial Sciences.

Cagnardi contributed actively to journals in the field. He edited the publication of *La riconversione urbanistica* (Dedalo 1976), *Belice 1980* (Marsilio 1982), *Strade, piazze e spazi urbani* (Franco Angeli 1983), *Piano e progetto* (Franco Angeli 1984). From 1987 to 1991 he was managing editor of *Terra*, a periodical on environmental and territorial sciences.

Pierluigi Cerri

Pierluigi Cerri, a graduate of the Milan Polytechnic, where he taught with Umberto Eco, was a founding member of Gregotti Associati. Member of the Alliance Graphique Internationale, he oversaw the image for the Venice Biennale in 1976. He supervised the design of a number of editorial series for the most important Italian publishing houses, including Einaudi, Bollati Boringhieri, Fabbri, Bompiani, and Skirà, and he was responsible for the image of the Kunst- und Ausstellungshalle in Bonn and of Palazzo Grassi in Venice.

Cerri was the art director of *EncycloMedia*, a collection of interactive texts on CD-ROM, and director of the graphic design series *Pagina*. He designed the visual identity of Electa, Italia 90, and Pitti Immagine and edited the image of Unifor, Ferrari Auto and of the new cultural center at Lingotto in Turin. He designed objects for Unifor, B&B Italia, Poltrona Frau,

Candle, Fontana Arte, and Fusital and planned scenic installations for RAI3. In addition, he worked with Alenia, Merloni, Pirelli, and Gruppo Shima Seiki, for whom he designed display systems and exhibition settings.

In 1994 he received the Award for Good Industrial Design from the Forum Design Hannover Industries.

In 1995 he received the Compasso d'Oro.

Editor of the magazines *Rassegna* and *Casabella* since 1982, Cerri also contributed actively to other periodicals like *Abitare*, *Domus* and *L'Espresso*. Editor with Pierluigi Nicolin of the Italian edition of Le Corbusier's *Vers une architecture* (Milan 1974), he also edited the publication of *Cinque graphic designer* (Venice 1976) and *Pubblicità di autore* (Milan: Electa, 1983).

Vittorio Gregotti

Vittorio Gregotti graduated in architecture in 1952 from the Milan Polytechnic. From 1953 to 1968 he worked in collaboration with Lodovico Meneghetti and Giotto Stoppino. In 1974 he founded Gregotti Associati, to which he still belongs, with Augusto Cagnardi and Pierluigi Cerri. Professor of architectural composition at the University Institute of Architecture in Venice, he taught on the faculties of architecture at Milan and Palermo and was visiting professor at the Universities of Tokyo, Buenos Aires, San Paolo, and Lausanne, and at Harvard, Princeton, University of Pennsylvania, and M.I.T.

He participated in numerous international exhibitions and oversaw the introductory section of the XIII Triennale (Milan 1964), for which he won the international grand prize. From 1974 to 1976 he was director of the visual art and architecture section of the Venice Biennale.

The writings of Vittorio Gregotti that have appeared since 1953 in architectural periodicals, magazines, weekly and daily papers, both Italian and foreign, are excluded from this bibliography, given their great quantity and the continual additions to the corpus.

In order to be able to construct a wider bibliographical apparatus, we refer to Vittorio Gregotti's editorial and journalistic activity.

From 1953 to 1955 he was the editor of *Casabella*; from 1955 to 1963, editor-in-chief of *Casabella-Continuità*; from 1963 to 1965, managing editor of *Edilizia Moderna* and responsible for the architecture section of the magazine *Il Verri*. Since 1979 he has been managing editor of *Rassegna* and of *Casabella* since 1982. From 1984 until 1992 he edited the architectural column "Panorama," and since 1992 he has been contributing to the daily paper *Corriere della Sera*.

Among Gregotti's published works are the following:

Il territorio dell'architettura. Milan: Feltrinelli, 1966.

L'architettura dell'espressionismo. Milan: Fabbri Editori, 1967.

New Directions in Italian Architecture. New York: Braziller, 1968.

Il disegno del prodotto industriale-Italia 1860–1980. Milan: Electa, 1982.

Questioni di architettura. Turin: Einaudi, 1986.

Cinque dialoghi necessari. Milan: Electa, 1990.

Dentro l'Architettura. Turin: Bollati Boringhieri, 1991.

La città visibile. Turin: Einaudi, 1993.

Le scarpe di Van Gogh. Modificazione dell'architettura. Turin: Einaudi, 1994.

Collaborators and staff
Gregotti Associati
1974—1995

Nicola Adami
Giuseppe Agata Giannoccari
Mario Agostini
Franco Ancillotti
Alfonso Angelillo
Antonio Angelillo
Corrado Annoni
Paolo Armellini
Paolo Asti
Annalisa Avon
Spartaco Azzola
Mauro Bacchini
Giorgio Baldessieri
Barbara Ballmer
Marta Bastianello
Fabrizio Barbero
Mariella Belli
Stefano Bellinzona
Alessandra Bencich
Anna Bettinelli
Alberto Berengo Gardin
Antonella Bergamin
Paola Bermini
Valérie Bergeron
Pietro Bertelli
Franco Bertossi
Monica Bianchettin
Marina Bianchi Michiel
Alberto Bianda
Paolo Bonazzi
Paolo Bogoni
Maddalena Borasio
Renzo Brandolini
Theo Brenner
Donato Buccella
Luciano Bucci
Sergio Butti
Francesca Cadeo
Cristina Calligaris
Giorgio Camuffo
Marina Candioli
Agostino Cangemi
Carlo Capovilla
Ginette Caron
Massimo Carta Mantiglia
Piero Carlucci
Massimo Caruso
Vera Casanova
Elvio Casagrande
Gaetano Cassini
Cristina Castelli
Rita Cattaneo
Maria Teresa Cavagna
  di Gualdana
Raffaello Cecchi
Alfonso Cendron
Federica Cescutti
Andrea Chiari Gaggia
Luciano Claut
Graziella Clerici

Paolo Colao
Aldina Colombo
Alessandro Colombo
Luisa Conte
Marco Contini
Davide Cornago
Luisa Corridori
Claudio Costalonga
Samantha Cotterell
Alessandra Dal Ben
Antonio D'Addario
Sylvie Donnadieu
Manolo De Georgi
Giulia Depero
Giuseppe Della Giusta
Marco Della Torre
Michela De Stefanis
Silvio De Ponte
Jacopo Detti
Giuseppe Donato
Carlo Donati
Carlotta Eco
Chiara Enrico
Anselmo Esposito
Marino Fei
Paolo Ferrari
Orietta Ferrero
Julia Fietz
Cinzia Francone
Simona Franzino
Francesco Fresa
Camilla Fronzoni
German Fuenmayor
Sean Gaherty
Mauro Galantino
Federica Galbusieri
Giacomo Galmarini
Chiara Gamba
Gino Garbellini
Paola Garbuglio
Claire Gazeau
Rocco Giammetta
Deidre Gibson
Valeria Girardi
Michela Ghigliotti
Raffaele Ghillani
Attilio Gobbi
Gaetano Gramegna
Claudia Groenebaum
Neil Gurry
Heidi Hansen
Marion Hauff
Paul Honhsbeen
Silvia Icardi
Nobuko Imai
Sylviane Kellenberger
Andrea Lancellotti
Beatrice Lancini
Jacopo Livio
Silvia Loreto
Elvira Losa

Lorenzo Lotti
Luca Lotti
Tomaso Macchi Cassia
Franco Maffeis
Carlo Magnani
Chiara Majno
Andrea Mambriani
Giuseppe Mantia
Monica Marchesi
Lorenzo Marchetto
Roberta Martinis
Michela Mascia
Laura Massa
Jun Matsui
Oliver Maupas
Augusta Mazzarolli
Costanza Melli
Antoine Menthonnex
Filippo Messina
Mariangela Moiraghi
Emanuela Monarca
Isidoro Montalbano
Luigi Montalbano
Claudia Montevecchi
Fabio Montrasi
Leandro Murialdo
Paolo Musa
Federica Neeff
Francesco Nissardi
Walter Arno Noebel
Sue O'Brien
Michela Pagan
Maria Rosa Palmieri
Marcelo Palozzo
Carla Parodi
Stefano Parodi
Sergio Pascolo
Giovanna Passardi
Maurizio Pavani
Claudia Pedacci
Anna Maria Penati
Anna Penco
Laura Peretti
Laura Pini
Martino Pirella
Carlo Pirola
Renza Pitton
Davide Pizzigoni
Peter Platner
Gianluca Poletti
Giulio Ponti
Ivana Porfiri
Giovanni Porta
Stefano Prina
Emilio Puglielli
Isabella Quinto
Cristiano Ravizzotti
Michele Reginaldi
Salvatore Regio
Silvia Ricca Rosellini
Cecilia Ricci

Marcella Ricci
Sara Ricciardi
Franco Rosi
Italo Rota
Eleonora Rovoletto
Gaetano Rubinelli
Gianbruno Ruggeri
Alejandro Ruiz
Umberto Saccardo
Tomas Salgado
Christiane Sattler Zicari
Fortunato Scocco
Paul Seletsky
Paola Seria
Donato Severo
Roberto Simoni
Susanna Slossel
Leila Smetana
Brenno Sonego
Frank Spadaro
Roberto Spagnolo
Stefania Spiazzi
Alessandra Spranzi
Christoph Stroschein
Elena Terni
Elisabetta Torossi
Milena Tortorelli
Antonella Torre
Gianfranco Trabucco
Monica Tricario
Maurizio Trovatelli
Alessandro Ubertazzi
Emanuela Uboldi
Pier Antonia Val
Monica Valdameri
Renzo Vallebuona
Carlo Vedovello
Isabella Vegni
Emanuela Venegoni
Claudio Ventura
Alessandro Verona
Bruna Vielmi
Paola Vignelli
Chiara Vitali
Giovanni Vragnaz
Massimo Zancan
Dea Zanitoni
Flavio Zanon
Maurizio Zanuso
Mirko Zardini